ANSWERING
ALASKA'S CALL

An intimate portrait of Alaska's legendary surgeon,
bush pilot, and legislator, Milo 'Doc' Fritz

LINDA FRITZ

ᴡᴡᴡ Epicenter Press

Kenmore, WA

Epicenter Press

6524 NE 181st St., Suite 2, Kenmore, WA 98028

Epicenter Press is a regional press publishing nonfiction
books about the arts, history, environment, and diverse cultures
and lifestyles of Alaska and the Pacific Northwest.
For more information, visit www.EpicenterPress.com

Cover and interior design by Scott Book & Melisssa Vail Coffman

Library of Congress Control Number: 2022946238

ISBN: 978-1-684920-94-5 (Trade Paperback)
ISBN: 978-1-684920-97-6 (Ebook)

Printed in the United States of America

*For my family
and in loving memory of
Milo and Betsy Fritz, my heroes*

ALASKA

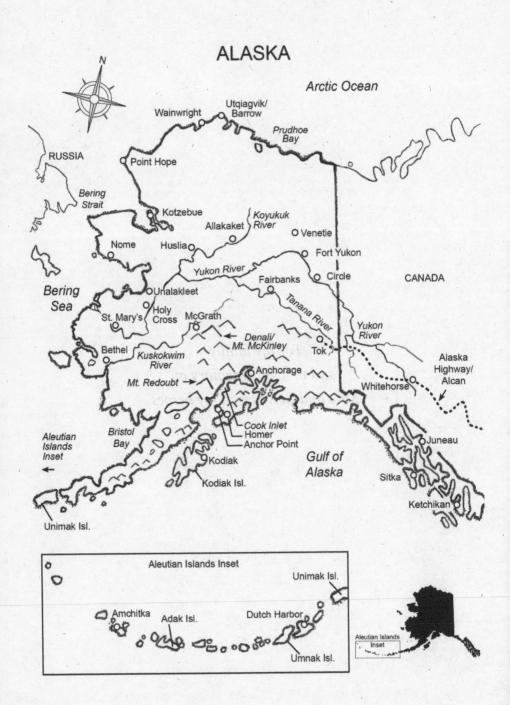

CONTENTS

*Only those who will risk going too far
can possibly find out how far one can go.*

—T.S. ELIOT

PROLOGUE

We need to know the history of the historian in order to understand the version that is being put in front of us.

—JULIAN BARNES, *THE SENSE OF AN ENDING*

ANCHOR POINT, ALASKA, 2008

IT IS THE LAST DAY OF SEPTEMBER, late in the afternoon, nearly cocktail time. I am behind the wheel of a rental car, trying to keep up with Aunt Betsy's friend Carol, who is rocketing northward in a blue pickup. I lower the driver's side window and crystalline Alaska air pours in. Its clarity was a wonderment to me during my first visit to Alaska over four decades ago. I still remember marveling at air so clear that I could look across to a far ridge and see individual leaves on trees, something inconceivable back in Pennsylvania. I inhale. Though warmed by the brilliant sunshine, the air still manages to feel brisk, invigorating, even intoxicating. Alaska. It feels good to be back, even for only a week, the amount of time allotted for a new challenge that has upended my fall plans, including plans to attend my high school's fortieth reunion.

This morning began at our farm on Maryland's Eastern Shore. By

early evening, I am to be at my aunt's Anchor Point home on the Kenai
Peninsula. It will be, almost literally, a coast-to-coast trip; at Anchor Point,
Sterling Highway jogs west, making it the westernmost stretch of highway
in the continental United States. Aunt Betsy lives on land just west of this
two-lane road, property that she and Uncle Milo purchased in 1949 from
the original Swedish homesteader.

In 1966, when I was sixteen, I received an invitation from Uncle Milo
and Aunt Betsy offering me a summer job as a nurse's aide in Dr. Milo H.
Fritz's Anchorage-based eye, ear, nose, and throat practice. It would also
include traveling and working with them in several itinerant clinics around
the state. I was prescient enough to appreciate that working for 'Doc' Fritz,
as he was known throughout Alaska, would be a once-in-a-lifetime experience. By then, I had a file full of weekly columns published in my local
newspaper and vague notions of a career in magazines. Anticipating lots
of rich story material, I kept a daily journal of my travels and experiences
throughout the summer.

As with that first trip to Alaska so long ago, I have no doubt that this
visit will also be memorable. No longer a burdensome teenager, I now
hope to be of real assistance. Memories of that event-filled summer com-
pete with feelings of nostalgia and sadness at the passage of time, as well as
a sense of impending dread. Uncle Milo died in 2000, leaving Aunt Betsy a
widow eight years ago. Jonathan, their older son, lived with her for several
years, but now at age ninety-five, Betsy has outlived both their children—
Jonathan and his younger brother Pieter.

In recent years, with her friend Carol's help, Aunt Betsy has managed
to live on her own. But now, well, I'm not sure what her situation is, which
is why I'm here. And, of course, I'm wondering if she even wants to see
me. Despite all the surface pleasantries—the periodic phone calls the photos, the exchange of letters—there is still that matter of "the book." Has
she forgiven me for the oral history interview I did with Uncle Milo back
in 1991? Oh, but things were frosty after that. Fritzes, especially fathers
and sons, have a history of fractiousness and long-held grudges. And Aunt
Betsy? She was first Elizabeth Berry before becoming a Fritz, but I can still
remember her stern, tight-lipped demeanor, the glacial eye, the pointed
silence directed my way after some known or unknown teenage misstep. I
know Aunt Betsy can be as starchy as her nurse's uniform.

Is she still mad at me?

My gaze is alternately being pulled right and left, like a tourist's, and I'm finding it hard to keep Carol's pickup in view as I try to take in the magnificent vistas as we roll northward. I don't want to miss the turn, but I don't want to miss any of this scenery either. To the west, across the glittering expanse of Cook Inlet, jagged-edged snow-capped peaks of the Aleutian Range push into azure sky. Outside the passenger window, swaths of evergreen forest blanket the ridges. Uncle Milo's words are memorably apt: "Alaska, where grandeur is commonplace."

Wilderness abuts the road. Later in the week, a stone's throw from this ribbon of asphalt, I will catch sight of a moose unconcernedly foraging in the tall grass. Today it still feels like summer on the Kenai, but signs of approaching winter are evident. Seed pods hang heavy on spent summer flowers lining the edge of the highway. A road sign advises drivers that snow-tire season starts tomorrow. Winter looms.

Weather is a serious topic in Alaska, as I was reminded during my plane ride from Anchorage to Homer. Above the steady thrum of the propeller engines, I caught the gist of a conversation between several sturdy-looking men in work boots and quilted vests who talked of contractors, divers, and some kind of project they were intent on completing before winter weather made it impossible. Snatches of sober-toned conversation had drifted my way, "—not a lot of time," . . . "—other projects," . . . "—freeze-up."

There were some twenty of us on the ERA plane that routinely makes that forty-five-minute flight from Anchorage to Homer. Out the windows we could see snowy glaciers, whose runoff flows into the ice-blue waters of Cook Inlet below, and spectacular views of Mt. Spur, Mt. Redoubt, and Mt. Iliamna as we flew by them, with Mt. Augustine visible to the south—all intermittently active volcanoes whose occasional burps of smoke and ash sometimes disrupt air travel.

This afternoon, flying conditions were near perfect—CAVU. I had learned the term from flying with my uncle: ceiling and visibility unlimited. However today, the clear, sunny weather and the lengthening shadows provided an unnervingly vivid view of the deep crevasses in the snow-dusted slopes we were flying over. As I looked down at the vast wilderness below, I was quietly gripped by terror that I had never felt as a seasoned traveler or even flying with Uncle Milo in a single-engine plane as a teenager. Now, as a mother, I have become more sensitive to the wonder and fragility of life, the potential for calamity. How would anyone find us if we crashed? Would being found even matter? This country has a way of making you feel both awed and insignificant. It has a way of forcing you to confront mortality—your own and that of others. Which is why I'm here.

"Betsy is failing," Carol had told me in the phone call that spurred me to action. "At times she's her old self, sharp as ever, other times she drifts off into her own world. Imagine that—almost ninety-five and beginning to show her age."

So, I too, have a time-sensitive task to be completed in the week ahead. Is a week enough time? Carol's help will be essential.

"Oh, I'll know you," Carol had assured me with a laugh when I started to describe myself over the phone. As Uncle Milo's secretary, Carol had been privy to the letters I'd written to him and to Aunt Betsy, as well as to years of photos chronicling our family life in Maryland. Carol would have seen many photos of me during that period, as well as of my husband—"Democrat" Bob, as Uncle Milo teasingly called him—and of our three boys as they grew from babies into young men. Picking me out at Homer's busy little airport was easy enough. There were few women on my flight, and I was the only passenger claiming a hefty hard-sided suitcase.

Carol's vigilant and discreet management of Aunt Betsy's household makes it possible for Betsy, now wheelchair-bound, to live alone—which, Aunt Betsy has made clear, she is determined to do. No Pioneer Home for her. Carol oversees Aunt Betsy's finances and is executor of her estate. Until now, Carol has been able to handle the minor and not so minor crises as they've come up, but a few weeks ago she ran into something unexpected: "There is no will," Carol informed me. That was the news that scuttled my reunion plans. Instead, I booked a trip to Alaska.

We pass the sign for Anchor Point. Thankfully, Carol slows and signals a left turn. As we ease onto the gravel road, I read the name on the sign: Milo Fritz Road—I had forgotten that detail. What else had I forgotten—or never known—about this remarkable man who had intrigued me from my earliest days? I smile as I crunch along, alert for potholes. Thinking about Uncle Milo always makes me smile. I loved his black, often self-deprecating humor. During my summer working for him, in addition to my daily journal, I began keeping a list of Milo's witty quips. A favorite I overheard when he was taking the history of a new patient with a long list of medical problems: "What brought you down to my level?"

In 1966 this road was just a weedy, two-lane path into the homestead.

Graded and graveled after Milo and Betsy finished building their combined house and medical office in 1974, the improved road has ushered
in much change. Now, as I follow Carol, we pass a VFW building, a senior
center, and a tiny public library—in the same building as a bar—which
have sprung up along Milo Fritz Road during the intervening decades. I
get a quick glimpse of Cook Inlet's shimmering waters before making a
hard right, following Carol's lead as she swerves to avoid major potholes
in a section of road that runs parallel to the Inlet. Modern homes line this
stretch. They sit on what is now prime residential real estate—once part
of the original 160-acre homestead—lots that my aunt and uncle sold off
periodically during lean times, which allowed them to hang on financially.

The road peters out at a cul-de-sac and I follow Carol's pickup into
Aunt Betsy's drive, past the three silvery log buildings built by the original
homesteader. Ice, snow, and winter winds barreling across the Inlet have
taken their toll on the rough-hewn cabin, barn, and outhouse, now sag-
ging into the verdant grass. Missing shingles have left gaping holes in the
roofs; small plants have gotten toeholds in the deteriorating wood. These
picturesque vestiges of another era are silhouetted against the steele-gray
expanse of Cook Inlet and the distant peaks of Mt. Iliamna, aglow in the
waning sunlight.

I park in front of the three-car garage extending from the modern
frame house, long and low, with cedar siding, a shake roof and white trim.
Carol is already out of her truck. With my wheeled suitcase clattering after
me, I follow her inside. Carol heads straight down the stairs to the former
patient waiting room and medical offices. "There was flooding down here
a while back and we had to move everything off the floor," she explains,
leading me through the jumble of office desks, chairs, and tables piled with
papers, records, photo albums, news clippings, and all kinds of memorabilia sorted into cardboard boxes, labeled year by year in Aunt Betsy's
handwriting.

We weave our way to the sanctum of Uncle Milo's office—now with a
freshly made rollaway cot—my quarters for the week. It's a large cheery
room, brightened by afternoon sunlight, and wall-to-wall burnt-orange
industrial carpeting. Rays of sunlight are filtered through a mass of spindly
saplings that have sprung up outside the wall of windows, obscuring most
of the view. A huge black-and-white portrait of Doc Fritz gazes benignly
from a far corner of the room. Nearly as tall as I am, it must be an old

campaign poster from one of his runs for the state legislature. It's a serious
countenance—his eyes steady, intelligent behind his glasses, his shaved
head, his mouth set resolutely—but I feel welcomed, his presence still per-
meating the room. Framed photos, books, memorabilia, and beautifully
crafted objects of ivory, fur, and basketry are all around the office, reflect-
ing the enduring loves of Milo's life—medicine, Betsy, Alaska, and flying.

Before we head upstairs again, Carol opens a door we had passed at the
foot of the stairs. She flips on the light, revealing a room with a concrete
floor that is the size of the three-car garage overhead. It is filled, nearly
floor-to-ceiling—on shelves, in filing cabinets, on tables—with documents
collected for "the book," the autobiography that Uncle Milo intended to
write after he retired. Aunt Betsy described these archives in a letter-to-
the-editor that was published in *Alaska Medicine* in 1987:

> *Seven 4-foot shelves of Milo's publications and reprints;*
> *42 shelves four-foot-long of mostly business correspondence,*
> *dating back to the 1920s or perhaps earlier; eight file draw-*
> *ers pertaining to Milo's political life; . . . 64 years of carefully*
> *kept diaries. In addition, there is a four-drawer file of the*
> *activities of the Eye, Ear, Nose and Throat Foundation and*
> *its Eye Bank which we began in the early 1950s. . . . more*
> *than 60 scrapbooks of memorabilia of the life and times of*
> *Betsy and Milo Fritz . . . a considerable number of slides and*
> *photographs of one man's 47-year medical career in Alaska*
> *as a private physician from Ketchikan to Barrow and from*
> *the Canadian border to the Pribilof Islands.*

I stand there for a moment taking it all in. Carol points out the massive patient register in a far corner. Nearly a foot high, it is a hand-written
chronology, listing the names of Doc Fritz's patients from all over Alaska.
Gone are the 57,526 patient files—the ones I had helped pull and refile
daily as part of my summer job—which Carol says were shredded for pri-
vacy reasons. The physicality of this remaining material is staggering. How
could one man have accomplished so much in one lifetime?

Upstairs is another world—tidy and serene. A massive two-sided
stone fireplace dominates the expansive space, dividing it in two. On the
living room side, a giant picture window offers a spectacular tableau of
water, clouds, and mountains. To either side are shelves of Alaskana and
books about flying. On the walls not given over to bookcases I recognize

oil paintings by my grandfather Henry E. Fritz and his friend and fellow Pelham, New York artist Rudolf C. Mueller, the man my uncle called "Uncle Rudolf" and had revered since childhood. There are landscapes of Maine, New York, and Europe. Unquestionably, Alaska reigns outside. Inside, the traditional furnishings—the Steinway, the classic simplicity of comfortable, upholstered chairs, the mahogany dining table and breakfront—reflect lingering East Coast sensibilities.

Aunt Betsy awaits us in a cozy alcove on the other side of the fireplace. The windows on this side face a small patch of lawn that has been carved out of woods of spruce trees and dense underbrush—all beginning to fade into shadow with the approach of evening. A wall of books—I see titles about art, history, politics, and biographies—extends nearly to the ceiling behind Aunt Betsy's wheelchair. What I didn't notice were the three identical urns, lined up across the mantelpiece over the fireplace. Carol would pointedly call my attention to them later that week.

I walk over to Aunt Betsy, not quite knowing what to expect. A picture of serenity, my aunt looks up at me from her wheelchair. Her eyes are steady, calmly fixed on my face. In them, I see no sign of the muddledness that had prompted the recent phone call from Carol. But as I lean over and greet Aunt Betsy with a careful hug, I am struck by her evanescence. She feels as frail and light as a bird.

Carol has made us each a cocktail, and we sit, drinks in hand, in this den-like area and begin to feel out common ground—the weather, family news, Aunt Betsy's health, which is fine she says. "I have no pain. I'm very comfortable here." To look at Aunt Betsy now, sitting primly erect in her wheelchair, her long hair loose and streaming down the back of her flannel robe, she looks almost girlish. Even at this stage of her life she is a handsome woman. I can see why Uncle Milo fell in love with her so many years ago at The Brooklyn Hospital.

"Why are you here?" Aunt Betsy asks me a few minutes later, fixing me with an unwavering gaze. It's a simple sounding question, yet I hesitate, trying to deduce from my aunt's face and from her voice the exact nature of the question that has brought an end of our initial pleasantries. It's been twenty-five years since we've talked face-to-face.

Why am I here? The will, a chance to reconcile, to revisit a major milestone of my youth? Myriad reasons have propelled me back to Anchor Point. I pause. I want to avoid any missteps. Aunt Betsy is awaiting my response. I expect she's noticed my hesitation. I decide to keep things simple for now. "I'm here to celebrate your ninety-fifth birthday!" I offer, with a raised glass and a smile. Carol joins in my salute, "Cheers!"

As our cocktails take hold, the conversation begins to drift effortlessly into the past. Aunt Betsy talks animatedly about her memories—about Milo and all he did for Alaska, the wonderful life they had together. Betsy's reveries sometimes wander and repeat themselves that night and during the days that follow. There will be mood swings—clarity and vagueness, reasonableness and petulance, enthusiasm and exhaustion, serenity and agitation, and many moments of nostalgia and reflection. Each day will bring its new challenges and adventures. I didn't expect otherwise. This is Alaska, after all.

As Aunt Betsy and I feed each other's memories over the next few days, the years and any lingering dissonance slip away. Her memories of older times are the default topic of conversation and seem to give Aunt Betsy the greatest pleasure. Our conversation is companionable, warmer than any I remember during my summer with them when she was always so stern, the moments of light-heartedness few and noteworthy. During this week, with Carol's help, we will settle the matter of the will so Betsy's wishes are legally documented. The extensive Fritz archives and Alaska Native artwork will go to the appropriate institutions when she passes away, which she will do peacefully during a night in mid-April.

But that's still six months away. During that final fall visit with Aunt Betsy, she and I have plenty of time to reminisce about old times. One evening, I ask her if she might like talking into a tape recorder, much like Uncle Milo did, maybe tell the stories behind some of the pieces in their exceptional collection of Alaska Native art. She considers this. She's willing to give it a try, she says. Then she pauses, looks squarely at me and says, "You do it. You tell Milo's story." Her fingers gracefully sweep the air as she gestures vaguely at the floor below us. "It's all down there."

PART I

The Call

KETCHIKAN, 1940 – FIRST TASTE
OF THE LAST FRONTIER

I was rather young to be so far north, but there is a period
near the beginning of every man's life when he has little to
cling to except his unmanageable dream, little to support him
except good health, and nowhere to go but all over the place.

—E. B. WHITE

FOR NEARLY TWO DAYS NEAR THE end of January in 1940, the S.S.
Alaska, the 200-passenger flagship of the Alaska Steamboat Company,
threaded its way north past mist-shrouded islands verdant with primal
forests of huge cedar, spruce, and hemlock trees. Two of those passengers were Dr. Milo Fritz and his wife Betsy, a registered nurse. The voyage
by steamship, following the Inside Passage from Seattle to Ketchikan, was
their introduction to the magnificence of the Last Frontier and to the reali-
ties of the young couple's Alaska dream.

The scenery through the heart of the immense Tongass National Forest
was every bit as spectacular as E. B. White had described when he, then a

man in his twenties, had steamed northward in 1923: "I was young enough to absorb with gratitude and wonder the vast, splendid scene of Alaska in the time before the airplane brought it to our door and when it was still inaccessible and legendary."

Dr. Fritz had been invited to Ketchikan to join the general practice of Dr. Henry Turner and Dr. Arthur Wilson, who were looking for a partner who was an eye, ear, nose, and throat specialist. Dr. Fritz, a Columbia- and Duke-educated EENT surgeon with itinerant medicine experience gained during his residency at Duke, fit the bill.

Milo Herbert Fritz, born ten years after E. B. White, was raised in a modest but culturally rich home in Pelham, NY, just two miles from White's home in Mt. Vernon. As boys, they would have roamed similar turf in an area still sleepy and rural despite its proximity to New York City. Both treasured memories of childhood summers in Maine and of messing about in boats; both felt the lure of Alaska and its implied promise of freedom, adventure, and pristine expanses. In time, Milo would become an avid reader of White's writings. Among my uncle's papers I found a yellowed reprint of White's piece on Alaska. Their sensibilities and experiences echoed each other.

As the *Alaska* approached Ketchikan, Milo and Betsy watched as contours of the town came within view. Milo's blue eyes, steady and perceptive behind wire-rimmed glasses, blazed with intelligence and intensity. He had been anticipating this day for a long time. At age thirty, Milo was still lithe and athletic. He had worked summer jobs as a farm laborer and lifeguard to put himself through college and had gained valuable experience with car and boat engines from tinkering with them since he was a teenager. A man with abundant energy and drive, he was prepared, he thought, for the adventure ahead. His usually serious countenance could give way to a boyish grin in a flash. His face must have lit up as they approached the dock. "Man o' man," was a favorite expression of his. Perhaps he was saying it then.

Betsy, then twenty-six, was a willowy, dark-haired beauty, her long hair expertly twisted and secured with combs. Unlike Milo, who was given to volatility, Betsy's ladylike demeanor was notably calm; her excitement and anxiety, if any, tended to be carefully contained. Both she and Milo had read as much as they could about Alaska and its desperate health needs. Both had optimistic but untested dreams for this uncharted Territory, but unlike so many other adventurers drawn to Alaska, Milo and Betsy intended to give—not take—from this land.

They were greeted by the view of hundreds of fishing boats that crowded the town's harbor. There was Ketchikan—derived from the original Indian name for the town, Kach Khanna, meaning "spread wings of prostrate eagle." In the 1890s, the fishing village had served as a supply point and center for miners during the Gold Rush. Ketchikan's buildings, most constructed of spruce or cedar, lay nestled against the base of 3,000-foot Deer Mountain; the town's weathered wooden sidewalks ran along the waterfront and on into the center of town. Stepping off the steamship on January 29, 1940, as Milo later recalled, "It was love at first sight."

THE VOYAGE FROM SEATTLE HAD CAPPED off a three-week, cross-country road trip—"The Great Trek" in Milo's words. After ringing in the new year with their families, the young couple had left Pelham, New York on a sub-zero day, driving a 1931 roadster they called Sally. They were provisioned with a thermos of hot coffee and the gift of a buffalo robe from a friend of Milo's who had interned with him at The Brooklyn Hospital in New York. "Besides warmth," Betsy remembered, "the buffalo robe proffered its own bit of medical history: it had once belonged to the friend's grandfather who had used the robe as he made house calls on his patients in New England."

After crossing the country and before heading north to Seattle, Milo and Betsy had stopped in San Francisco to call on a Miss Yetter, a nurse, whom Milo had managed to track down there. Milo wanted to personally thank her for the exceptional nursing care she gave him at the time of his birth, some three decades earlier.

In August of 1909, Milo's parents, Henry Fritz, an art teacher and artist, and his very pregnant wife Amelia, also an artist, were vacationing in a rustic cabin in the Berkshire Mountains of Massachusetts. The couple had gone there to paint.

The story, as related by Betsy:

> Amelia went into labor and was taken to the House of Mercy Hospital in Pittsfield, Massachusetts. Amelia's labor was long and difficult. Henry stayed at the cabin and during the waiting period he did one of his best paintings, The Berkshires in Summer. Communications there were primitive: To reach Henry, a telephone call was made to a neighbor

> who had a telephone and also a fish horn. The neighbor blew on the fish horn to let Henry know that the baby had been born and it was time for him to take the bus into town. The baby had arrived and the joy was great, but there was sadness too. Henry and Amelia's new son Milo was born with a paralysis of his left side.
> ... As an infant Milo was a problem to his parents and, with his constant crying, a nuisance to neighbors. He weighed less at six months than he did at birth. No formula seemed to satisfy him until he was fed malt liquor. Then he began to improve.

Betsy recalled their visit with Miss Yetter in San Francisco: "She told us she had spent so much time massaging Milo's left arm and leg in hopes of overcoming the paralysis. At night she would pull his bassinet up close to her bed and fall asleep massaging and exercising the left arm and leg."

Miss Yetter's nursing care and the many hours she devoted to massaging strength into Milo's tiny limbs—perhaps facilitated by the malt liquor—had allowed the weakly infant to blossom into the robust man—a surgeon, no less—who came to call on her in 1940. Milo would continue to champion nurses—particularly the Alaska public health nurses who were often the sole sources of health care in rural areas—his admiration perhaps colored by Miss Yetter's dedication.

KETCHIKAN'S PRIMARY INDUSTRY IN 1940 WAS fishing—halibut, salmon, cod, and herring. One of Milo's new colleagues, Dr. Wilson, recalled the town of those days in an oral history: "Roads were all wooden or gravel. Very, very little cement. You made lots of house calls. . . .The fishermen either worked at the canneries to put up the fish or they trolled and brought in the fish that they caught on a hook and line and sold them. Or the seiners came in with theirs, so some group, generally two groups, always could pay some bills."

Betsy soon fell in love with the busy waterfront community and its mild climate, writing:

> Even in winter there is much rain, but very little snow. . . .
> We had read so much about the then-Territory and felt we knew about it. Not so, every day brought a new surprise—the sweet-smelling air, the sunrise and sunsets, the business of

the waterfront, and most of all the friendly people. The lo-
cal paper always commented on who was leaving or arriving
by ship. It also published who was admitted to the hospital,
and sometimes 'why' and how successful the treatment was!
A new custom for us.

Upon his arrival, Dr. Milo Fritz became one of a half-dozen physicians serving the town of 3,000, Alaska's second largest community. He was Alaska's first board-certified ophthalmologist. As a partner in practice with Dr. Wilson and Dr. Turner, Milo did a considerable amount of eye, ear, nose, and throat surgery. The eye procedures he performed regularly included fixing crossed eyes, cataract extractions, corneal transplants, repairing retinal detachments, and plastic surgery of the lids, in addition to basic refraction. Procedures for the ear, nose, and throat included removal of tonsils and adenoids, submucous resections (to treat deviated septums) and rhinoplasties (commonly known as "nose jobs"). He also routinely removed foreign bodies from eyes and from kids who had inhaled all sorts of things.

Milo immediately began attacking the myriad health problems he encountered among the Alaska Natives. "Terrible," he said of the health conditions they faced. "For instance, right near Ketchikan there is a place called Metlakatla [an Indian community on Annette Island]. I went over there one Sunday. Almost every kid had a draining ear, for the love of Mike, and one was also choking to death on his adenoids and tonsils, so I arranged for him to come in" [to the Ketchikan hospital].

THOUGH ANTIBIOTICS HAVE RENDERED TONSILLECTOMIES AND adenoidectomies rarities now, between 1915 and the 1960s, these operations—referred to as "T&As"—were the standard solution for a child dealing with persistent ear- and throat-related ailments and were the most frequently performed surgical procedure in the United States. From 1921 until 1946, there was even a Tonsil Hospital in New York City, established to remove the tonsils and adenoids of poor children. In Alaska, Doc Fritz had seen how the severe climate and inadequate medical attention could transform routine colds into a chronic condition that, when untreated, left many Alaska Native children deaf and even blind. Milo's mission was to treat these problems.

Milo's clinic work took him throughout Southeast Alaska. "Wrangell and Petersburg were two places I went while I was in Ketchikan. I picked up case after case there. You didn't have to be smart. I'm not trying to pawn myself off as a guy with great acumen who could figure these things out; any medical student in their fourth year could have made the diagnosis. I only did the cases that were simple; complicated ones I'd take into Ketchikan; the more complicated ones would go to Seattle."

"This guy is ambidextrous," Dr. Wilson marveled, recalling Milo's unusual surgical abilities when he first joined their practice in Ketchikan:

Of course, we got him everything he wanted. He wanted a set of instruments and we got them for him because he knew how to use them. He knew what he wanted from the beginning of that patient to the end. He was a hard worker. He didn't ever try to make it easier for himself. Just went about his work. He is a character, that guy . . . an outspoken person. He is careful in his work. He is a little impetuous and he sure steps on some people's toes you know.

Milo and Betsy acquired a cabin. Betsy soon had second thoughts, as she wrote her in-laws, Amelia and Henry, that spring:

Naturally, the day I first saw it with the sun shining through the trees and on the garden and water, like anyone else I fell in love with the place. For two days we debated and then decided to not take it. If we had only left it at that but no, we changed our minds once more and now we are stuck with the place. There are so many ifs. If we could go out there now as it is and live in it, we would save so much money, we would be able to enjoy the out-of-doors, go fishing, have a garden. All in all, have a home of our own. But there is no such a thing as a bargain. You only get what you pay for. So, we have exactly what we are paying for. A nice piece of land on which is a tiny, little cabin in very poor condition, an overrun garden, and a dock whose piles are rotted away. . . . There is no plumbing, nor water piped to the house. . . . It is not furnished and we have no furniture. Milo seems to think that we could go there and live on boxes and the like until we can afford to get some furniture. We could not at this time afford to buy at one time the necessary pieces of furniture without going into debt. We both agree to not do that.

When their first winter was well behind them, Betsy wrote:

We are having many days of sunshine now. I never before realized what wonderful stuff it was. Most of the days are very warm, occasionally a north wind makes it cool enough to wear a sweater or light coat. The leaves on the trees and shrubbery are out in full. The early spring flowers such as tulips and daffodils are fading. Lilacs, daisies, pansies, and marigolds are lovely. It is impossible to see the ground (in the country or on our property) for the foliage that is so luxurious. It is not a question of what to plant or where but what to unplant and where. When you leave the road and walk up the path to our cabin it is, I imagine, rather like the tropics. Waist-high ferns on either side, millions of small ferns, and plants, wild lily-of-the-valley everywhere, moss hanging from the trees, as in the southern part of the U.S., but not as lovely, and moss of various shades of green on the rocks, trees, and logs. . . . I never see darkness now. . . . Good bright daylight remains until nearly 10:00. The sun is up and busy again (I woke up at 5:00 this morning and it was out; it is light at 3:00) very early.

Milo had comparatively few night calls in Ketchikan but was busy most evenings. One Sunday afternoon when Milo had some free time, they went out to the cabin, taking "the little Turner boy" with them. Dr. Turner's son and Betsy "climbed around on the rocks and caught crabs while Milo repaired the dock," Betsy wrote, and then, looking ahead:

My plan is to work on the land and make the sort of a garden that we dream about and then when our one year's probation is up, see how things are going to work out and then, if we stay, if we can afford it, start from the ground up on the sort of a small house that we would like to have.

Ever the realist, Betsy came to see "how really absurd it was for us to go out there to live. We moved into a smaller but more pleasant apartment here in town." It was on the south side. "And so, I have sunshine, on the days that it shines, nearly all day. Also, I have a fine view of the channel looking south. [The apartment] consists of a fair-sized living room, the same-sized bath and kitchen, one large closet." The feature that intrigued them was the Murphy bed. "Milo likes to make it so that he can fold it up and put it away."

Then there was Ketchikan social life. Betsy described it in a letter to her in-laws:

> *It is the very best thing in the world for me to meet the*
> *people, alone and without Milo to fall back on. I have to talk.*
> *I can't just sit there with my teeth in my mouth and grin.*
> *However, it seems as though I never shall get all of my calls*
> *paid back for the first round. At least once a week I don a*
> *hat, white gloves, and dress shoes, arm myself with cards and*
> *something to talk about and start. Only to return and find*
> *another pile of cards under my door. Being one of the doc-*
> *tors' wives I was asked to pour tea at the hospital last Sunday*
> *afternoon in conjunction with the Hospital Day exercises. I*
> *am glad that I don't play bridge for that would give me less*
> *time than I have now to play with my husband.*

Betsy also began her role as the couple's business manager. She kept the books, did the banking, paid the bills, and tried to save money. She also decided to go to work.

> *I put my name on the registry to do private duty. It seems*
> *there is quite a demand for private duty nurses and the ones*
> *here work if they want to or if they have no bridge game for*
> *that evening. I also requested night duty as that is the time*
> *that the others hate to work. It will work out fine for me be-*
> *cause: I work from midnight to 8 AM and then I am home*
> *in time to have breakfast with Milo. He will go to work and*
> *I to bed. If I get up at four there is plenty of time to do what*
> *housework there is in this tiny apartment before dinner. Then*
> *we will have the evenings together. That arrangement will*
> *also allow me to keep whatever social engagements we may*
> *make. It will enable us to pay for the house more quickly. If I*
> *find that it will jeopardize our happiness or that I am losing*
> *weight of course I shall stop.*

Betsy joined the Ketchikan Nurses Association, "for the good of myself and my country." It helped her to keep abreast of the ever-changing nursing field and made it more convenient for her to work. She also dutifully joined The Hospital Guild, "composed of the doctors' wives who meet once a month and sew for the hospital," as well as the St. John's Episcopal Church and the church Guild. Betsy also learned about homemaking through the

University of Alaska Home Extension Group. She attended lectures by the home demonstration agent from the University at Fairbanks to learn new skills and "at the same time get my mending done."

She also wrote: "The one group that has the most interesting meetings and would be the most beneficial to me is the American Association of University Women for which of course I am not eligible." This comment was probably an allusion to her father-in-law's misgivings about Betsy's lack of a college degree. Henry, with a PhD in education from New York University had expected a suitable mate for his son the doctor would have a college degree. Milo's mother Amelia, a graduate of Hunter College, was well educated for the times.

Nevertheless, Betsy's East Coast nursing training and two years of living and working in Durham, NC while Milo was at Duke, had provided her with skills that Alaskans recognized and found pertinent, which must have shored up Betsy's self-confidence. She wrote:

> At the Home Extension meeting I heard a fine talk on vitamins. Thought of Belle-Mere [as Betsy called Amelia] the whole time. When the agent was finished, one of the ladies said that, as I was a member of the medical profession, perhaps I would like to add a word. I surprised myself by saying that I did have a word to say. Milo still doesn't believe that I really got up and spoke to the group. The lecture had covered the history of the vitamins and the sources of each, how to prepare the foods that we may best obtain the various vitamins. She had also told of the various deficiency diseases resulting from improper diet. She described in detail all of them except pellagra and admitted that she had never seen a case of that. So, I talked about the condition in the South where the poor white people live on fat back, cornbread, and occasionally some turnip greens. I told them of the really dramatic response that these persons ill with pellagra showed when they were given proper diet and nicotinic acid or vitamin B in the hospital.

Betsy, already an expert seamstress, also learned how to make pigskin gloves while in Ketchikan.

> After 1 June, I am going to send for a skin and make myself some. Gloves are a bit difficult to buy here unless you care

for cotton ones in fancy patterns and gay colors. Nearly all of
the members have made more than one pair, one person was
finishing her ninth one. They fit perfectly.

Summer found them celebrating the Fourth of July, Ketchikan-style.
Milo described the high-spirited celebrations in a letter to his parents:

> The Fourth up here is a combination of Christmas, Jewish
> New Year, and a Chinese wedding. Nobody does any work
> and the day is typically American. On the 3rd, at about
> 12:00, those who are going to get drunk begin to do so. All
> office workers and clerks get a half holiday. At the junction
> of the two main streets in town is erected a wooden plat-
> form. The local airplanes & all the small fishing boats carry
> in passengers from the outlying settlements –Klawock, Port
> Alexander, Metlakatla, Kasaan, and Craig. Everyone gets
> out of his working clothes and into his store suits. The Indians
> dress up in their best white men's costumes and tank up with
> his liquor. There are boxing matches on the wooden platform
> and we hang from our office windows to get a good view of the
> fun. What the boys of different weight classes lack in train-
> ing and ring knowledge they make up for in earnestness and
> toughness gotten by felling logs or fishing from small boats.
> There is a lot of wild swinging and every once in a while, a
> blow lands and the blood spurts. Once or twice, there is a
> knockout when one boy ducks into instead of away from a
> wild and uncontrolled fist. The fights only last three rounds
> so the damage is slight.

> The night of the third, Betsy and I had Lt. George Synin
> and his charming wife Eleanor in for supper and a fine time
> was had by all talking about the war and the national situ-
> ation. George is the commanding officer of the Coast Guard
> Patrol Boat, the Nemaha.

> The Fourth dawned overcast, but at least there was no
> rain. At 10:00 every man, woman, child, and dog was down
> on the business section of town. There was a parade led by
> George Synin very straight and military with drawn sword
> and his small crew behind him. Next came the men of the
> "Cyane" with rifles on their shoulders. Following next was

*the Shriners Band, much improved since it performed at the
cemetery on Memorial Day. Then there were veterans, Moose,
Elks, Sons of Norway, longshoremen, guys who just wanted
to parade, various ladies auxiliaries, kids on bikes festooned
with gay crêpe paper, the Wingren Brothers' (groceries) new
delivery truck, boats of sundry local patriotic organizations,
Miss Ketchikan (one of the local Fancy Girls but, nevertheless Queen for a Day) riding with her two Maids of Honor
(daughters of two of our leading families) in the cockpit of a
small cruiser that was raffled off by the Elks. Bringing up the
rear was a mad assortment of kids and dogs.*

As DR. WILSON OBSERVED, MILO'S VIEWS on the Territory's medical needs
sometimes differed markedly from established government and medical
authorities. Milo did indeed start stepping on toes:

*Somebody came up here from the AMA and said, 'What
the hell! You don't need an eye, ear, nose, and throat man
in Alaska.' If you can imagine anybody saying such a stupid
thing. . . . In my innocence, I brought up books that I would
read while I was waiting for the occasional patient to come
in. . . .But in Ketchikan, I was like a guy who was the only fellow selling life preservers at a shipwreck. I mean, I was busy
from the word go, and I still haven't read those damn books.*

In December of 1940, Milo, a Reserve Officer in the U.S. Army, received
notice that he was being called to active duty in New York State. He wanted
to serve his country but requested permission to first take his otolaryngology boards at the end of his stipulated period of practice. This was granted.
By that time, too, Betsy learned she was pregnant. With mixed feelings,
they began preparations to leave Ketchikan and return to the East Coast
in the spring of 1941. By then, despite some satisfying work and fondness
for Alaska, a sense of disillusionment with Ketchikan had begun to set in.

As Milo would later explain:

*In Ketchikan, this was a village of 3,000. . . . It was re-
ally a waste of a person with the talent that I had amassed,
not because I'm so smart, but because of the training that I'd
had and the six years of post-graduate training from medical
school, to bury myself in a hamlet like Ketchikan, drawing on*

*a population of perhaps 10,000 people. I decided I wanted to
leave and this was a graceful way out. It was kind of a waste
of time. But since no one had been there before, there was
a hell of a lot of work to be done initially, so we were very
happy there. We were young and in love and it didn't matter.*

Their son Jonathan was born in Ketchikan on May 12, 1941. After the
usual two-week hospital stay, Betsy went from the hospital directly to the
ship. They left Alaska with their new baby and went back to New York
State where Milo reported for active duty.

Milo's reflections about Ketchikan faintly echoed the earlier ones of E.
B. White: "Ketchikan was our first Alaskan port of call and the scene of the
passengers' first disillusionment. . . . The village 'a warm mosquitoey place
smelling of fish.'"

The parallels are there—the unmanageable dream, the restlessness, the
limitations of Ketchikan—but when Milo took leave of Ketchikan, unlike
White, he was no longer young and unencumbered. Milo, a husband and
new father, was now facing military service in a war that soon would
greatly impact Alaska, as well as his own life.

MILO'S EARLY DIARY –
HIS FRIENDS, HIS HEROES

*A hero is simply someone who rises above his own human
weaknesses, for an hour, a day, a year, to do something stirring.*

—BETTY DERAMUS

AT THE AGE OF FIFTEEN, MILO began keeping a diary, a practice he
kept up until three weeks before his death. His first entry on April
20, 1925, offers an early glimpse of an adolescent trying to establish his
moral compass:

> *Things to Remember*
> *1. Develope [sic] an elephant's hide*
> *2. Remember that there is always a man better than you are*
> *3. Honor thy father & thy mother*
> About a year later Milo added:
> *4. Be a gentleman.*

Subsequent diary entries, anecdotes from letters and other archival
material paint a youthful portrait of a principled and disciplined striver, a

boy doggedly determined to overcome perceived weaknesses and achieve the goals he set for himself, however lofty or outside the mainstream. It was a heroic path, all but ensuring disappointment along the way.

From most standpoints, the neighborhood of Pelham, NY provided an idyllic environment for Milo and his younger brother Larry, always "Laurens" to their parents, Henry and Amelia, who were major influences on them both. "They used to read stories to us," Milo recalled. "In fact, my first language was German. But World War I came along and German became extremely unpopular, and so they stopped talking [German] and I never did complete my basic education in the German language."

Their father was "very strict about manners and table manners and the way we spoke to people and how to behave when we were introduced to folks." In later years both brothers could wax entertainingly about one shared complaint. "Mother was very lovely," Milo said, "but she had this artistic tendency for dressing my brother and me up in weird costumes that we hated and we didn't look like other boys. We called these outfits "dingwaddlers." In family portraits, Milo's brown hair and Larry's blond curls spilled down well below their ears, Prince-Valiant-style. Wearing their despised dingwaddlers, Milo and Larry look like little princelings. In those photos, Milo is a picture of decorum . . . and good health. More clues about Milo's partial paralysis as an infant would surface years later.

Their father's fall from an ice wagon as a boy was an oft told family tale. It seemed to explain why one leg was shorter than the other, making it necessary for Henry to wear a heavy, built-up shoe. It perhaps explained Henry's inclination toward artistic and intellectual pursuits, and even, as some family members speculated, why he had difficulty getting along with others and caused so much unhappiness at home.

But apparently there was more to Henry's leg problem than a childhood fall. Betsy noted that Milo's father came to Duke University Hospital in the 1930s as a patient and Henry told the orthopedic surgeon that he had recently learned that as a very small child in Germany he'd had surgery on his hip for osteomyelitis. Additionally, according to Betsy, doctors thought Henry might have had phocomelia (defective development of arms, legs, or both.) Pictures of the sturdy young boy in his dingwaddlers attest to Nurse Yetter's success in overcoming what may have been Milo's unfortunate genetic inheritance.

Stories that the brothers would later tell about their childhood adventures were invariably funny and entertaining, however, an undercurrent of unhappiness flowed through the Fritz household at the time. Milo had no memory of being in either his maternal or paternal grandparents' homes. His maternal grandmother would occasionally come to spend the day with her daughter Amelia and her grandsons Milo and Laurens. One time, that grandmother brought him a birthday present, a secondhand bike very much in need of repair, but nonetheless a thrill for Milo to receive. He also remembered other times, when his paternal grandfather Heinrich used to walk back and forth in front of Milo's home shaking his fist at the house because he did not approve of Amelia, the woman his son Henry had married.

A spouse not good enough for a Fritz? That, and uncompromising men with unhappy father-son relationships were ongoing family traditions that went back several generations.

Milo's grandfather Heinrich, born Karl Heinrich Fritz in 1851, grew up in the court of Kaiser Wilhelm I in Berlin where his father, Wilhelm Karl Heinrich Fritz was an interior decorator for the royal residences and those of the Kaiser's friends. Milo's grandfather became an interior decorator also but rebelled against his father's wishes for a proper arranged marriage with a lady of the court. Instead, he fell in love and married Hedwig Krause, descended from French Huguenots, who was a farmer's daughter from the Spreewald section of Germany. He was promptly disowned. Heinrich and Hedwig settled in Lubben, east of Berlin in the Spreewald, where Milo and Larry's father Henry Eugene Fritz was born in 1875, followed four years later by his sister Selma. Henry would later enjoy telling his sons, "I was born on the Spree!"

When Henry was seven years old, the family moved to the United States. Family stories about why they left Germany vary. According to one, Heinrich did not wish to join the German army. Selma's son Harry offered another version to Milo and Betsy when he visited them at Ft. MacDill Airfield in Florida after World War II: Heinrich, a difficult man to get along with, was high on a ladder one day, installing heavy red velvet drapes in a castle, when he became very angry with his assistant below him and "dropped" his hammer on him. That, Harry said, was the reason they left Germany so hurriedly.

A third version was offered by another cousin, Eleanor Chandler,

the daughter of Heinrich's youngest child, Pauline, born after the family
arrived in New York. Eleanor wrote that because Heinrich had a beautiful
baritone voice, he was able to immigrate to the United States as a member
of the Metropolitan Opera House chorus. Eleanor's version:

> *After the family's arrival in New York City in 1882,
> Heinrich's time with the Met was short-lived—Heinrich
> felt he deserved a more leading role and the opera manage-
> ment didn't. He left indignantly and took a job with Sloan's,
> a very upper-class furniture and interior decorating firm on
> Fifth Avenue. This was a time when the socially elite adored
> anything imported from Europe, so Heinrich was in his ele-
> ment. He was given three floors of studio space to oversee
> a large staff. Of course, he hired only German decorators
> and forbade any employee to speak English. "German is the
> language of culture," he declared, "not that polyglot English
> which is further mangled by American accents and slang."*

An old saying would continue to ring true through many generations:
"You can always tell a Fritz but you can't tell him much."

For two summers, when their parents were off painting in Europe, Milo
and Larry attended Camp Talcott, a YMCA sleepaway camp in Huguenot,
NY approximately ninety miles northwest of New York City. Their much
younger cousin Larry Hayes also attended this camp, thanks to Milo's
intervention. "Cousin Larry," the son of Henry's sister Pauline, was only
seven years old at the time, but Milo persuaded Larry's parents to let him
go to Camp Talcott under Milo's supervision and they relented. By the age
of fourteen, Milo had become a mentor and role model for his younger
cousin who ultimately would become a neuropsychiatrist.

The Fritz family spent several summers on the coast of Maine which
the two young brothers liked to explore in a rowboat that, as Milo later
reminisced in a letter to his brother, "was made of wood and heavy as hell,"
with a brass half-round running along the keel from the stem to the rudder posts. "We used to joke that we had a boat on which there was a brass
band—the keel, if you recall."

Their teenage maritime adventures included making an exhausting
trip in their rowboat around Spruce Point from Linekin Bay to Boothbay
Harbor. Milo was "amazed that we rowed so far from shore and neither of
us had ever heard of a life jacket, much less owned one." Milo was hesitant

about diving into the icy water to cool off until Larry told him to pretend he had to rescue Alice, his dream girl of the moment. Milo pretended and over he went, right through a giant red jellyfish. Milo was blind for about an hour thereafter.

During Milo's high school years Amelia took to her bed. He and Larry did most of the household chores and carried trays of food up to their mother. She claimed to be ill and perhaps she was. Amelia visited many doctors with vague complaints. These visits became costly but perhaps they helped satisfy her craving for attention. She lay in bed hour after hour listening to her radio, especially to claims about cures for this and that from all sorts of home remedies.

Many years later, Amelia told Betsy that she was angry with her husband at the time. Henry was spending money on antiques to beautify their home when Amelia felt the money could be better spent on the family. Amelia also confided to Betsy about the time she returned home to find Henry in ardent embrace with a model. Once, maybe twice, Henry went on a trip to Europe in the summer, leaving Amelia to deal with things as best she could.

Milo's differences with his father were usually minor, but on one occasion, because Milo had displeased him in some way, Milo was forbidden to attend a high school party. However, after pretending to go to bed, Milo got up and climbed out his window, went to the party, and had a fine time. Henry was so furious that he ordered his teenage son out of the home and out of school, which would have happened, had it not been for the intervention of friends and neighbors.

RUDOLF CARL MUELLER, A GERMAN IMMIGRANT and accomplished artist, was the one particular older neighbor and family friend whom Milo could reliably turn to throughout his childhood and teenage years. Though not a blood relative, Milo and Larry always called him, "Uncle Rudolf." He remained a loving father figure to Milo all his life, and Uncle Rudolf's approval was frequently sought on weighty matters. "Home" to Milo was Uncle Rudolf's combined house and small studio at the back of the lot at 327 7th Ave., just a few blocks from the Fritz house at 4 Poplar Ave.

As Milo later wrote about Uncle Rudolf:

> One of the biggest Americans that I have ever known
> was only 5'6" tall. He was born in a German village that is

now part of Poland and came over here around the turn-
of-the-century, . . . impelled to come to the United States
by his youthful reading of James Fenimore Cooper, attend-
ing the wild West shows of Bill Cody and his yearnings to
meet the American Indian. He spoke with a German accent,
mixed with a Brooklyn accent which made him difficult to
understand until you got used to it. He came to our house
frequently, and my brother Larry and I used to go over to his
place all the time to look at the paintings in progress and talk
to him because he was a very friendly uncritical man and
didn't demand great things of children. He loved them and
we loved him.

Milo's friendship with Uncle Rudolf would endure until the artist's death at age 100 in 1967. By then Milo, had been an eye surgeon for nearly thirty years and had been elected to the Alaska House of Representatives. After Uncle Rudolf's death, his paintings and those of his wife Angela were shipped to Alaska. Milo and Betsy had bought all the paintings previously to ease the old man's financial burdens. The Mueller paintings would join those by Henry E. Fritz on walls of the Fritz home and medical office, which became chockablock with art. It gave Milo great pleasure when a patient commented that a visit to Milo's office could seem like a visit to an art museum.

Milo had two other great friends throughout his childhood—Harold Johnson and Donald McKenna—neighbor boys who also attended YMCA camp with him. Milo would stay in close touch with both friends all his life.

Harold was the son of Swedish immigrants. He and Milo acquired an old canoe that required extensive repairs. "If we put many more brass screws in it, it wouldn't have floated," my uncle claimed. "I got a set of wagon wheels and took it by hand through the streets of Pelham and New Rochelle to a place called City Island on the outskirts of New York City and we used it there for the summer."

Donald McKenna was a year older. "He had in his family two cars – a Peerless, which was something like a Cadillac, and a Mitchell touring car. . . . He taught me how to drive. He was a very meticulous teacher, and in fact in my life, three of the great teachers that I had, had almost no education. One of them was Donald who was a high school graduate."

Between them, Milo and Donald earned enough money to buy a second-hand Ford roadster—and later a sailboat—which they enjoyed for a couple of years until Milo earned enough to purchase a Stutz Bearcat on his own—not new, of course—a car he would speak of with great fondness.

From his earliest days, Milo seemed to have a keen interest in and appreciation for the females in his life. His first diary was prefaced by dedications to two close friends at the time, one, a girl named Carol, "whom I honor, and who furnished, in many ways, the thoughts and feelings that started me writing this book . . . and because I admire her more than any girl I know for her candidness and truthfulness in everything she does or says. Such people are hard to find now anywhere."

In the spring of 1926, at age sixteen, Milo attended his first dinner dance with a girl named Natalie. The list of girls who were Milo's friends and romantic interests would grow long over the next few years, despite Milo's retrospective lament to his brother:

> *In those days, the thing to be was a football player. Whether or not you could use "is" and "are" correctly didn't matter—it still don't. And I wanted to be "popular" and felt that my goddam eyeglasses interfered. But I couldn't see what was written on the blackboard (now known as the chalkboard) without them.*

They all attended Pelham Memorial High School. In 1927, *The Pelican* yearbook, listed graduating senior Milo Fritz, as "A Macbeth in ambition, a Paderewski in coiffure, a genius in the making, and a 'bear' with the ladies." A photo of Milo then, shows a handsome, serious-looking young man in owlish glasses. His "goddam eyeglasses," apparently were not a major handicap in his social life. "One time, Yvonne and Celine came over to see us," Milo would recall in a letter to his brother many years later. "You and I and they sat in that garden swing between the Brown's bungalow and our house. One of the girls sat on my lap and of course I had a terrific erection—all wasted of course. I don't think the other sister sat on your lap, but you were there. In those days there was no such word as sex."

Milo was active in the dramatic club all four years, on the staff of the school newspaper, its business manager the fourth year, and art editor of *The Pelican* yearbook. He was also on the track squad, in the literary club, president of the junior class, and secretary of the Executive Council. A strong swimmer, he passed his junior life saving test in high school, later becoming a senior lifeguard.

To earn money during his senior year of high school, Milo worked as a clerk at Ware's department store during the busy Christmas season of 1926, receiving his first paycheck. Following graduation, Milo and Harold Johnson, hitchhiked up into the Adirondack Mountains area of New York State looking for summer work. They stopped at a farm near Elizabethtown called Roaring Brook Farm where they were given jobs, a place to sleep in the hay loft and fed huge meals by Mother Brown, the farm owner's wife. John Denton, the foreman, directed their work and taught them much about cultivating, carpentry, and caring for livestock, including two horses. After work, Milo tried shooting under John Denton's watchful eye, but usually they went swimming, fishing, or mountain climbing. Both boys had a wonderful summer, so much so that the next year they decided to work as farmhands for another summer.

It was during that second summer that Milo met Anne Pitkin, "a peach of a girl and sweet 17." From then on, he saw her almost every day and liked her more and more. He became friends with her father. Milo repaired an old radiator for him and put it into the father's 1913 Ford. Again, he would go fishing with John Denton, sometimes cooking their catch on the spot. Milo claimed it was the best fish he ever ate. One day, Milo put his life-guard training to use when he rescued little Hugh Denton from drowning in an old swimming hole. Suddenly, Milo was a hero.

HEROIC FIGURES WERE AN IMPORTANT PART of Milo's boyhood and he admired and was influenced by several in his local community. In addition to Uncle Rudolf, with his Old-World aesthetics and talents, there was another man whose early influence on Milo was enduring. There was no medicine in his family background "as far back as we dare trace either side of the family," Milo once quipped, but there was Dr. Augustine C. McGuire. Six years after retiring from medicine, Milo described their pivotal encounter this way:

> At that time, we had a family physician called Augustine
> C. McGuire, and whenever we got sick, he would come over
> to the house and take care of us. In those days, doctors made
> house calls, and I thought he was great. One time after we
> had moved into the last house that I'd ever lived in while I

was in Pelham, we were cleaning the place out and there was
a trash pile used to burn up the stuff that they took out of
the house. And there were some broken beer bottles in it and
somehow as a kid I fell down and cut my wrist. Dr. McGuire
came over and sewed my wrist up. I thought that was a ter-
rific thing to do and I decided that's what I would like to do
the rest of my life.

Milo carried that memory with him all his life—as well as the little scar on his wrist, still visible in 1991when he pushed up the cuff of his sleeve to show me.

Though Milo had set his sights on becoming a doctor in junior high, his goal was briefly diverted during his freshman year at Columbia University. Charles Lindbergh's spectacular solo crossing of the Atlantic the previous May had ignited in Milo a passion for flying. He now wanted to pursue "the goal of aviation," as he wrote in his diary in January 1928. In efforts to emulate his hero Lindbergh, Milo "swore off coffee, tea, tobacco and liquor," but not for moral reasons. Physical fitness was of utmost importance to Lindbergh, who believed that caffeine would reduce the steadiness of hand and eye. Though Milo's aspirations to become an aviator were short-lived, he incorporated his hero's philosophy into his own life. Lindbergh's abstemious regime would continue to serve Milo well in future years as a surgeon and later as a pilot. Extremely self-disciplined, Milo made it a rule to eat moderately, to walk or use a bike for transportation when he could, and to opt for the stairs rather than take an elevator.

In fact, it was in a stairwell where Milo and Betsy first crossed paths. As she remembered, it was the young doctor's first day of his internship (following his graduation from Columbia University College of Physicians and Surgeons in 1934) and he was taking an exploratory tour of The Brooklyn Hospital.

CHRISTMAS AT
THE BROOKLYN HOSPITAL, 1934

Eventually I even addressed him by his first name.
—Betsy Fritz

"BY DECEMBER 1934 MOST OF MY classmates had already finished their training and left," Betsy wrote of the time just prior to her graduation from nursing school at The Brooklyn Hospital in New York City. "But I was still in my student uniform making up the time I had lost when I had been hospitalized with possible rheumatic fever and aching knees." The delay would prove fortuitous. Betsy described how the romance between Dr. Milo Fritz, then six months into his two-year residency at the hospital, and nursing student Elizabeth Berry had begun:

> Now I was assigned to night duty on the acutely ill side of
> the pediatric ward. The department occupied the entire top
> floor of the old building. It was divided into two parts with
> the front half for older and convalescent children and the
> back portion was divided in half—one side for tiny infants
> and the other half for acutely ill children.

At Christmas time, as was customary, a floor-to-ceiling tree appropriately decorated was placed in the front half of the Ward for the older children. As a night nurse assigned to the back part of the department, I felt it seemed too dreary for this time of the year. The young patients were either too young or too ill to take much notice of tinsel or red bows but for the rest of us and especially for the visiting parents it was certainly lacking in seasonal cheer.

After I had given the last feeding, medication, diaper change and all was quiet I took matters in my own hands to remedy this lack of Christmas spirit. I called the Engineering Department and asked them to send somebody up with a saw for cutting a tree. When the man arrived, I boldly took him to the other end of the Ward and asked him to cut about three feet off the top of the big, decorated tree. As a result, I at least had a dandy little tree for our area albeit undecorated.

Not having any money with which to purchase some decorations I had to make do with what was at hand. This was back in the days before individually packaging, dispensing, and charging the patients for whatever was needed for his or her care. Every floor had quantities of whatever might be needed, from medications to dressings, to soap. For instance, on this Ward were large boxes of safety pins for diapers and these I strung together to make a bright chain to drape on the boughs. The same for paper clips. It was the custom to place on the patient's chart cover a red, green, blue, gold, or silver seal indicating whether the patient was surgical, medical, obstetrical, orthopedic service, etc. By placing two of these seals back to back with a bit of black surgical thread protruding from the top for a hanger I had what looked to be a round traditional Christmas tree ornament. Charting was done in those days before computers, by writing on the patient's chart with "dip" pens using blue ink in the daytime and red during the night. The "gold" pen nibs turned upside down and hung from the tip of a tree branch by almost invisible surgical silk appeared to be tiny golden candles. There was plenty of cotton for "snow" around the base.

It was fun to do, satisfying to me and I was glad that I had been so brave as to "steal" part of the big tree and I am sure that the missing part was hardly noticed.

Many hospital employees came to see the little tree. One attending surgeon brought his young son to the hospital to view it. It seemed to cause unwarranted commotion and more and more people visited the Ward. These visitors came in the daytime and I never saw them as I was off duty, sleeping. One person in particular, an intern, wanted to meet the nurse who had done this and he was told that it was the night nurse.

After "bedtime" and the bright overhead lights were turned off I would take each infant out to the desk where I could sit while I was giving them their late evening bottle. I was comfortable and so were they being held and in the soft light from the desk lamp. This is how that curious and very charming intern found me when he came to meet the night nurse. After that he came each evening to sit and talk to me while I carried on my duties. This intern was Milo Fritz who had passed me on the stairs on July first when he had just arrived at The Brooklyn Hospital.

He asked me to go Christmas shopping with him but I refused. He asked me to go out more than once but I continued to say no. I found him friendly and charming, very much so, but I did not want to start something that would not be special and lasting. I did not want to risk a brief acquaintance and then be dropped as he had done with so many other nurses. I was very shy and very, very inexperienced. I hardly knew him and yet I felt very much in love with this stranger. He kept on asking and I kept on declining. He persisted and finally won by asking me to go to The Bronx Zoo to see the blood sweating hippopotamus. Eventually I even addressed him by his first name.

At The Brooklyn Hospital it was customary on Christmas morning for all of the nurses not on duty to get up very early and parade two by two through the hospital corridors singing carols. And to end up in a circle out of doors in front of the main entrance singing. The interns were encouraged to join us and their customary place was at the rear of the procession. Not so with this intern who with another, Joe McConnel, kept racing about to be right behind or next to me. I am sure that my face was as red as the lining of my cape which we wore with the sides folded back showing the red lining for Christmas cheer.

Fraternization between student nurses and the house staff was not exactly forbidden but it certainly was not encouraged. As students we were well insulated from the real world and though it was not a religious institution, life for the student nurse was much the same as life in a convent. One was either on duty, in class, studying or asleep. We were over-trained and under educated. So, imagine my surprise when the caroling was over and Miss Anna Bentley, our formidable Superintendent of Nurses said, "Doctor, would you like to come into the Nurses Dining Room and have breakfast with Miss Berry?" Of course, he would and did. We nurses sat at round tables of six, so one of the girls gave up her place and this brave man in white, afraid of nothing, got in line, picked up his tray of breakfast and braved the female sanctuary.

PART II

Duke

PART II

Duke

RESIDENCY: DUKE MEDICAL
SCHOOL, 1936

Duke, you know, was set down in a place where the medical care was about 100 years behind the times in the early '30s.

—MILO FRITZ

Aᴄfter completing his two-year internship at The Brooklyn Hospital, Milo decided to do another residency at Duke Medical School. In a 1982 interview with medical historian Kenneth Kastella, Milo described what led him to follow up his Columbia General Surgery Residency with a second residency at Duke:

> *I had a wonderful teacher named Alexander Gutman whose work on gout is only now being recognized as having been significant. I thought the world of him, so as I neared the end of my medical school career, I went to him and said, 'What would you suggest as postgraduate education?'... He said, 'I think you should take what we call a rotating internship, two years. Go through OB/GYN, surgery, medicine,*

*pediatrics, and specialties as it happened to be so you get an
overview of the whole thing.' And I have never, never regret-
ted it.*

*. . . I wanted to get into the Mayo Clinic, so I went out
to the Mayo Clinic: no dice. They missed their opportunity.
. . . I soon discovered—this was stroke of genius you might
say—that in order to get what you want, you have to go in at
a lower grade. Duke appealed to me.*

Milo had planned to stay just a year to "finish out the gaps" in the excel-
lent training he had received at the Columbia College of Physicians and
Surgeons, then "go to Europe for as long as $500 will last, get married
in October and open up soon after somewhere in Westchester [NY]." He
also planned to become an obstetrician and gynecologist. However, Milo's
experiences while at Duke changed all that.

Duke School of Medicine and its hospital opened their doors in 1930,
just six years before Milo's arrival in the summer of 1936. Duke's teaching
program was run by clinical chiefs who were graduates of Johns Hopkins,
and the new medical school was already ranked by the American Medical
Association as one of the top twenty schools in the country when Milo
entered its general surgery residency program. Located in the picturesque
town of Durham, North Carolina, Duke was the only major medical facility serving the Carolinas. Its hospital and outpatient clinic drew people
from all over this poor, rural region, from the Appalachian foothills to the
remote enclaves dotted along the Atlantic coastline.

Even though Milo already had two years of postgraduate training, he
applied as a general surgical intern for the only spot available—available
because one of the surgical interns had contracted tuberculosis. But he was
in. And Duke, as Milo explained in our 1991 interview, prepared him for
what he would face in Alaska:

*Dull as I was about the ways of the world in those days,
I somehow realized that if I could just get in the place, at
any level, that I could go on and get specialized training
when a vacancy on the house staff occurred. So, I took an
internship and, in a manner of speaking, started all over
again as an intern at Duke. . . . In the surgical first year
you rotated through the various services, one of which was
urology where I learned a great deal about that important*

*specialty. And the other one was orthopedic surgery, which
did me no harm in my wanderings through Alaska later on.*

MILO'S INTERNSHIP AT DUKE BEGAN ON JULY 1, 1936. In a letter to his
parents about a week later, Milo described the health and living conditions
prevalent in the region beyond Durham:

> *Many live in the most appalling poverty. It seems so un-
> necessary. The earth will grow anything. Their position is like
> that of the early Arctic explorers who cooked the seal and
> bear meat thus killing the substances in the meat that would
> have prevented scurvy. If these folks would just grow a few
> vegetables instead of entirely tobacco, pellagra (a horrible
> disease caused by vitamin deficiency characterized by sores
> on the places exposed to the sun, diarrhea, and various forms
> of dementia) would be wiped out.*
>
> *The doctors at first were antagonistic to this place
> [Duke], feeling it was taking the bread out of their mouths.
> But it does quite the contrary. They send a patient in, we
> work him up, treat him and send the patient back to him
> (if he can be treated on the outside). We also send letters
> to these doctors describing what we found and what we
> did and what they should do. So slowly the ill feeling is
> disappearing.*
>
> *My duties at present consist of the admission and pre-
> and post-operative care of white and colored urology females
> and of colored surgical males—a motley bunch of almost
> unbelievable low mental and moral level. I have one feeble-
> minded white girl of 15 who had a baby 10 days ago.*
>
> *Yesterday I had a 16-year-old colored boy in clinic who
> had both syphilis and gonorrhea! Cases in children of 5 to10
> are not uncommon. The tragic thing is that we treat them but
> what good is that since they spread the disease far and wide
> among themselves? No public health or preventive measures.
> Too awful—but lots of practice for us!!!*
>
> *. . . My room is about the Brooklyn size but it has a nice
> large closet and a wash basin with a built-in medicine cabi-
> net. There are also built-in cockroaches of tremendous size*

and extreme squishiness. If they bit, they would have a bite like the kick of a mule. They are friendly, literary creatures and are most often found reproducing cozily between my books.

At Duke, in the tradition of Johns Hopkins, an intern was responsible for his patients 24/7. Though used to lack of sleep and hard work, Milo worked from July 1 to November 15 without one day off and by the fall of 1936, the grind was taking a toll on his spirits, as Milo wrote in a letter home:

> *The leisure I thought I'd have is just a joke. There is no specified time off, there is no piano, and there is not the remotest possibility of taking up either German or boxing—alas.*
>
> *. . . I've not been away from this place for more than 2 hours at a stretch since I got here. I'm slowly going nuts. If it were not for the weekly movie and the beauty of the campus, I'd go nuts. . . . The work here is easy enough but the intolerable part is that there is no time off. I miss Betty [as he originally called her] very badly and hate to wait another year before getting married.*

Milo was also becoming increasingly worried about contracting tuberculosis (TB). Following another practice the senior doctors brought with them from Johns Hopkins, Duke did not isolate its TB patients from other patients in the surgery ward, which was why, as Milo told his parents when he was accepted at Duke, the spot in general surgery had suddenly opened up for him.

Milo was on the verge of quitting when Dr. Anderson, Chief of Ophthalmology, and Dr. Eagle, Chief of Otolaryngology, said, "Look, our internship in those two specialties is free and it will lead to a residency. If you'll take it, we'll promise you that you can go through the residency."

Finding a way to transfer out of his unhappy general surgery internship into a specialty with less fraught working conditions was a huge relief to Milo. Years later, he explained:

> *It was medicine and—it's like falling in love in those days—you fell in love with the nearest girl to you. What the hell! EENT sounded interesting to me, so I went into it. And since ophthalmology and otolaryngology had not been part of my rotating internship, it sort of rounded out*

*my education. And during the three-and-a-half years that
I was on the service, I learned a great deal about those specialties. In those days it was possible for one mind to grasp
the fundamentals of both specialties whereas nowadays you
have people who do nothing but ears, nothing but plastic
surgery of the lids, or just cataract extractions, let alone doing all of those things.*

Shortly after his transfer to EENT in November, Milo wrote home,
and continued to keep his parents updated on his progress with frequent
letters:

Nov. 29, 1936

*I am really accomplishing something. . ." I expect to be
asked to stay another year in EENT . . . and if I do, I'll get 20
D a month so I'll be financially independent of your generosity. I want to stay here if I can because the work here is on the
very frontier of EENT, because it will give me expertise in a
very lucrative specialty—all before I'm 30.*

Dec. 6, 1936

*The nose and throat business is doing nicely and I keep our
service going well by fixing the noses and throats of all the patients I previously had on Urology & Orthopedics. We Fritzes
leave no stones unturned. The eye work (ophthalmology), the
E of EENT, has me baffled though because the refraction end
of it, i.e., fitting glasses to you, is tainted with mathematics
and physics—two subjects that have always thrown me for a
loss. However, I rassle with Brother Thorington's well-known
classic [Refraction of the Human Eye and Methods by James
Thorington, 1916] on the subject for at least an hour or two
a day and am slowly and painfully learning the hocus pocus
of fitting glasses.*

*There is no doubt that ophthalmological surgery is re-
ally the most delicate. One slip and, by gum, you've blinded
your patient in that eye. I haven't done any eye ops yet, but
I will soon, and now as never before am I glad that I have
assiduously avoided liquor, tobacco, and coffee because my
hands after a good night's sleep are just as steady as a couple
of jolly old rocks. I've even given up beer—nature's noblest*

drink—because I notice I have a little tremor the next day—
even after the one or two glasses I drink.
    . . . Pop, this year is far from futile. It would have been
had I not changed to this service. I am not quite as thick as I
look and would have quit Jan. 1st had I not got a break.

THE ALLURE OF ALASKA

Adventure is a sign of incompetence.
—VILHJALMUR STEFANSSON

DURING THE SECOND YEAR OF MILO'S RESIDENCY at Duke, Larry traveled to Durham and briefly became a patient in the Duke EENT department, as Milo described in a letter home:

> The week was made eventful by the arrival of good old
> Larry. No sooner did he get here than I sat him down on an
> examining chair and had a look at the schnozzle that has
> caused him so much trouble. It was in bad shape to begin
> with and was made worse by getting socked a few times
> while he was at Virginia. Glenn Slayer operated on him the
> next day and it was the second most difficult operation of
> this type he had ever done, but he got an excellent result
> and Larry should be much more socially acceptable than
> heretofore. . . . He stood the operation well, had a cocaine
> jag after it, but no pain to speak of. [Cocaine was com-
> monly used as a topical anesthetic for EENT operations at

this time. A "jag," or period of sleeplessness/restlessness, was a listed side effect.]

Milo had recently stayed with his brother in New York City, a visit that would change the course of the young doctor's life.

By 1937, Larry had moved to Manhattan after graduating with honors from the University of Virginia in 1933. The golden-haired Yankee had majored in economics and French and enjoyed his life as a Virginia gentleman, photographing Charlottesville's Southern charms as well as gravitating to other aspects of its culture.

This was the time of Prohibition. Through experimentation and ingenuity, Larry, like many of his UVA classmates, became proficient at the craft of fermentation, creating alcohol from "anything," he later claimed, "—including old socks." Though generally courtly, even shy, Larry had apparently gotten into a few not-so-gentlemanly scrapes during his college years, judging by Milo's letter about his brother's "schnozzle," or Larry may have taken up boxing, an interest he shared with Milo, and one of the few sports popular at the University during the Depression.

Like Milo, Larry had been steeped in the arts growing up. Both brothers had developed an appreciation for painting, poetry, drama, and classical music; both had learned to play the piano as children. Larry had a fine singing voice and near perfect pitch. At Virginia, his musical tastes were broadened by his friendship with a professor named Howard Lee. The professor, an avid collector of traditional American folk songs, loved to sing and play the guitar and threw "wonderful parties," according to my father, whose friendship with Howard would endure for decades. During that time, Howard's appreciative audience would continue to grow. In the late 1940s, dozens of songs sung by Lee would be recorded by the Library of Congress, and, in 1962, the professor's reputation in this arcane area of American music would draw a young Bob Dylan to his door.

Larry took up the guitar and the recorder to play for fun at Howard's parties and other social gatherings, but his abiding interest was classical music. Larry had fleetingly considered pursuing a master's degree in music, but his father squelched that idea. "You're not a good enough musician," Henry wrote him. "You'd never be able to support yourself." Get a job, he instructed.

By the time of Milo's visit, his younger brother had gotten a job writing advertising copy for J. Walter Thompson. Larry was living in a sparely furnished apartment in a three-story brick townhouse in the heart of Greenwich Village while casting about for something more adventurous to do. He continued to strike up friendships with interesting and unusual people. One of these was the celebrated Icelandic explorer Vilhjalmur Stefansson, an accomplished, charismatic figure who lived in New York City when not away on one of his periodic expeditions to the polar regions of Canada and Alaska. Then in his mid-fifties, Stefansson was a man of great energy and persuasiveness who liked to regale audiences with his amazing stories about "living with the Eskimo" and thriving in what he saw to be the "friendly" wilderness of the Arctic. Stefansson gave lectures promoting himself and his books, while extolling the virtues and promise of life in Alaska and the Arctic. He also frequented Greenwich Village cafes, the cultural and intellectual hubs of the time, and was quite a sensation.

Larry became an admirer of Stefansson, whom he described as a "great explorer" and a man with "impeccable taste in women." Among the books on Larry's bookshelf during his "Barrow Street days" was Stefansson's *The Northward Course of Empire*, one of the explorer's numerous popular and scholarly publications about the Arctic and its peoples. On the flyleaf, Stefansson had inscribed: "To Laurens Fritz who thinks of practicing the preachings of Vilhjalmur Stefansson, Sept. 18/37."

Larry was deep in the throes of Stefansson-induced "Arctic Fever" when Milo arrived from Duke. In one photograph of the interior that has survived, Larry's Spanish guitar rests between a stylish but well-worn settee and a bookcase crammed with books. I had long remembered that photo, recognizing the guitar that my father had passed on to me along with his interest in folk music. Returning to the photo in recent years, I noticed an overlooked detail: pinned on the wall over the settee is a huge map of Alaska.

Milo's trip to New York was prompted by a malpractice suit, extremely rare in those days. The Brooklyn Hospital was being sued and Milo was asked to testify. As he recalled:

> *A patient, when I was at The Brooklyn Hospital, had been brought in to have something done on his nose, and somehow got on the tonsil list. I started taking out his tonsils and he rebelled, which was perfectly proper, and decided to sue the hospital. . . . But the suit didn't come up for trial until after I*

had moved my activities to Duke University. . . . The insur-
ance company needed my testimony, and so they offered to
pay my way. . . . That was at the depths of the Depression, and
to have your way paid to and from Durham, North Carolina,
and New York, that was like pennies from heaven—more
than that—dollars from heaven. . . . I was glad to do that
since life was pretty tough down there and pretty restricted.
So, I went up and went to visit my brother Larry. . . . Spread
on his desk was The Governor's Report on the Territory of
Alaska *by John Troy, who was the governor. It described the*
condition of health among the Eskimos and the Indians up
there. Prominent among their difficulties, besides tuberculo-
sis which was rampant, were those frightful afflictions of the
eyes and ears.

Previously, Milo had considered going to China after completing his residency at Duke. During that same trip to New York, he was interviewed by the Presbyterian Board of Missions with the idea of going to the Peking Union Medical College. As he described the experience: "I wanted to go there because the people of China were benighted and lacking in medical care, but when they got to the religious angle of it and began to pray for me right there in the interviewing room, I felt that wasn't for me. And then I saw this stuff on Larry's desk and read the governor's report, I said to myself, 'Why worry about taking the mote out of the Chinese eye, when we have a beam to take out of our own?' And so, I decided then I was going to Alaska when I got through at Duke."

Milo and Betsy had talked about going north before—on vacation, a float trip down the McKenzie River in Canada. But *moving* to Alaska? What did Betsy think of that? "She required no persuasion at all," Milo recalled, years later, adding:

She was an old-fashioned girl and went along with the
admonition in one of the Old Testament books that said,
'Where thou goest, there go I,' so she didn't give a hang one
way or another where we went. When I got books from the
library on Alaska, she read them too, and so she became
very familiar with not only the medical problems, but also
the economic and cultural problems that existed up there.
So, she was an enthusiastic participant. She didn't weep and

cry and carry on about leaving her family or the South '48,
she was glad to go.

The seed for Milo's lifelong fascination with Alaska had been planted. And Larry? His dreams of Alaska and the Arctic faded when he realized that he could not realistically hope to support himself as a copywriter in the Far North. In the fall of 1938 Larry boarded the *Edinburgh Castle* and sailed off to South Africa, where he had landed an advertising job promoting oil for a firm in Cape Town. Larry was well settled into his new life in the British colony, enjoying the cultured and privileged lifestyle of an American ex-pat, when Milo's letters began arriving from Alaska in 1940.

MARRIAGE TO
"AN OLD-FASHIONED GIRL"

*If I wait till I can afford to get married it will be another
5 years. And that just won't do. . . . two years without
Betty will be very tough indeed.*

—MILO FRITZ, APRIL 1937

O N JUNE 15, 1937, MILO AND Betsy "committed matrimony," as Milo phrased it, in Betsy's hometown of Tioga, a small rural community in upstate Pennsylvania. The wedding was held in St. Andrews Protestant Episcopal Church, a church started by Betsy's great, great, great grandfather. Younger sister Margaret was Betsy's maid of honor; her brother Thomas an usher. Milo's brother Larry was best man.

Henry and Amelia did not attend the ceremony. Perhaps their absence was due to their own deteriorating marriage; within a few years they would be living apart. Perhaps it was Henry's way of expressing his disapproval of Milo's marriage to a woman without a college education. Once again, a Fritz patriarch deeming an offspring's choice of spouse unacceptable?

Predictably, Milo kept up a parallel Fritz tradition—sons did not follow their father's wishes. Later in the summer, Henry sent the newlyweds a fine painting he had completed of the Duke Chapel. Milo wrote back that he and Betsy were "both nuts about it" and equanimity seemed to prevail.

As a young girl, Betsy had been introduced to genealogy by her grandmother, and this interest would continue to occupy her spare time throughout her life. Was this avid interest in researching her family tree perhaps partially fueled by the early Fritz family slight? It's hard to know, but Betsy's diligence bore fruit. She would later trace her lineage back to Plymouth colony governor William Bradford and another ancestor who fought in the Revolutionary War. This documentation would qualify Betsy to become a member of the Daughters of the American Revolution. Perhaps by tracing her family's roots back to colonial patriots, Betsy was reaffirming her worthiness—to herself, at least, and perhaps to her father-in-law.

Born Elizabeth Mersereau Berry in 1913, Betsy was the daughter of Thomas J. Berry and his wife Margaret. A string of ancestors named Thomas J. Berry had made their home in Tioga since "the first Thomas Berry arrived there in 1792," according to Betsy's account. "He had a roadhouse in his log cabin and also in it was the first school, post office, voting place, and the organization of the county."

Betsy's early forbears were on their way north to settle in New York, but stopped overnight at the town's inn, which served as the local pub and public house. All their plans changed that night when Tom Berry won the inn in a poker game. As a result, the Berry Family remained, becoming one of Tioga's prominent nineteenth-century families, developing their farm with great success and eventually building a lovely Greek-revival home, the focal point of Betsy's childhood.

As a young teenager, Betsy attended Ashley Hall, a private all-girls boarding school in Charleston, South Carolina. In addition to academic coursework and appreciation for the arts, Ashley Hall offered sewing and other domestic skills that would serve Betsy well in the future. She would occasionally spend weekends with classmates and ride horses on their plantations, enjoying a privileged lifestyle. However, when Betsy was about sixteen, her family's finances suffered a major setback. During the Great Depression, her father became ill and their fine house and 800 acres of land had to be sold—bought by a family friend, Albert Kreiger. Following her parents' reversal of fortune, Betsy returned to Tioga where she completed her last two years of high school, graduating from Tioga High School.

The effects of Betsy's time at Ashley Hall—brief as it was—would prove lasting. Throughout her long life in Alaska, Betsy would continue to have a distinct air of gentility about her, often in marked contrast to her surroundings. In deportment, manners, and temperament Betsy retained the quiet grace of a lady.

AFTER THEIR TWO-WEEK HONEYMOON AT MONHEGAN ISLAND, Maine, Milo and Betsy returned to Durham and prepared for the remaining two-and-one-half years of Milo's Duke residency. Betsy found a nursing job at nearby Watts Hospital, but finances remained tight, a situation the couple seemed to face with cheery resourcefulness. They had been impecunious since the early days of their courtship while at The Brooklyn Hospital, as Milo elaborated:

> I earned nothing a month and some people said I was worth every cent of it! And so, we took advantage of the many things around New York City that you can enjoy that cost nothing, or very little, like going on ferry boat rides or taking a trip out to the Statue of Liberty, or going to the Bronx Zoo, or visiting the Metropolitan Museum of Art, the Museum of Natural History, the Hispanic Museum, the Numismatic Museum, going swimming out at Jones Beach, things like that.
>
> We never thought that we were poverty stricken, but we were. Once in a while my mother or my father would slip me a few dollars. That's the only money I had since there was no way of earning money at that time since the internship was extremely demanding. As I look back on it now, we must have worked 16 to 18 hours a day sometimes, and occasionally would go a day and sometimes as long as 36 hours without more than a catnap on a stretcher or something like that in between the demands of the job.
>
> . . . but I always had an afternoon off a week, and Betsy and I would go on one of these expeditions together, and once

in a while somewhere one of us would get a little money and
we'd go to the movies, but we couldn't afford that very often,
not even in those days, which was during the depths of the
Depression.

As Milo wrote his parents in 1937 during the newlyweds' first fall at
Duke:

Let me tell you that we do our cooking thru our own ingenuity and by such arrangements as would make Houdini
jealous. We cook on the electric stove you helped us to get on
a series of boards on the floor. We get water from the john
and ice cubes from our landlady. We have one small room
that a bed 1/3 fills. If you are willing to come and enjoy Xmas
with us, we'll guarantee that you'll have fun and lots to eat
(Betsy's as fine a cook as she is a dressmaker). But if you can't
eat in a bedroom from fine dishes washed in water from the
bathroom, you'd better not come.

Betsy was proving to be a prudent and resourceful mate, Milo an attentive and appreciative husband. In those early days, Milo even helped Betsy
with the task of washing her long dark hair, which he so admired. He wrote
an anecdote about it in a letter to his parents that same fall:

Monday night I was stripped to the waist and Betsy was
kneeling over the bathtub in which I was vigorously washing
her hair when Uncle Elb (Mr. Smith of Brooklyn) came in
and visited us. I finished my job and put on my shirt while
Betsy unwrapped the towel she had around her neck to protect her dress (even tho it was an old one) and then we talked
to him over a pitcher of lemonade. It was good to see someone from home. He was tickled over my washing Betsy's hair
tho it is a self-appointed task which, I say with all modesty,
I do very efficiently, if you can accept a certain amount of
splashing of the walls and ceiling and the semi-submerged
state of Betsy when I finish.

Milo also took an interest in Betsy's creativity with a needle and thread
and in women's fashions in general, writing in 1937:

Friday nite was the first med school dance and the problem was an evening dress for Betsy. I had my 12 yr. old tuxedo which still serves and the remnants of a dress shirt of

doubtful vintage. Three days before the dance Betsy started
making a dress of silver with a red trailing scarf and by golly
it was a beautiful piece of work. She fixed her hair elaborate-
ly. I kicked in with an orchid and the effect was devastating:
she really was quite the most distinguished looking girl at the
dance . . . and am I proud!

And in 1938:

For the Senior Dance of the Graduating class of Watts
Hospital. Betsy wore a dress of flowered lace, flowers in her
hair and was as usual the most distinguished looking woman
there.

Such detailed observations of women and how they dressed would
continue to punctuate Milo's correspondence throughout his life, often
to the surprised delight of his readers, leaving no doubt that Milo was
an unabashed admirer of attractive, well-turned-out women. For several
years in the early 1950s, Milo was Alaska's American Medical Association
president and, often accompanied by Betsy, attended the AMA's annual
conventions "outside"—as Alaskans call the lower forty-eight states. In his
newsletters, Milo's commentary would range freely from his experiences
inside the lecture halls to the dinners and peripheral social events attended
by his medical colleagues and their spouses. Milo's lively accounts would
invariably include details about the host city and the fashions worn by the
women he observed at these events.

Henry Fritz, also a connoisseur of beautiful women, took a while to
warm to his degreeless daughter-in-law, despite her charms and talents.
Milo, however, expressed no such qualms, writing home enthusiastically
shortly before their first anniversary:

[Betsy] is a generous creature and she shows this trait
more every day . . . Boy what an asset she will be to me in
whatever community we set up in to practice. She's a plum if
there ever was one. This PM we played tennis and walked in
the sunshine in the forest after I had scandalized the neigh-
borhood by cleaning the car dressed only in my swimming
trunks. Sally needed the cleaning, I needed the sunshine, and
the neighbors needed a good scandalizing.

During that summer of 1938, they jumped at the chance to housesit
for friends who lived outside of Durham, as Milo wrote in a letter home:

We're living in the country in the style of #4 Poplar of the old days. There are no neighbors and the only sounds are those of bird and beast as they potter about their multitudinous tasks in the shrubbery, in the garden and the nearby woods. Woodpeckers machine-gun the dead trees and rabbits peer into the garage as I minister to Sally's morning wants, smoke curls from the chimney and there are no neighbor's brats and radios to befoul and besmirch the otherwise pure air. We are both healthier and happier and ever so much cooler.

On the Frontier of EENT
Training at Duke

My God, the time I spent down at Duke University interning I had the time of my life. I worked like hell and I was so tired sometimes I couldn't think straight. I've read my diary and I never read any beefs in it.

—Milo Fritz, 1982

Excerpts from Milo's letters to his parents offer a glimpse of the medical skills he was acquiring during his remaining two-and-a-half years at Duke. He was candid about the "ups" as well as the "downs."

Oct. 10, 1937

> Last week I chased a peanut around a kid's lung with a bronchoscope a la Chevalier Jackson, whose instruments we use, and finally emerged triumphant with the peanut in the forceps. I also started teaching my elective course in EENT. I am learning a great deal by this teaching and shall, as a result, be much better qualified to pass the American

Boards of Ophthalmology and Otolaryngology than I otherwise would be.

Nov. 7, 1937

Professional life goes on much as before. The only triumph is the modest success of the elective course I'm giving in EENT. Attendance is high, but the course is pretty basic. It will improve with each quarter I give it. I also gave one lecture to the nurses in EENT without preparation—I got 15 minutes' notice.

Dec. 20, 1937

Last Thurs. did my 1st major eye operation—just another step up the ladder—successfully.

Milo's previous "beef" about working conditions in general surgery erupted again in a letter home that winter—though it may not have made it into his diary and perhaps subsequently faded from his memory:

Feb. 12, 1938

You may also recall that I got the place because one of the interns came down with TB. You remember also that I was going to quit, but instead got a break and transferred to the ENT service. Well, conditions have not improved, for the day before yesterday one of this year's crop of surgical interns got TB! He is the fourth. And each one has been of the same service. It's so unnecessary and that's what makes it so awful. The chief, unlike Drs. Eagle and Anderson, doesn't seem to give a damn about his men. Please keep this to yourself. My last year here—when I don't care whether they can me or not—I'm going to do something about this if I can.

May 14, 1938

I can get a lot of operative work to do at Watts Hospital on two mornings a week under the aegis of Dr. Anderson, our professor of Ophthalmology here at Duke, providing I get the license [which Milo did—the cost to practice medicine in North Carolina then: $50]

July 14, 1938

Tell the folks that I am an instructor in EENT Surgery and House Staff Surgeon in that Specialty. I am now second in command.

Aug. 29, 1938

Did a radical mastoid on an 11-year-old kid yesterday and the operation was a success.

Sept. 25, 1938

The resident in surgery, Max Schiebel and I were sent to a Vet Hospital—i.e., veterinary, and there I removed the eye of a pretty little Pekingese who had a rare and malignant tumor in his left eye. You see my fame is spreading. . . . The high spot of the week however was an operation I was able to perform on a 72-year-old woman for cataract. In addition to the fact that she had been blind for twelve years, she had an over-ripe cataract and had increased intraocular tension. I did a combined cataract operation and decompression. And I was successful. I take the bandage off tomorrow and if she did not bleed into the eye, I will have really accomplished something against considerable odds.

Jan. 25, 1939

I have made three brilliant diagnoses judged not entirely by myself—which have made up a little for the poor job of two weeks ago when I messed up a cataract operation on a most uncooperative old Negress. The uncooperativeness is not an excuse. After all, the cooperative patients anyone can operate on successfully. It is the tough ones that show whether or not one is a hot surgeon or just a mediocre one.

That is how it goes with me. Just when I think that I really am good, I completely nullify something really brilliant by something abysmally stupid or clumsy. I do hope that the average will be good. Good intentions are not a substitute for good vision, however. And while on the subject, cataracts and other diseases of the eye are found most often in old eyes and therefore in degenerating eyes. That is what makes it so hard.

Aug. 29, 1939

I saw a two-year-old colored girl who stuck a pair of scissors in her left eye this p.m. and now has a prolapsed iris, a lacerated cornea, and a traumatic cataract. I had to get the operating room set up to do what I could to save the eye and while waiting for the wheels to go around I am attempting to finish this. I am not trying to impress you with my importance, but it is my delightful job to do all the operating that I can get hold of from June till I finish and since all the operating cannot be scheduled – much of it is emergency as in this case—I am on call most of the time for operating at all hours and seeing patients in consultation on the other services.

. . . Well, since the last paragraph I have done the operation on the little kid. I think that she will have a useful eye when the cataract is taken off later. A cataract, for your information, is any opacity of the lens. The kind most people think of is the senile type. It is just as though the lens of a camera instead of being transparent gradually became opaque—like ground glass. We remove the opaque lens (cataract) and the light rays can again reach the retina at the back of the eye. Since the lens of the eye is gone, we must supply one in the shape of a very thick glass in front of the eye. In the case of this incident the lens was traumatic—caused by the points of the scissors penetrating the lens. In the course of a few hours, it becomes opaque and the eye stays useless till some brilliant young ophthalmologist removes the cataract.

Tonight, I clipped off the iris that had stuck in the hole the scissors had made in the cornea. If no infection sets in, she has a potentially useful eye and a cosmetically inoffensive eye if, as soon as the effects of the scissors and my operation wear off, she has the cataract removed.

Sept. 9, 1939

This a.m. I operated, among others, on an 81-year-old white man who was as deaf as a fish. His left eyelid rolled out and made the eye look angry red. This is due to the loss of elasticity of the skin which happens in old age. In addition, he had a membrane growing over the eye—which you, of course, since you know what a cataract is would not call a cataract—called a pterygium. I transplanted the latter and did a plastic operation on the lid—the latter is the hard part; the former is a minor procedure. Enclosed is a rough sketch of what I did. It looked pretty good too.

Sour note. A few months ago, I removed the eye of a three-year-old colored girl for what I believed was a congenital glaucoma—hard eye. The microscopic sections of that eye were not rushed through because we thought it was just that. Imagine my chagrin to find only three weeks ago that the cause of the hardness of the eye was a glioma of the retina—a very malignant tumor which soon spreads to the brain.

I wrote to the doctor who sent the case and I find that the little girl is dying of spread–metastasis. If I had sense enough to suspect that tumor, I could have perhaps saved her life by X-Ray. This is the worst mistake that I have made in a long time. I hope that I will not make many more like it.
Oct. 22, 1939

Did a lot of work this week and feel that I have at last perfected a painless way of doing a complete removal of the ethmoid sinuses. Doing it is hard enough, but doing it painlessly is what I have been striving for since I learned the operation. I got an idea of how to do it from a French man named Laurens. I modified the idea and one of the other boys here is using it successfully and Dr. Eagle is going to begin to use it himself. My last two cases were women who had had previous operations that were very painful. They were very apprehensive so that since the method worked on them, I feel that it is good. They were the 10th and 11th consecutive cases. I had a few failures in the beginning because I was afraid to do too much, but now that I have studied the anatomy of the region and had a successful run of cases, all is well.
Oct. 22, 1939

Last Thursday while I was very busy my nurse told me that there was a young girl in the clinic to see me. I knew there must have been something unusual about it since she knows that I do not like to be interrupted. So, I quit what I was doing and went out. It was my little girl whose nose I had fixed the week before I came home. She came all the way from Elizabeth City by bus (175 miles) just to let me see her and to thank me. And I must say that she is now a little beauty. She is small, blonde, and shapely and I added

*what turned out to be a very nice little turned up nose. I
just could not think of anything to say. Her entire attitude
had changed. She was poised and confident. She wore inex-
pensive but tastefully selected clothes and a little go-to-hell
hat that was most becoming. To date this is the case that has
brought me the most satisfaction. It is fun to do all the other
stuff that comes in our specialties, but somehow changing
this girl from one who shuns her fellows on account of her
face to what she is now, normal, and really pretty, makes
me feel pretty good.*

MILO ALSO FOUND SATISFACTION IN ANOTHER ASPECT of his EENT residency—seeing patients at itinerant clinics in rural North Carolina for the
State Department for the Blind. Examinations were done in the field and
eyeglasses prescribed; minor surgical problems were taken care of at the
time if suitable conditions were available. All other patients needing surgery or extended treatments were sent back to Duke Hospital where Dr.
Fritz did the surgery.

"I learned my itinerant medicine at Duke, where I was also crazy
about going into the western hills of North Carolina, or to the little forgotten towns on the eastern shore of North Carolina, down toward Kitty
Hawk and Cape Hatteras." . . . "Most of the house officers, that is the
interns and residents and assistant residents, didn't like to go on these,
but I did!" Milo recalled. "And you also got paid a little bit for it and that
would give us a few dollars to add to what Betsy made, since she supported us while we were at Duke—supported herself, rather—I just had
my room and board and laundry at Duke. I learned how to do good work
on an itinerant basis."

Milo began doing these clinics in April of 1937, writing his parents
about it with great enthusiasm, "These clinics are godsends and not in dis-
guise either. We get them thru the kindness of the Prof. of Ophthalmology,
Dr. Anderson, who really has the welfare of his Housemen at heart."

In the fall of 1937 Milo wrote home, describing eye clinics held
in two tiny towns, 200 miles east of Durham in the coastal region of
North Carolina: "I got a sudden call to hold eye clinics at Manteo on
a Friday and at Camden on Monday, Oct. 25th. Here was a chance to
make 50 bucks minus 25 for expenses and see the country." Milo drove to

Elizabeth City where he met up with Mary Williams, the North Carolina state Public Health Nurse, at 7:00 the next morning. Convoying in two cars through unrelenting rain, they arrived in Manteo about 9:00. From his Nov. 7 letter:

> *Mary has her own Chevrolet sedan—"Lucy-Belle"—in which she runs all around in charge of the Eye Clinics held by the commission. They try to get local ophthalmologists to take the job at 25 D a day but in these counties there ain't no such doctor so they asked us. Nobody qualified would take the job, even here—i.e., nobody but me. "Sally" was loaded with $3,000 worth of equipment and at Kitty Hawk her rapidly disintegrating top began to blow off. The situation is a peculiar one—if you go 45-50 M.P.H. the force of the slipstream blows the top off and if you go less than 25 M.P.H. the top stays on but you don't get anyplace. I decided to put the top down because I had to get there by 9.*

> *The clinic was very large. There were 53 kids that I examined from 9 am to 7 pm. I was only required to see 25, but some of them had come all the way thru wind and rain from Hatteras Village—below Buxton.*

> *. . . My darkroom was the vault in the county courthouse. Of the 53—39 needed glasses, 10 had conditions which lenses would not correct and 4 were normal. The kids were not the sniveling type I had at Oxford last month. The boys were all very well developed intelligent and upstanding; the girls were all rugged also. There was one imbecile and one psychopathic personality but between these 2 and the other 51 there were no gradations. These kids get their strength fishing and farming and are the direct descendants of Elizabethans many of whose speaking mannerisms are still retained with a very pleasant accent.*

> *After the clinic I was almost blind myself, so Mary Williams and I stayed with a Mrs. Evans all nite after playing on the piano and got up in a sun-drenched Saturday am with nothing to do till Monday.*

> *Mary decided that she was willing to try to get to Hatteras in her car even tho we were told the road, such as*

it was, was washed out by yesterday's rains. So, we filled the
car with gas, oil and water and let all but 18 lbs. of air out
of the tires and set off.

As Milo wrote his family, he and Mary explored the Outer Banks, brav-
ing flooded roads, driving along the hard-packed beach, and getting stuck
in the sand several times—once with an incoming tide. Along the way they
were assisted by a variety of people they met—a couple of sailors from the
ferry, a fisherman, and two men with the Coast Guard—"fine red-cheeked,
healthy people whose generosity served us all the way down, saving us
from sea and sand."

We arrived . . . via the beach instead of "inside" and came to
the Wright Memorial at Kitty Hawk at about 3. There Orville
Wright made the first flight (100 yards) in a heavier than air,
motor-driven machine on Dec. 17, 1903. The monument is
a very beautiful airplane beacon (see photos). [Milo sent his
parents snapshots from this trip, one labeled: "Kitty Hawk -
Wright Brothers Memorial.] *This is a place that I've always*
wanted to see. I am seated in the rite foreground. In front of the
door is one of the Wright brothers who just dropped his teeth.
[Orville perhaps; Wilbur died in 1912.]

That night we stayed in a cabin at a closed-up tourist
camp (I'd meantime got my car from Manteo). We had a
woodstove fire and were comfortable.

Next am we drove to Camden where the clinic was held in
a dusty school building. My darkroom was improvised in the
alleyway between the girls' john and the hall. There I couldn't
help but observe along with my ophthalmic work that little
girls are just as obscene as little boys.

I saw 23 patients of not nearly the high type as those at
Manteo and fitted 18 pairs of badly needed glasses. 2 sets of
eyes were normal and 3 were not amendable to correction
with glasses.

That pm at 4:30 I left for Durham arriving there at 9:30—
which is not bad time. It was a fine trip and just two days ago
I received a check for $90 from the state, which combined
with the $25 from the Oxford clinic (received 10 days previ-
ously) made $115 - $27 or $88 profit which represents the

first jack I ever got out of being an M.D. It also came just in the nick of time as we were pretty badly bent financially. But the stuff I saw in these kids' eyes was of incalculable value from a professional standpoint and the only thing I could find wrong with the trip was leaving Betsy home.

PART III

Alaska Still Beckons

WORLD WAR II ALASKA AND THE ALEUTIAN CAMPAIGN

Conditions make the man and not man the conditions.
—ABRAHAM LINCOLN

IN THE SPRING OF 1941, AFTER OVER A YEAR of private practice in Ketchikan, Milo's life was abruptly impacted by world events. Milo, a reserve officer in the Army, was called up by New York State. At the end of May, Milo, Betsy, and their two-week-old son Jonathan returned to New York, where Milo promptly took his otolaryngology board exams, after reporting for active duty. As he recalled:

That was the time when Roosevelt got the Selective Service Bill passed by one vote, and it made it possible to call up reserve officers for a year's active duty. . . . And since there was no war going on, they asked—they didn't command—they said, 'How many of you fellas would like to go to Alaska?' And before they could change their mind, my hand shot up . . . before my hand could come down, they had my papers cut.

Dr. Fritz returned to Alaska as a first lieutenant with the Army Air

Force. Betsy and Jonathan stayed with her folks in Tioga, Pennsylvania. Milo's turnaround on the East Coast was quick, as Betsy noted:

> *While the ship was docked in Ketchikan, he not only had a chance to say goodbye to our friends, but to check on his last post-op patients before continuing north. When the ship reached its next port of call, he received mail which arrived in Ketchikan after he had left and some kind person in the front office put the mail on a northbound private plane to be delivered to Milo at the next stop. True Alaskan thoughtfulness. In this mail was a notice that Milo had passed his ENT board exams.*

Milo had now passed both the oral and the written exams for both ophthalmology and otolaryngology, returning to Alaska as its first board certified eye, ear, nose, and throat specialist.

Milo went on active duty at Fort Richardson and Elmendorf Airfield, a military base near Anchorage. Since June of 1940, the base had been undergoing dramatic enlargement in response to the growing threat from Japan in the Pacific. By the time Milo arrived the following summer, the population of the Anchorage area had swelled to over 8,000—more than doubling in eighteen months. Military personnel and construction workers for the base continued to pour into the area. The airfield would play a vital role as an air logistics center and staging area during the Aleutian Campaign.

Milo was classified as a flight surgeon, a misnomer since a flight surgeon traditionally neither flies nor does surgery but serves as a primary care physician for aviation personnel. The colonel, who oversaw all medical service in Alaska, permitted Milo to spend as much time as he wished at the base hospital—at that point just a cluster of low wooden buildings—after he completed his routine chores on the flight line. During his "office hour" he examined, treated and, where indicated, operated on many of the Army personnel.

Anchorage doctors began asking if Dr. Fritz would examine and treat civilians in need of his care. The Army not only approved this but encouraged him as well as other military doctors interested in caring for local people. When surgery was indicated, as it was with one of the town's leading citizens, Milo was permitted to operate in Providence Hospital after becoming a member of the staff in 1941. That was Milo's introduction to

Anchorage. "I resolved, more or less, I remember: If I survive this thing, I'm going to come back here later."

The military also sent Milo to remote parts of Alaska. After Milo had examined, treated, or operated on military personnel, or made arrangements for those needing extensive surgery and care to be shipped to Anchorage for surgery when he was back on base, he was free to care for civilian patients. Milo explained:

> Really, your medical skills during the war time went to pot, but there were various calls for ophthalmology and otolaryngology in the peripheral areas like Nome, or Valdez, or Kodiak, or Sitka, or Juneau, and so my commanding officer, a wonderful fellow named Colonel Luther Moore, would send me to those places, because I learned my itinerant medicine at Duke.

"These orders gave Milo an opportunity to travel over much of Alaska and to meet many Native patients," Betsy wrote. "He became more and more enamored with these remarkable, patient people and more and more in love with the then-Territory."

Milo's proclivities as a maverick and humorist were becoming apparent. A story about Milo soon found its way back down to Dr. Wilson, Milo's former partner in Ketchikan, who related it:

> They told this story about Milo when he got moved up there to Ft. Richardson. The war came along and on Washington's Birthday the general put a copy of Washington's Farewell Address on the bulletin board. So, Milo came along and looked at it and then he let out one of his cracks, "I always knew it took a long time to get word from Washington but I did not think it would take this long!"

ON A CLOUDY, FOGGY JUNE 1 IN 1942, an airplane en route to Elmendorf Airfield crashed on the formidable and unsurveyed flanks of volcanic Mt. Redoubt on Cook Inlet, 110 miles southwest of Anchorage. The plane crash drew now Major Milo H. Fritz into a heroic rescue mission. Nearly fifty years later, Milo described it to me this way:

> A pilot was coming back – I've forgotten his name – from out on the Aleutians and instead of taking the minimum en route altitude, he decided to fly at 7,000 feet on instruments.

*And he banged into Mt. Redoubt, which was 10,000 feet
high. The only reason we ever knew anything about it was
that his copilot was badly injured—one leg and one foot—
but [the pilot] wasn't hurt. It was an empty C-47 or DC-3.
He worked his way down to the beach and thumbed his way
into Anchorage and told us what had happened, so they sent
out a party in an airplane to spot the plane on the southeast
slope of Mt. Redoubt. Then they selected me as a volunteer
to lead a group of, I would say, about 20 men up there to
get the copilot. We went from Anchorage by boat to Harriet
Point and walked in through the most Godforsaken, mos-
quito-infested bunch of alders that you can imagine until we
got above the timber line, where of course, we found that the
service ceiling of the Alaskan mosquito is about 7,000 feet.
After that we didn't have any insects.*

*We found the pilot emaciated and dehydrated and unbe-
lieving that somebody was finally there to rescue him. I don't
know how many days he'd been there, but he'd been there
quite a while. We had brought along a device called a Stokes
litter, which was a litter that was shaped like a man with his
feet stretched out and his arms beside him, which would keep
him from rocking around. We put a splint on his leg—we
had brought along the necessary materials—gave him an in-
travenous shot of saline and fed him and got him down the
mountain in great shape to the lake where the float plane had
landed us before we'd walked to Mt. Redoubt.*

*We got letters of commendation and all that. I wrote the
thing up for my wife. She decided that it would be a darn
good article for* The Saturday Evening Post *and went over
it and ironed out some of the things that had no business
in there that were of a personal nature, and, by God, they
bought it.*

Milo's full account entitled, "Ambulance Case on Mt. Redoubt," was
published in *The Saturday Evening Post* Oct. 2, 1943. The dramatic rescue
story still resonates with Alaskans; it was reprised in a 2010 article by Clark
Fair published by *The Redoubt Reporter*, a Kenai Peninsula newspaper.

Two days after the plane crash on Mt. Redoubt, the Japanese bombed

Dutch Harbor in the eastern Aleutian Islands, the one-thousand-mile chain of volcanic islands that divides the Bering Sea from the Pacific Ocean. A few days later, Japan invaded and occupied the islands of Attu and Kiska in the western Aleutians in an attempt to get a toehold on the North American continent and divert American forces away from the main Japanese attack at Midway Island. The U.S. Army and Air Force responded and the Aleutian Campaign was underway. Though little known, Alaska's "Forgotten War," was the only World War II campaign fought on American soil.

Milo was moved out to the Aleutians as flight surgeon for the 343rd fighter group. "I was out on Amchitka and Adak. I also went to some of the other islands along the way, like Dutch Harbor and Umnak where there were Air Force bases."

The foggy, rain-drenched Aleutians were long renowned for their inhospitable terrain and treacherous flying conditions—"It's too thick to fly if you can't see your copilot" was a favorite wisecrack—adding to the difficulties of the Aleutian Campaign. As daunting as those rugged volcanic islands were for combat, they held a unique appeal to Milo, as he recalled his wartime service there:

> Speaking about the Aleutians, they are one of the most beautiful places you can imagine. They have a bad rap. People think it either rains all the time or that they're covered with ice and snow. They have no trees. The grass grows 6 ½ feet tall, and the air is clean and pure. And sure, it rains and blows and is clear and snows a little—all within a few hours—never-the-less, except for flying an airplane, it was a great place to be. Nobody was shooting at me, and when they had the battle of Attu, instead of taking those of us who were acclimated to the terrain and had the proper equipment, they took troops from California to fight that frightful battle. They wore leather shoes and they got frostbite and immersion foot and all that in addition to having to fight off the Japanese who were very determined.

To Milo's surprise and delight, Bob Hope brought his first-ever USO show to Alaska, even out to some of the desolate Aleutian Islands during the height of the Aleutian Campaign. For a week in September 1942, Hope and his intrepid entourage of singer-actress Frances Langford, comic Jerry Colona, guitarist-singer Tony Romano, and "one guitar" travelled 1600 miles throughout Alaska. They braved the war and bad weather to lift the spirits of troops who were, Bob Hope stated, "the loneliest guys in the world. Also, the coldest."

"Some of our toughest shows were around Unimak," Hope wrote in his book, *Bob Hope: A Life in Comedy*.

> At one place we had a lot of guys sitting on cold wet ground. Boy, were they rugged! I took cold shots before I left Hollywood, but that weather was too much for me. I caught a cold that I still haven't been able to shake. But I was happy there, and I told them so. You never heard such laughs, such cheering, and such applause. "I'm happy to be here where the action is," I told them. . . . The boys went for Frances in a big way.

The uplifting effects Hope's shows had on morale were confirmed by Milo, who attended one of the shows during the troupe's island-hopping trek out the Aleutian Island chain. Milo wrote his parents, describing the event while purposely self-censoring exact locations. An excerpt from Milo's letter was published soon afterward in his hometown newspaper, identifying the writer as "Dr. Milo H. Fritz, who is in charge of a traveling clinic somewhere north of Seattle," and "the elder son of Dr. Henry E. Fritz of Chester Park." Milo wrote:

> You have, no doubt, heard how Bob Hope the comedian and Frances Langford the singer came up here to entertain us. We're grateful for the time the men put in for us and we appreciate the inconvenience they are put to. But to see a real live girl and a celebrity, that was something none of us had ever hoped for. If ever one came, we expected she would call at the big posts and leave the smaller places, where they are still living in mud and tents, for the men.
>
> Well, there may be prettier girls than Frances Langford and without question there are better singers than Frances Langford but I know very well that there is no better loved girl in the world than Frances Langford—and not by two or even 10 men, but by a large number that is a military secret. Any one of them would gladly have died for her there and then. At this particular post when she stepped on the stage, the applause was deafening and rolled back and echoed and

re-echoed from the tin walls of the theater in great waves of sound. Then, just as suddenly as it had started, it stopped and there was absolute silence. Even "Consumptive Row" was silent—as she began to sing.

Out farther from here – much farther – where all there is is mud, tents, wind, and rain, we heard of their party and knew that they would not come. They might come as far as XXXXX we thought, but no further surely than XXXXX, but to the stunned surprise of everyone they came right out to XXXXX. It seems hard to believe that the girl could be more appreciated anywhere than she was at XXXXX, but that is true. As one big Georgian pilot said: 'To see that lil' old girl out here singin' to us in the mess hall, just about made me cry.' And, believe me, that guy is tough – combat pilot, squadron leader, and holder of the Distinguished Flying Cross. I saw common soldiers in their mud-stained fatigue dress – fresh off the 'cats' they were using to level the field, stand there rapt, with tears making streaks down their faces as quiet as men of stone. I saw sick and wounded men and officers seem to blossom as she sang. I saw kids who hadn't smiled for weeks, laugh and shout after the program was over and the small, courageous girl had sat down and eaten with the men out of a mess kit on a bare board table in the Quonset hut.

So, there may be better, braver, more beautiful, and more musical girls than Frances Langford – but you'd better not say it to any of us up here unless you want to die suddenly and painlessly.

As Frances Langford would later quip, "Bob said he would never take a woman up there again. They got all the attention." Frances certainly got Milo's—ever appreciative of bold and comely women.

IN 1943, THE HEADQUARTERS OF THE ELEVENTH AIR FORCE was moved to Adak and Milo was stationed there for a while. The Japanese bombers bypassed Adak. "I never heard a shot fired in anger in all the time I was there," Milo recalled. "That was just the grace, you know, when the list came out, I could have been sent anyplace."

Milo did see action of a different type following an airplane crash on Davis Field at Adak. An account of the incident was included in an interview of Milo that was published upon his retirement from medicine in 1985 by the *Homer News*:

> *Two planes taxiing onto the runway from different directions collided. And one burst into flame. Inside it were live ammunition and more fuel. Dr. Fritz and four others extracted the wounded pilot from his parachute harness and removed him to safety.*

Recalling the incident, Milo said, "It was crazy. If you had a minute to think about it, it's something nobody in their right mind would do. Gas and burning airplanes with ammunition in them is a tricky mixture."

For his heroism, Milo was awarded the Bronze Star Medal.

FOLLOWING THE ALEUTIAN CAMPAIGN, MILO WAS SHIPPED to Venice, Florida in 1943. Once again, he was able to live with Betsy and Jonathan, now two years old. Shortly after the birth of their son Pieter on June 30, 1944, until the end of the war, Milo was assigned to MacDill Army Airfield, near Tampa where he was in charge of eye, ear, nose, and throat medicine at the station hospital. While there, Milo met Dr. Phillips Thygeson, already one of the country's leading ophthalmologists, who held a similar position at a base nearby. Dr. Thygeson's postdoctoral research at University of Colorado was of great interest to Milo.

Dr. Thygeson had studied blinding trachoma among the Apache Indians at Ft. Apache in Arizona. The infectious disease causes the roughening of the inner surface of the eyelid that can be terribly painful and is a leading cause of blindness around the world. Working with another doctor, Dr. Francis I. Proctor, the two had discovered the cause of trachoma—a filterable microbe, now known as Chlamydia trachomatis—and, in 1939, had discovered that sulfonamides could cure trachoma.

While serving in Florida, Phil Thygeson and Milo used to meet weekly, alternating bases, when they would discuss patient care and medical matters at the two facilities. From these meetings developed a close personal and professional friendship.

Near the end of World War II, Dr. Thygeson was reassigned to Valley Forge Army Hospital where all of the severely injured eye care patients were being sent, either for treatment or to learn how to cope without sight if they could not be helped. He urged Milo to try for a temporary transfer to Valley Forge as it would offer Milo an opportunity to learn more and newer techniques. Milo opted not to follow that path, though the friendship endured throughout their lives, deepened by a monthly exchange of letters.

A troubling sense of time slipping away hit Milo when he was finally discharged in 1946. By then, Milo was nearing thirty-seven—approaching middle age. With a wife and two kids to support and his medical skills "gone to pot," as he put it, after over four years of military service, the doctor was at a professional crossroads. Where to now?

Milo always seemed to be a man acutely aware of the ticking of the clock. During the summer I lived with him and my aunt, he would often return home for lunch or dinner after an intense session of surgery or patient care, and hail us with, "Busy as a man killing snakes today!" A humorous remark was a favorite foil to make light of his problems or veil his concerns. In later years, the pressures of fleeting time seemed to intensify, driving every waking hour as Milo relentlessly tried to pack as much work into each day as humanly possible. "Collapsed into bed," "pooped," "tumbled into bed, exhausted," "utterly bushed," were common entries in his diaries in the years to come. These entries were in marked contrast to what Milo had written in a letter to his parents during the final months of his EENT residency at Duke, "I am satisfied to be an obscure surgeon off in the woods somewhere where I can be comfortable and raise a family."

Upon Milo's return to civilian life, that line of thinking no longer seemed to be the case. A keen sense of urgency seemed to drive him professionally.

PARK AVENUE DOCTOR, 1946

In Boston they ask, how much does he know?
In New York, how much is he worth?
In Philadelphia, who were his parents?

—MARK TWAIN

WITH THE WAR AND ALASKA RELEGATED TO THE PAST, Milo accepted a position in Hanover, New Hampshire. It was a decision he came to regret a year or so later. "They had something called the Dartmouth Eye Institute, which was based on some cock-eyed idea the man had concerning something called aniseikonia, which meant different size images before each eye—an entirely theoretical and nonsensical concept. After I'd been there for a while, I'd had it."

In 1946, Milo moved back to New York. He stayed with Uncle Rudolf at his spartan studio-house in Pelham. Betsy and the boys lived with her parents in Tioga, shuttling back and forth, until Uncle Rudolf offered them the use of his house during the winter months when the artist went to Florida to paint. Eventually they would find a house they liked and could afford in the Westbury area of Long Island—one of the first tract homes

built by Levitt & Sons in a suburb soon to be famous: Levittown. As Milo
explained:

> *I got a chance to go to New York City with a man named*
> *Townley Paton, and we got a house through the Veterans*
> *Administration out on Long Island, which is near New York*
> *City, and I practiced in his office which was at 927 Park*
> *Avenue. I would get the people that he didn't want to see. All*
> *the fashionable and all the rich people he would see, except*
> *when one slipped through, and I would see peasantry. But I*
> *earned a living for my family and that was fine.*

For a while, that was enough. Professional and financial success was
presumably just a matter of time for the decorated World War II veteran
returning to the peace and relative prosperity of civilian life. Milo was a Park
Avenue doctor now; Betsy's ties to her family in Tioga were renewed. Sons
Jonathan, aged five, and Pieter, two, had access to both culture and countryside. Betsy was sometimes dressing the boys in clothes from Best & Co.

Milo's mentor, Dr. R. Townley Paton, was a prominent ophthalmologist who had trained with the famous Dr. William Holland Wilmer at
Johns Hopkins in Baltimore. Dr. Paton, now affiliated with the Manhattan
Eye, Ear & Throat Hospital, was particularly interested in sight restoration
through the use of corneal transplants, leading him to found the world's
first eye bank in 1944. Milo was one of seven ophthalmologists awarded a
scholarship to receive special training in the technique of corneal grafting
at the Eye-Bank for Sight Restoration in New York City.

The mission of the eye bank was to encourage eye donations so ocular
material was available to replace damaged corneas—the clear, protective
lens covering the eye—and to treat other eye ailments. Dr. Paton's efforts
were helped tremendously by a wealthy and well-connected socialite, Mrs.
Aida Breckinridge. She had previously raised millions of dollars to establish the Wilmer Eye Clinic at Johns Hopkins in 1929 after Dr. Wilmer had
saved one of her eyes from glaucoma.

Aida's husband, Henry Breckinridge, was Charles Lindbergh's lawyer and had come to fame during the highly publicized kidnapping and
murder trial that had transfixed the country a decade earlier. Like the rest
of the public, Milo would probably have known Henry's name from the
newspaper accounts of the tragedy that had shattered the life of the world-
famous aviator—Milo's longstanding hero.

Perhaps Milo learned that Aida, too, had played a minor role in aviation history. At the age of 18, when still a student in Paris, Aida de Acosta
became the first female to pilot a motorized aircraft when she made a
solo flight over Paris in a balloon in 1903. The incident was immediately
hushed up by her well-to-do parents who were worried that such publicity would ruin their daughter's chances for marriage. Now in her 60s,
Aida was nearly blind and still dealing with glaucoma. She remained a
dynamo, however, and was tireless in attracting money and publicity for
Dr. Paton's Eye-Bank and for the treatment of eye problems. Aida and
Milo went to Brooklyn together in March of 1946 where Milo addressed
100 science and biology students about the Eye-Bank and the need for
donor eyes.

While Milo was trying to establish himself at Dr. Paton's Park Avenue
practice, his brother, coincidentally, was on the fringes of that same upper-
crust strata of society that sometimes, drifted Milo's way, and Larry played
a minor role in sending a clutch of socially prominent and well-heeled new
patients to Milo's door.

By 1946, Larry was living in Ardmore, a town in the tony Main Line
suburbs west of Philadelphia. After two idyllic years in South Africa, the
impending war had eliminated Larry's job in Cape Town of promoting oil
products. He had returned to the States in the fall of 1940—nine months
after his brother's and Betsy's departure for Alaska—with his new wife,
Edith, a vivacious British South African. For a time, the newlyweds lived
near Hartford, Connecticut where Larry had gotten a job in public relations at the Sikorsky division of United Aircraft. There, his work brought
him into occasional contact with the courtly Russian engineering genius
himself, Igor Sikorsky, whose vision of a vertical-flight machine would
soon result in the first practical helicopter manufactured in the U.S.

After six less-than-idyllic years of a marriage, Larry and Edith divorced.
Edith returned to South Africa with their little red-headed daughter Karen.
Larry took a job with the Sun Oil Company in Philadelphia. His new digs
were a garage apartment at Hillcrest, an estate owned by Mrs. H. Ridgely
Bullock, a wealthy widow from a family that, for generations, had been
listed in the Social Register, the preeminent directory of the wealthy and
well-connected. Though sixteen years older than Aida Breckinridge, the
Eye-Bank's devoted benefactor, Mrs. Bullock and Aida moved in the same
social circles.

Mrs. Bullock, Larry's new landlady, then in her late-70s, invited Larry for cocktails at the manor house one evening. What began with pleasantries over cocktails with Mrs. Bullock, quickly blossomed into friendship. Eventually it evolved into an almost filial relationship between Larry and the elderly lady—"Gammy," as she was called by her family and friends.

Gammy was nearly blind. From dealing with her own eye problems, Gammy was quite conversant in the field of ophthalmology. After meeting Milo during one of his visits to Hillcrest to see his brother, Gammy was so impressed with the accomplished Dr. Fritz she began recommending him to her friends. Despite Gammy's age and failing eyesight, she was still very socially active. Milo's practice on Park Avenue benefitted from its association with Gammy and her influential friends.

That first year back in New York was a hectic but professionally productive time for Milo, as Betsy described it—commuting into New York City from his temporary quarters at Uncle Rudolf's house in Pelham very early each day, making hospital rounds on his post-operative patients, examining patients in the Park Avenue office until noon, then—often lunchless—back to the hospital to do surgery, followed by seeing free clinic patients, and rounds again. Evenings were spent in the laboratory working on his research and dictating his findings. "There was little room in his life for a wife and children at this time," Betsy noted, continuing:

> Milo had previously considered and turned down professorships at two medical schools, which would require administrative work and university politics, as well as the teaching he loved. In such places his surgical skills would soon rust out. Other offers were at large, well known medical clinics where he felt he would be just a cog in big machines with restrictions in scope and freedom. His desire was to keep up his work with living people, live with his family, take time off when he wanted to and at fifty or so take a teaching job. Milo had seen too many others driven to coronary and or nervous collapse goaded on by ambition, increased need for money and bigger jobs. They set impossible goals for themselves to make up for the uncertainly they felt inside.

Milo's research was going well. On January 16, 1947, he had a major breakthrough, writing in his diary: "I did it at last after thinking about it for 7 years—I put [a patient's] spinal fluid in his vitreous chamber. Did it at

5:30 after everybody else was through mucking about. Very much relieved to see the previously invisible retina. Home happy but pooped."

Immediately after surgery Milo could visualize the retina which he had not been able to see previously due to the murky vitreous. Nor could the patient see for the same reason. This was a blind eye, but after the vitreous replacement, the patient's vision became 20/50.

Milo's subsequent paper about the results of that research was published in the prestigious *American Journal of Ophthalmology* in August 1947. The novel procedure was also reported in the lay press, which helped publicize the Eye-Bank and their efforts to raise more funds for research.

Milo's research papers were now being published in medical journals with satisfying regularity. During this time, he also was asked to write the ophthalmology section for the next edition of the *Merck Manual of Diagnosis and Therapy*, the textbook of medical knowledge used by doctors worldwide. Dr. Fritz's professional standing was on the rise and he was pleased with his success.

Initially, New York seemed to offer Milo a promising future. However, early in 1947, as they were preparing to move into their new house in Westbury, things began to change with R. Townley Payton, the doctor with whom Milo was an associate. Dr. Townley was "suddenly fretting over income taxes, family problems and possibly jealous of Milo's accomplishments and notoriety," according to Betsy, and "began acting in an unusual manner. Not angry, just no longer friendly. He still assisted Milo in surgery when asked and Milo assisted him." But in mid-February 1947, Dr. Payton informed Milo that he could no longer keep him on as an associate, even though they had two more years on their agreement. He would keep Milo on as an assistant, but for much less money. "It was a big blow to Milo," Betsy wrote.

The blow was cushioned somewhat by an intriguing invitation. In the spring of 1947, Milo was contacted by Conrad Earl Albrecht, a doctor he had befriended in Alaska during World War II when they were both posted at Ft. Richardson. Dr. Albrecht, now the Commissioner of Health for the Territory of Alaska, asked Milo if he would like to become a member of a nutritional survey team among the Eskimos and Indians of Western and Southwestern Alaska. "Gosh, here I had a chance to go back to Alaska, get paid for it and have my passage paid," Milo remembered, "so I just took off—took a leave from Payton's office, and went."

Falling in Love Again, 1947

*I went with the idea of getting Alaska out of my system
once and for all, but like a drunkard who takes just one
more drink I am worse off than before. Indeed, I see the
insuperable amount of work that is to be done. I've just
about made up my mind to return and to Anchorage.*

—MILO FRITZ

"ONE OF THE MOST WONDERFUL PEOPLE to deal with," Milo said,
"was this man Dr. Albrecht."

Dr. C. Earl Albrecht had been the medical director of the hospital for
the Matanuska Colony, a farming community outside Anchorage that had
been set up by President Roosevelt in 1935 as part of the New Deal. Just
prior to World War II, Dr. Albrecht was called up to serve at Ft. Richardson,
arriving there in 1941, soon after Milo. By war's end, Dr. Albrecht was
chief of surgery and commanding officer of the 183rd Station Hospital at Ft.
Richardson, just eight miles from Anchorage. Milo, who reported to him,
came to revere Dr. Albrecht for his skills as a doctor, as a leader—a man
who could get things done.

Following the war, Dr. Albrecht was asked by Governor Gruening to become the Territory's first full time Commissioner of Health. In transitioning from clinician to administrator, Dr. Albrecht's foremost challenge was fighting Alaska's massive tuberculosis epidemic. In 1945, when he took over as Commissioner of Health, the death rate for TB among the Indigenous populations was as high as anywhere in the world, some 600 per 100,000. Within ten years, under Dr. Albrecht's skilled leadership, it was down around 60 per 100,000. The dramatic decrease was evident, as illustrated by this anecdote recalled by Dr. Albrecht in an interview years later:

One of the missionaries in Bethel I used to visit quite often said to me, "Earl, your tuberculosis program is working." I said, "Why I'm glad to hear that. How do you tell that it is working?" She says, "My Sunday school is getting bigger and bigger. The children aren't dying."

As the TB epidemic was being brought under control, the next most pressing medical issues in the Native villages were mastoiditis, caused by repeated ear infections, and phlyctenular keratoconjunctivitis, scarring of the cornea, caused by eye infections or infections in other parts of the body. A large percentage of Alaska Natives along the Arctic Slope and the Bering Sea region had opacities of the cornea resulting in loss of vision. Clearly, the situation cried out for the skills of an EENT specialist such as Doc Fritz. The ambitious itinerary for Dr. Albrecht's survey team was to include visits to Anchorage, as well as Nome, Kotzebue, Deering, Sheshalik, Wainwright, Point Hope, Unalakleet, Holy Cross, Bethel, Aniak, Seward, and Cordova.

Milo shared Dr. Albrecht's sense of mission and urgency, so of course, when his old friend asked him to return to Alaska, Milo was eager to go. He arranged for a six-week leave of absence from Dr. Townley's practice and the Eye-Bank.

In 1947, so soon after the war years, it was difficult to obtain the basic ophthalmological equipment necessary for this proposed trip to Alaska, but with the help of friends, doctors, and optical companies, Milo was able to assemble what he thought he would need and ship it ahead. When Milo landed in Anchorage in mid-June, he was relieved to find that his equipment and luggage had arrived and was in good condition.

MILO CAUGHT UP WITH THE NUTRITIONAL TEAM in Kotzebue. He and two team members then flew on to Selawik, an Inupiaq village of 350 people, of which thirty-seven were examined. These patients were all full-blooded Eskimos with normal vision, but with visual difficulties due to corneal opacities, or vision impairments due to advanced age. Milo concluded that the opacities were due to poor hygiene and avitaminosis A, B, and C (insufficient amounts of these vitamins) from birth to age five. Milo found that cases of phlyctenular conjunctivitis (PKC) and blepharitis (crusty eyelids) cleared up rapidly with atropine and sulfa medication.

In Selawik, the Inupiat used canvas kayaks and lived in sod huts. They went up the river for muskrats and lumber, Milo learned, making rafts of the logs that they floated down the river. The logs then were used to build their huts. During his few days there, Milo braved swarms of mosquitoes to walk about the village, admire the beautiful children, pet the least ravenous dogs, and have Eskimo tea. One day Milo had reindeer meat for lunch. He learned how the Inupiat tanned muskrat skins. Milo became acquainted with the many blooming wildflowers and picked a collection, which he packed with cotton, pressed between discarded Alaska Department of Health schedules and sent to Betsy. Milo also tried paddling different types of kayaks, which he later described in a letter to his son Jonathan. The villagers brought the team samples of their food, herbs, plants, and white fish oil for a specialist to examine. Another doctor, a bacteriologist, was studying blood groups, and Milo drew blood from them for examination.

When the team returned to Kotzebue, Dr. Stewart Rabeau of the Public Health Service offered them living and working accommodations at the hospital. One evening, Dr. Rabeau took some of the team for an outboard motorboat trip to the mouth of the Noatak River where ice still clung to the shore of Kotzebue Sound in late June.

Milo also visited Eskimos who were assembled at a beluga whale camp on the beach at Sheshalik. Their dogs were all staked out there; muktuk and whale meat were drying on racks. Milo examined thirteen families in tragic need of T&As (tonsillectomies and adenoidectomies) as well as abd (vitamin) guidance on what to feed the children from birth to age five. Milo ate both raw and cooked muktuk while there. On June 23, the team flew out of Sheshalik at 2:00 a.m. and arrived back at Kotzebue at 5:00 a.m. Because of the long daylight hours, days and nights often ran together.

Milo enjoyed talking to the pilots that flew him to these Alaska outposts, encountering one he had known during the war. Once airborne, some of these pilots would let Milo fly part of the way to their destination, which was exciting and fun for a man with a long-running interest in becoming a pilot. Take-offs and landings were another matter. At Wainwright, it took the pilot four tries to take off with the payload of freight and passengers on board. To Milo, the aborted takeoffs were less frightening than the landing on Wainwright's short muddy bank. Back in Kotzebue, Milo helped Bill Peterson, a pilot who had previously flown him in and out of Point Hope, change the spark plugs on his plane. Later, "Pete" let Milo fly the whole way to Nome, including the approach. However, the experienced bush pilot took over the controls again for the tricky landing.

Milo described his Nome experiences in a letter to six-year-old Jonathan on July 3, 1947:

Dear Jonathan,

The Old Man is pretty tired after examining eyes all day, so he is back in his little shack of a hotel which is no larger than Dinny's [Jonathan's grandmother's] house. But my room was small and the sound of the Bering Sea waves right at the back of the building made such a lonesome sound that I, that is, the Old Man, decided, in spite of the rain, to walk out of town about a mile or so to where the Eskimos from King Island are camped.

These Eskimos come across 60 miles or so of open water in large open boats about the size of the crash boats at MacDill Field. They have ribs and a keel just like the outboard motorboats that we used to go out in, but instead of boards for the side and bottoms, they are covered with the hide of walrus stitched together by the Eskimo women with strips of reindeer gut or hide, with some kind of wax or grease to make the seam waterproof. They use the walrus hide because the walrus are plentiful and lumber is very scarce—no trees at all growing in this part of the world which looks a good deal like the land around Jones Beach.

Near the stern of the large skin boats which are called oomiaks [umiaks], there is a square shaft like a chimney. The top is level with the side of the boat and the bottom is open, with the hide tacked tightly to it so there is no leak. The Eskimo puts his outboard motor in this well and makes the whole long trip that way from King Island loaded with ivory from tusks of "animidles" that died and were buried many years ago, extra gas, seal stomachs tanned and used to hold drinking water, the women, babies, tools, and tents. It is really a heroic trip and they make it to spend the 4th of July in Nome, sell their ivory carvings, have a few slugs of fire water, visit their relatives and generally have a holiday.

In the daytime the men sit under the upturned skin boats and carve things from ivory and the little children run about the beach or try to copy what the men make using pieces of driftwood.

In a town called Kotzebue the Old Man met a very nice young pilot named Bill Peterson whom everyone calls Pete. Pete took me all over in his little plane and let me do all of the flying except the landings and take-offs which, of course, is the very hardest part of flying. I don't get sick at all as I did before the war and almost did on my first trip from Nome to Kotzebue. You'd love travelling like this.

When I came back from Nome the other day, Pete showed me hundreds of small white whales in the water. They are hunted by the Eskimos who make things from the bone, eat the hide, drink the oil, use the oil for light and fuel. The meat is called muktuk and it tastes like a pair of old sneakers boiled in sowbelly. You'd have to be awfully hungry to enjoy it.

While the Old Man was in Selawik the Eskimo men let him try using a kayak. First, they let me use a woman's kayak which is kind of wide and easy to use like a canoe. Then I used a man's kayak which is a little narrower and a whole lot crankier and tippier. And the next day I tried a hunter's kayak which is like going to sea on a razor blade with edge down without tipping over. I did not spill, but it was no fun.

I'll be home in four Sundays and maybe you can show me how to swim.

Love,
The Old Man

In Kotzebue, Nome, Bethel, and Seward there were hospitals where Milo operated and assisted with surgeries. In the smaller Native villages, he briefly became part of the community, trading sheets for a sleeping bag and staying in spartan accommodations, often shared with another team member or the pilot who would be flying him to the next village the following day.

On July 9 Milo flew from Unalakleet to Holy Cross, a fifty-one-year-old Catholic mission on the Yukon River with 137 Eskimo and Indian children. These waifs, Milo learned, were taken in, raised, and educated until they were adults. Then, they were free to leave or stay and help if they wanted to.

The plane was met by Father Spils and Father McIntyre, who, with the Brothers and Sisters, worked to get Milo's equipment set up. Milo found a spirit at Holy Cross that was much different from what he had observed at the government schools. The mission was organized to be as self-sustaining as possible. Milo visited its massive vegetable garden, an impressive machine shop, and a fish wheel up the beach. He also inspected the simple dormitory, the kitchen, the serving room, and "Heaven," the salvage room for clothing and the sewing room for older girls, where they were allowed to entertain their boyfriends.

Terrible eye, ear, nose, and throat conditions prevailed at Holy Cross, Milo discovered, not only with the children, but with the Fathers, Sisters, and Brothers as well. After assessing the immediate medical needs at Holy Cross, Milo radioed a request for more ether to a former World War II colleague, Dr. Fred Langsam, in Bethel. With the additional ether and equipment sent from Bethel and the superb help of the two priests and Sister Superior and Sister Mary Edward, Milo was able to do tonsillectomies and adenoidectomies on fifteen of the children over the next couple of days.

Because of their familiarity with the surroundings and the love of the staff for them, these trusting children went to sleep without a sound, Milo observed. "Not one cried. One bled a little and all were in good shape that night. Sister Superior held the tongue blade, Father Spils held the suction rod which he made by using welding tubing, and which he kept free and clean with water after each case."

The Sister who was cook and first base coach wanted to know if there was anything that Milo or the children needed. Milo teased her and said what they needed was watermelon. That night at dinner the Sister produced a cake shaped like a watermelon and iced with green icing. When cut open the cake was pink inside and had "seeds" of chocolate drops. Full of admiration for these people where everyone helps, nobody rides free and nothing is wasted, Milo would continue to tell that story for years.

On Sunday, Milo dressed up and attended Mass. In the afternoon, when the steamer *Nenana* came in, Milo found that some of the crew members had typhoid. "Because of four cases of typhoid on *Nenana,* I "shot" the whole crew with typhoid vaccine. . . . then everyone helped move 36 tons of freight from the ship to the mission storage shed. Heavy work but the spirit of fun was there and the kids seemed to love it."

Milo then spent seven days in Bethel. He reconnected with Dr. Langsam who ran "a wonderful 50-bed hospital," as Milo wrote Betsy, "where he does pneumothoraxes, fractures, obstetrics, plastic surgery, proctology—and all of it superbly. . . .A great man and a Godsend to this community . . . egg-bald, beautiful teeth, gentle ways, stout, and a damn good doctor. . . . He also speaks Eskimese and has a pathetic and funny collection of fan mail."

During his time in Bethel, Milo identified and treated a range of ailments. He saw two cases of tuberculosis of the larynx and refracted scores of patients. Milo did numerous T&As and other eye, ear, nose, and throat surgeries, pulled molars, did a circumcision and various other procedures, including appendectomies, with Dr. Langsam. At the end of their productive week, Milo was spent, but, as he wrote Betsy, "No matter how tired one is nor how dirty they may be, there is a shining beauty and disarming charm that dispels fatigue."

These letters to Betsy were signed, "Springtime," an endearment I often heard Aunt Betsy use when talking to my uncle at home during my summer with them. In the office, of course, he was always "The Doctor." My father often called his brother "Mushmouth"—the name of comic strip character—but apparently never knew the origins of "Springtime" until he raised the question in a letter many decades later. Milo's response:

> *Springtime is a term of endearment used by Betsy when she wishes to attract my attention from whatever was occupying it to her. It is like the name Mushmouth you use and the origin is way back in my young days when the term was not so much at variance with things as they are now with me. . . . After a little research I find that Springtime was the name of a cowboy in a Sat. Eve Post yarn of the 30's. As a joke I asked Betsy to call me that. Then I insisted on it and so*

*an affectation became a habit and incongruity has been the
end of the affair that began so innocently so far away and so
long ago.*

After holding final clinics for Albrecht's survey in Seward and Cordova,
Milo returned to Anchorage at the end of July and prepared for his return
to the East Coast. A prophetic diary entry reads: "Wanna come back but
will Betsy?" And, then on Aug 2, Milo wrote: "Took off at 6:00 pm and I
never saw Anchorage looking more beautiful. I hated to leave, except for
Betsy and the kids."

ALASKA – OPPORTUNITY OR OBSESSION?

> *All great and honorable actions are accompanied with*
> *great difficulties, and both must be enterprised and*
> *overcome with answerable courage.*
>
> —WILLIAM BRADFORD

WITH ALBRECHT'S SUMMER SURVEY CONCLUDED, MILO was expected home on Sunday, August 3, 1947. The flight that was to bring him back from Alaska arrived, but he wasn't on it.

As Betsy recalled:

> *The boys and I, all dressed in white and as fixed up as*
> *we could be, went to LaGuardia to meet Milo. We stood on*
> *the observation deck and watched the people deplane but no*
> *Milo and so we went home very dejected since we had missed*
> *him and looked forward to his return.*
>
> *The next day I received a telegram saying he was going to*
> *be a day late.*

> *When Milo reached Minneapolis and was to change planes Milo was found to be completely amnesic and stuporous from medication taken to sleep because he was so excited. The personnel took him to Swedish Hospital where he was put on a plane at 6 pm. He reached New York at 4 am.*

Early that next morning, Betsy, alone, was waiting for her husband. She remembered Milo's first words when he came off the plane—"I'm going back, I don't know about you." Then he kissed her and told her he was glad to be home, though he hated to leave Alaska.

Milo's diary entry on Aug 5, the following day:

> *Betsy agrees that it is Alaska for us. The move can be called cowardly or heroic, brave or foolish, selfish, or noble, depending on the point of view. But then I'll be where I love to be, with the boys and Betsy near at hand, and loads of work to be done. I'm fed up to the gills with New York.*

After covering for Dr. Townley during his vacation at summer's end, Milo told him he would be leaving the practice to get ready for his move to Alaska in the spring. Milo's final day as a Park Avenue doctor was Oct. 11. Soon after, Milo established a small practice on Long Island. He kept occupied by reading medical journals and writing articles that would be published in several medical journals, Betsy recalled. "In the afternoon he would go into New York City and to the Manhattan Eye, Ear and Throat Hospital whereas a staff member he would diagnose and treat patients in the clinic and operate on those cases needing surgery that did not have or could not afford their own surgeon."

Larry came out to Long Island for a weekend visit that fall. He brought with him Helen Wahlberg, an attractive and accomplished new girlfriend whom he wanted Milo and Betsy to meet. The two had first met in Chicago where Helen worked as a home economist for the appliance manufacturer Hot Point before and after World War II. During the war, Helen had joined the U. S. Marine Corps, soon graduating from its Officer Candidate School as one of its first female officers. By war's end, Helen had risen to the rank of first lieutenant. Since returning to her job at Hotpoint, she had taken an editorial job at the *Ladies' Home Journal* and moved to New York City, where she and Larry crossed paths again. They would marry in Chicago, a year after their visit with Milo and Betsy, becoming my parents in 1950.

Some sixty years later, I asked my mother about her first impressions of Milo. Her recollections of meeting Milo, Betsy, and their young sons were vivid, but not for the reasons I had supposed. She remembered that one or both boys had some slight cold or ailment, and what still bothered her was that both boys were given considerable medication that evening to ensure they would not be a problem for the babysitter. That weekend, Helen also learned that Larry and Milo's parents were all-but-divorced, of particular concern to her, given Larry's marital track record.

And the former Marine officer's take on the adventuresome doctor who would soon be returning to Alaska? Oh, she replied in a memorable remark that perhaps revealed more about my mother than Milo, she was "well acquainted with men and their narratives."

That winter, Helen phoned the Fritz home to say goodbye and to wish Milo and Betsy well on their trip to Alaska. After conveying this to Milo, who answered the phone, Helen asked to speak with Betsy. Milo told Helen that Betsy was "still making her mind up about Alaska" and was not available to talk. Perhaps Betsy's former "wither thou goest sentiments" were being tempered by other considerations, such as her responsibilities as a mother of two small children.

After winter set in, Betsy and the boys came down with colds. Betsy developed a sinus infection with pain severe enough to keep her in bed, so Milo's days were stretched further as he took on care of the boys, cooking, shopping, laundry, and cleaning. "Both boys were well behaved," Betsy wrote, "and would amuse themselves without disturbing me too much while Milo was at the hospital or office."

After a snowfall, there was some time for fun. "Nearby was a slope where Milo took Jonathan for coasting." And for reasons not explained in her account, "Jonathan was a most embarrassed child when he and his father built a snow man which turned out to have been the largest snow man ever." And, perhaps in anticipation of their upcoming move to Alaska, "they built an igloo with a tunnel entrance" next to the monstrous snowman.

Years later, Betsy would recall those final months on Long Island:

Milo's professional skills were not being adequately used in his "pityingly small but growing practice," as Betsy termed it, where he sat in his "dismal, second-hand office waiting for a patient to wander in . . . his surgical skills wasted, since this area was in such close proximity to the large medical centers of New York City. . . . It was a trying period of waiting, waiting, waiting. How soon could Milo unload the practice, such as it was, find a buyer for the house, get packed and on our way to Alaska where he wanted to be and where he was needed?"

There was an unmistakable air of finality in their activities and extended leave-taking. Perhaps Betsy felt she and the boys were seeing their last glimpse of culture and civilization, of East Coast gentility. Both parents took Jonathan into New York City for what Betsy termed, "a final look around," hoping that six-year-old Jonathan would be old enough to remember the experience. They rode the "El," they viewed the city from the top of the Empire State Building, and ended their day of touring with hot cocoa at what they called "Uncle Rudolf's Schrafft's" at 556 Fifth Avenue, where the artist "had spent many hours lying on his back on scaffolding to paint the very lovely Michelangelo-type ceiling and the frescoes over the doors."

Milo's medical practice and their house were sold by March 1st and the next ten days were a frenzy of packing, shipping, and farewell visits for Milo and Betsy during which Jonathan, Piet, and Annie, their Dalmatian, were taken to Betsy's parents in Tioga for an extended visit. An article published in a local newspaper in April 1948, described their upcoming departure this way:

> *"Doing what I want to do instead of just dreaming about it," is the way Dr. Milo H. Fritz describes closing his practice in NYC and with their two small sons, to move to the Far North.*
>
> *"I am especially interested in the study of a certain eye disease among the Eskimos of the Arctic Slope," he declared. "I have never got Alaska out of my skin since I was there in 1940 and 1941. There is a tremendous need for trained medical specialists up there."*

"We sold our house and I remember I lost the check for the down payment," Milo recalled. "Since then, Betsy has taken care of our finances. I bought a Chevrolet sedan from my brother, for I think $700.00 or something like that, and we loaded that up and took off for Alaska."

MUD, SNOW, ICE... AND
A DALMATIAN

We belonged to the American Automobile Association, but
decided to go up in March and April, which was a damn
stupid thing to do, because that was the breakup—by breakup,
I mean the time that winter is changing into summer and the
ground is muddy and the roads are impassable, but the AAA
never told us that. Otherwise, we would have driven to Seattle
and gone up by boat. . . . It was one hell of a trip.

—MILO FRITZ

ON MARCH 23, 1948, THEY—Milo, Betsy, Jonathan, aged six, Pieter, aged three, and their Dalmatian Annie—drove away from Tioga, Pennsylvania on a swing south to Sarasota, Florida where Milo's father Henry was now living, painting, and teaching occasional classes at the Barnum & Bailey Museum. He and Amelia were now separated; the family's former home on Poplar Avenue had been sold. After pushing through the bleakness of an all-day rain, near the end of the first day, they rolled up a long sweeping drive to call on Gammy. Betsy's account of their visit:

> *We stopped at Hillcrest, the palatial home of Mrs. Ridgely Bullock in Ardmore, to have tea and say goodbye to 'Gammy.' We had a nice visit before a roaring fire. There were all sorts of cookies and goodies made especially for the boys. Jonathan took it all calmly but Pieter, not used to being served by a uniformed maid, got up from his chair and followed the maid with the cookie tray right out to the pantry and stayed there amusing and being amused by the servants until we collected him when we were ready to leave. Mrs. Bullock had the maid prepare a package of cookies for Pieter to take with him and it lasted until we reached Missouri.*

After a week-long visit with Henry in Sarasota, they turned northward. In Granada, Mississippi they briefly reconnected with Milo's cousin and protégé Larry Hayes, who as a result of Milo's encouragement and occasional financial assistance was attending the University of Mississippi Medical School. Then on to Memphis, Tennessee, and the Sears Roebuck where Milo and Betsy had stopped on their first trip to Alaska. This time, according to Betsy, they "obtained all of the required gear for driving over the Alaskan Highway—spending close to $31!"

On April 9, they reached Rochester, Minnesota where they were given a tour of the Mayo Foundation. Milo had met both Will and Charlie Mayo back in 1936 during Milo's final year at The Brooklyn Hospital, when he had unsuccessfully attempted to secure an internship at the Mayo Clinic. Milo recalled:

> *People wanting to get there, were so few in numbers that you would be interviewed by the Mayo brothers themselves. I shook hands with both of them. Not that that is anything, I suppose. There were ten thousand people that did that, but I thought it was a great day in my young life.*

By mid-April, the Fritz family had arrived at the Canadian border. Betsy wrote:

> *Leaving home was sad, leaving warmth and sunshine was hard, but leaving the good old U.S. on April 12 at 11:00 am, at a place named Sweet Grass, and crossing to a place named Coutts, on a cold, gray, muddy day was a low point.*

We had no difficulty in crossing the border other than Milo had to leave his gun in the U.S. at the guard house and they would mail it to Anchorage. Small arms were not allowed to be carried through Canada. The police were very much interested in how much money we had and in what form it was. They did not want to be burdened with stranded travelers down on their luck.

The sun came out and they were feeling better as they headed north to Calgary, Alberta. They were still twenty-three miles from their goal. Betsy wrote:

Suddenly there appeared a cylindrical black cloud ahead like pictures I had seen of approaching tornadoes. In seconds we were in a blizzard. We could not see anything because of the blowing snow—the wind was at least 50 mph. Though mid-afternoon, it was dark as night. We crept slowly into the village of Okotoks and very grateful for finding civilization.

They stopped at a small hotel and got the last available room. The lobby soon filled with others seeking shelter from the storm—the worst blizzard in seventy years according to the old-timers they talked with. People were soon gathering by a window with a view of the highway and began betting on which cars were going to make it up the steep hill just beyond the hotel. Most of the cars would slide back down.

Scenery the next morning was "perfectly beautiful" but the new, ungraded road between Okotoks and Edmonton was awful—potholes, mud, ice—no foundation and no road signs except where there was a bridge. Milo had found space for the car in a warm garage the night before. However, five miles out of town they discovered that, despite the garage storage, the car had frozen overnight. The muffler blew out. "Not only was the noise alarming, but the fumes coming into the car were awful. It was either freeze to death with the windows open or choke to death with them closed. We chose the latter."

Milo and Betsy had planned to stop over in Edmonton for several days so they would have time to get the car repaired and shop for the warmer clothes and sleeping bags they would need for the rest of the trip. But their stay was abruptly cut short. After getting the car fixed, Milo went to the AAA office for information about the road. AAA advised him to buy chains and to leave early the next morning in order to get across the

Smoky River before the ice went out. If not, they might be stranded on this side for a week or more, until the ice was gone and the ferry was back in service.

Milo returned with the unhappy news. The AAA-approved motor court where they were staying that night had a small store and a stove, of sorts, which had prompted the boys to ask for "a home-cooked dinner." With the laundry she had done earlier in the day hanging in the warm cabin, Betsy heated up canned spaghetti and worriedly prepared to take off into the cold and snowy dawn without the warm underwear, bedrolls, and food supplies they needed.

> By the time we pulled into Athabasca I was feeling bet-
> ter. The sun came out and the sight of a town helped. We
> bought fresh fruit, pasteurized milk, cookies, and chocolate
> in a spotless white Marketeria. We had often read of the ro-
> mantic place when we had been planning our trip down the
> McKenzie. Never did I expect to drive through here in a car.
> I took the wheel but after three good skids, for no apparent
> reason, I got the shakes and gave it to Milo.

They stopped to put chains on the tires and found the two rear fastenings of the Kari-top had come adrift. The top load was swaying back and forth, causing the car to skid. Between intermittent snowstorms they caught glimpses of the beautiful Slave Lake country and of a distant dog team, miles from anywhere. In the midst of another storm in another isolated area, they passed an Indian woman with a papoose on her back. Whenever the sun came out, the snow on the road would melt and the water would splash up under the car fenders and freeze, adding to the weight. The weight might have helped keep them on the road but the frozen mud acted like sandpaper on the tires. They stopped frequently so Milo could chop the ice from the bottom of the car—a futile battle costing them precious time—necessary when Milo could no longer turn the wheel because of the ice buildup. The running boards were almost dragging on the road.

> Exhausted, cold, and exasperated we pulled into High
> Prairie. . . . Milo found two beds on the second floor of a "ho-
> tel" that no civilized Easterner would have entered. The over-
> heated lobby was filled with smoke, filth, lounging Indians.
> . . . There seemed to be but one bathroom with the usual

*fixtures, but only the commode had running water. . . We
stationed one boy in the bathroom and gave the other an en-
ema in the bedroom and then rushed him down the hall and
vice versa.*

By the next morning, the heated garage had softened up some of the ice under the car and Milo was able to chop off what he estimated to be 600 pounds of it. The double-bitted ax they carried proved useful, but not for the purpose intended. Mud, snow, ice, more mud, snow, ice. About noon they reached the Smoky River.

*There was no bridge there in 1948 and in the summer a
ferry was used to get across. In winter, one skidded down on
a palisades-like bank and up the slippery slope on the other
side. We did. The overflow water on the ice was so deep that
it came in under the door onto the floor of the car. Seven
hours later, the crossing was closed to all cars until the ferry
could be used, probably a two-week waiting period.*

Relieved, they now thought they could take their time. They made it through Grande Prairie all right, but a few miles north of Beaverlodge, they became unsure of the way. Milo attempted to flag down a passing car to ask directions. Not only did it not stop, it didn't even slow down; Milo received a face full of muddy water and the spray went all over the ceiling of the car and even into the back seats. A missing road sign caused them to take a road that soon had their car and several other vehicles mired in mud like they had never seen before. They were right behind a party of seven men in an International one-and-one-half-ton pickup truck and a Chevrolet Carryall—both vehicles also bogged down.

*We tried to unload the car in order to lighten it.
. . .Everything had to be carried through mud to the snowy
field. Each foot had about ten pounds of mud on it. Even
then we could not move the car so we re-loaded it. You have
no idea how ludicrous a Guide to Good Eating Places Along
the Road looked . . . in the back window. . ., or the cast iron
popover pan. Equally silly was Milo having to carry the boys
or the dog over to the snow for airing purposes.*

Stuck in the mud ahead of them were miners heading back to a Yukon gold mine west of Whitehorse that they had bought two summers ago. Milo, who had spoken to the men in the hotel the night before, helped them as much as he could. As the men labored, Betsy and the boys sat watching in their car, now without a working heater. In chopping the ice off the car that morning, the ax had accidently gone right through the heater hose.

The men put chains on the trucks—jacking them up, taking off the wheels and carrying them to the snow where the chains were put on before replacing them. They had all gotten stuck around 3:00 and, as the afternoon turned into evening, Betsy wondered if they would ever get out of there. The men were getting colder as the temperatures went down with the sun. At 7:00 p.m. a man with a diesel tractor came along, pulling them and several other vehicles out for $3.00 each. After watching the men work so hard for so long, that little bit of money seemed like nothing to Betsy.

> We would never believe it had we not seen it ourselves.
> The mud was built up on the outside of the tires about 3 feet.
> It also piled up under the hood so that Milo could not shift.
> When he was supposed to help the tractor, he could only go
> in first gear. Our car was so low that we could not get over
> the ruts so Bill, an ex-woodsman, cut the ruts just as pretty
> as you please with an ax, right in front of each tire.

Milo and Betsy's car got stuck two more times, but by hooking up both trucks to the tow rope, it was pulled through. Their plan was to get out of the mud, wait until midnight, then drive on the frost, the term for frozen mud. But the mud showed no sign of freezing. They decided to form a convoy with the Fritz car between the two trucks and drive straight through the night to Dawson Creek, British Columbia, where the Alaska Highway began. That road, they hoped, would be high and dry. The miners even took some of their load. They had made the trip before and more or less knew the way.

> Both boys were asleep and we wished we were. Neither of
> us ever had so much trouble staying awake. Milo would ask
> me questions and I would give the silliest answers, so sleepy
> that I uttered the most terrible gibberish.
> . . . It was a beautiful night. Clear and cold. It was made
> complete with a beautiful display of Northern Lights and a
> little later two handsome deer out for a stroll. . . . At one place
> there was a choice of roads to take and no sign to help. . . .

> *The men got out and had a conference and decided to take the one with the most car tracks on it. It turned out to be the right one. I had begun to think that the lights of Dawson Creek would never show. Suddenly we rounded a curve and there it was.*

It was very, very late and everything was closed. There were 600 ammunition trucks stopped there and the drivers had all the beds. The seven men fanned out through the business section looking for rooms and reported that they had a found a room for the Fritz family in a third-class hotel.

> *It was third rate and no question about that. With fear and trepidation, but too tired to care I put the boys on a single bed that was made up with unbleached muslin that reached neither to the head nor foot of the filthy mattress and awful looking quilts that were so torn that the gray stuffing was coming out. I didn't dare look at the mattress. Milo and I piled into the other single bed whose springs were so worn out that we slid right down into the middle. So tired we fell asleep right away.*
>
> *I woke up early in the A.M. with a splitting headache. I went down the hall to the one and only bathroom and just stood there. It was so filthy that I could not even use the modern convenience. All these Canadian hotels at that time were built with holes large enough for the boys to crawl through at the top and bottom of each wall so that air and heat could circulate. . . . Lots of other things leak out of the holes as well. We got out as soon as we could dress.*

Milo was able to find a room and bath in the best hotel early that morning. While waiting for it to be ready, they all had a big breakfast and walked about while the garage men worked on their car. As soon as the seven men had the mud cleaned from their trucks, they set off for their mining camp near Haines Junction, nearly one thousand miles away.

While Betsy and the boys bathed and slept, Milo checked on the car and found that the men at the garage were not doing a very good job. Milo pitched in and was shoveling mud out of the inside of the car with an ordinary garden spade when he saw the seven men returning to town. Thirty-five miles from town the miners found that their overloading spring on the pickup was broken. They were back to get it fixed.

On the way to ask the foreman, Lou, to a thank you dinner, Milo met the foreman coming to see him; Lou thought he might have appendicitis. Glad to be of some help, Milo prescribed some medicine for Lou. Betsy described Lou and his companions:

> He was a giant of a man with a high order of intelligence and a sharp sense of humor, and quiet, well thought of by his crew. One was a high climber (a man who cuts the tops out of trees in logging.) His son Ray has a picture of him dancing on a treetop after a cut, smoking and even standing on his hands on the tiny space. He was a wonderful fellow. Ray had been in the Seabees during the war. Oliver was the real miner, and his son Irving, an ex-sailor, and Jesse, a menacing-looking, huge man completed the group. Except for Darrell—a very young, likeable chap, a skillful driver and a good sport. [The seventh, Bill, was mentioned previously as the expert with the ax.]
>
> They were a wonder of teamwork and cooperation. They got along well and not only spent the days together in the cars, but their evenings as well. This was their third summer of working a gold mine that they had purchased. The first year they just built the buildings and got ready to mine. The second year they did take out some gold over and above expenses. This year they hoped to make a real profit. We were all friends now and they took us under their wing.

COMING INTO THE COUNTRY

There's a land where the mountains are nameless,
And the rivers all run God knows where;
There are lives that are erring and aimless,
And deaths that just hang by a hair;
There are hardships that nobody reckons;
There are valleys unpeopled and still;
There's a land—oh, it beckons and beckons,
And I want to go back—and I will.

—ROBERT W. SERVICE, "THE SPELL OF THE YUKON"

FOR THE NEXT 900 OR SO MILES OF THE ALASKA HIGHWAY, from Dawson Creek to Whitehorse, Yukon Territory, the miners were always around to lend a hand—loading the boys and Betsy, loading baggage, helping to refuel the car. "If Milo stopped to put on or take off chains or adjust something, at least two men were at his side and the job was done."

Betsy drove the first 100 miles of the Alaska Highway, "90 per cent dry, fairly smooth and the driving easier than any day so far since we left the border." The Fritz family would have been among the first civilians to travel the road, as it had just opened to the public in 1948. The 1600-mile gravel road linking Dawson Creek and Fairbanks had been carved through Canadian and Alaska wilderness as a military supply route during World War II. Spurred by fear of a Japanese invasion, the Alaska Highway (Alcan) was completed in an incredible nine months and was an engineering marvel. As the Fritzes headed ever northward, weather was increasingly a challenge.

Milo and Betsy planned each day's travel with care, as gasoline, food, and lodging were only available at places roughly a day's drive apart. There were emergency shelters along the road for travelers caught in bad weather or for those without funds to pay for lodging. The emergency shelters were old road-building camps or parts of such camps where one would have to cut wood and build fires to stay warm. Late in the day they ran into a blizzard, but managed to creep along to that day's goal of Fort Nelson and their lodging, which Betsy described:

> The "hotel" at Fort Nelson was made of three old Army
> barracks fastened together to form an H. In the sleeping por-
> tion there were 70 beds, and two washrooms for each sex. In
> another portion there was a small office, small kitchen, and
> a dining room. It certainly was not lavish, but clean, warm,
> good food and well run by a spare, firm man from Montreal.

Their room, "more than adequate," had a double bed with a studio couch and "plenty of nice clean woolen blankets." However, since the hotel had to haul all its water and the supply was low, they were not allowed to bathe. Their seven friends, who had loitered along the way, arrived while they were having dinner. After the boys were tucked in bed, the adults sat in the lobby and talked. Betsy described the next day:

> All of us were up early and on our way in a convoy.
> During the night about six inches of snow had fallen and it
> was also much colder than the day before—below zero. We
> had not gone far when a truck stopped us and told us there
> was 18" of snow ahead at the summit and the road had not
> been plowed yet, so we all turned back to Fort Nelson.
>
> There, Jonathan and Pieter tried to play in the snow but
> it was too cold, so they sat inside where the boys colored and
> played with a French girl about Jonathan's age. After lunch,
> they learned that the road was open and we started out again.

Betsy and Milo soon discovered that their car had a broken leaf spring, so the heaviest of their baggage was put on the pickup truck, which certainly helped as they made their way up the summit and across the Canadian Rockies, which, Betsy noted, "towered above and all around us as we went to the highest point of the trip. The scenery was magnificent. I cannot describe how beautiful and how wonderful it was. Nor could I take a picture that would do it justice."

Along the way, they hit a snowstorm and then a small blizzard that dropped sixteen inches of snow on the travelers, slowing them down. They could go no farther than Coal River, which they reached when it was nearly dark. Their lodgings that night were at a place both small and rustic. Off the dining room was a short hallway leading to four rooms with no doors, just panels of flimsy printed cotton across the doorways. Truckers were already there and in bed. The owner Mr. Kennedy made two of the men get up, giving the two-cot room to Betsy and the boys. Betsy wrote:

> Jonathan and Pieter went right to bed and to sleep. The
> adults sat around the U-shaped counter and ate dinner and
> talked. . . . Mr. Kennedy seemed to be the only person work-
> ing there. He was so full of pep, personality, and enthusiasm
> for the North that he equaled Milo in this respect. He amused
> us for ages with his plans for horse packing trips, hunting
> trips, and telling us about the hot springs nearby where veg-
> etables could be grown, of coal deposits, of gold deposits. . . .
> The men all went to the storeroom and got cots, making beds
> for themselves in the dining room. Mr. Kennedy practically
> tucked them in.

Though Betsy didn't think Mr. Kennedy had changed the sheets in their room after the truckers were rousted out that particular night, she found that hotels along the Alaska Highway generally "had clean, comfortable beds and towels. Most places were heated in some fashion. Food was usu-ally adequate and plentiful. No fresh milk. Mr. Kennedy served us half a fresh orange as dessert which was a real treat."

And she had praise for the condition of the roadway:

> As far as the Alaska Highway goes, there is nothing the
> matter with it. It is kept open all of the year. It is graded
> frequently. Most of it is higher than the surrounding terrain

so that it is well drained. It is wide also. . . . The road is
well marked. . . . There are "filling stations" sufficiently well
located so there is no need to carry extra fuel, though we
did carry some. It would have come in handy had we been
stranded out in the wilds. At these filling stations you more
or less take care of yourself. In some places you could get
some food and sometimes there were snacks and candy bars.
Sixty-five cents was the most we ever paid for a gallon of
gasoline and that was in the Yukon Territory. . . . The weath-
er was something else.

. . . In the convoy the next day a flat tire on the pickup
was only a matter of seconds with two men carrying the flat
tire around the truck one way while two others brought the
good tire around the other way. Real teamwork resulting in
nobody having time to get cold.

They discovered that their heavy-duty chains had stretched from all
the grinding in the deep mud at Beaverlodge. Lou and Milo removed five
links from each to make them fit again. The weather became so bad that
Milo felt Betsy should not drive, so Lou drove their car and Milo got a rest
in the pickup for half a day. Lou "was a very nice person. Being a father, he
understood and didn't mind when the boys had to wee-wee or when they
were carsick. The hazardous conditions required the most careful driving
at all times." A moment of carelessness in a remote area or in bad weather
meant disaster. Betsy continued:

Bill spotted three wolves crossing a lake and we all got out
to look and photograph. . . . Probably there was much more
that we missed in many ways due to bad weather and all our
worries. . . .Driving was often too hazardous to look about.

. . . At the end of the day we looked down from the high-
way and saw the lights of historic Whitehorse. The men knew
exactly the place to stay: the Regina Hotel. We arrived there
in time for a late dinner of Olympic oysters, huge, cracked
Alaska king crab and black cod. You can imagine how much
we enjoyed this meal. With my strong, hot tea I asked if I
could please have some lemon. They did their best to accom-
modate me and brought in a tiny slice of a dried-out lemon.
I was very appreciative.

> *This hotel is owned and operated by an elderly Swedish*
> *couple, Mr. and Mrs. Erickson. It was as clean as only a good*
> *Swede could make it. It was like coming home to find such*
> *warm, clean, comfortable rooms with lovely clean warm*
> *blankets and quilts. It was so nice and we were so tired that*
> *we decided to stay over a day and rest.*
>
> *This first night it was -26 degrees, so after the boys were*
> *in and their warm outer clothes off, I took Pieter's snow suit*
> *out and put it on the dog.*

Other times, "Milo made a nest for Annie each night and buttoned her into Jon's snow suit"—theirs unquestionably the only Dalmatian in the Yukon so devotedly outfitted against the cold. "In Canada," Betsy wrote, "no dogs are allowed in hotels. Annie ended up spending much of this month in the car," continuing:

> *After sleeping as long as possible and with dawn at 3:00*
> *AM, we got up and went for a walk before breakfast. We in-*
> *spected the old Yukon River ships pulled up on the shore for*
> *the winter. Then we drove all about town. My feet got cold,*
> *I was discouraged/tired and we went back to the hotel and I*
> *went to bed again and cried myself to sleep.*
>
> *After the nap and dinner of more black cod I felt better.*
> *I went out and bought paper and started my letter while my*
> *washed hair dried.*
>
> *Time and time again I would have given a great deal for*
> *a drink at the end of a long, hard day. The Canadians make*
> *it too difficult to bother with. A lady has to drink in the lady's*
> *parlor with but one escort; otherwise, she is not a lady and is*
> *not allowed in. The seven men, eight with Milo, could not go*
> *in with me, and as we did not know seven ladies, the seven*
> *men went one way and Milo and I another.*
>
> *. . . In the evening in Whitehorse we sat around the lobby*
> *and talked. Two of the men had colds and all of them needed*
> *a laxative and so Milo was practicing medicine.*

The Fritz family left Whitehorse the next morning after saying goodbye to the miners who were checking their mail and attending to other business in town. They parted on warm terms, with the miners inviting the Fritzes for a summer stay at their gold mine camp. Later that morning, just beyond Mile Post 1104, the turnoff for the miners' camp, Milo and Betsy had a flat tire. Milo had to change it himself. Betsy noted, "We missed the seven friends for their help and their company."

A more dangerous situation awaited them in Alaska. Two miles after crossing the border they were driving around an outside curve with a precipitous drop into the ravine below when the car went into the worst skid of the trip.

> *I felt sick as I saw the cliff whizzing past for the third time. Fortunately, the snowplow had left one little pile of snow and our back wheel caught in it. I got out and watched Milo pull out of it. Fortunately, there were no cars coming in either direction. At the time this happened I was holding a knife and cutting some chocolate for an afternoon snack. I sat like a statue for some miles still holding the knife and shaking like a leaf at the same time.*
>
> *The broken spring leaf caused the back end to be out of line and consequently it whined and buzzed. The clutch made a terrible sound when shifting. We crept along slowly hoping that the big bulge in the front tire would not blow out.*

It was supper time before they reached the first community and U.S. Customs in Tok, ninety-three miles from the border, where they were "charged a terrific price for a barren room with no heat and $3 each for a horrible plate of stew." After a cold and sleepless night, they left at dawn. Betsy wrote:

> *Milo's cheerfulness and enthusiasm kept us going and helped me at least from feeling sorry for myself. I guess the boys felt as I did during that cold, early morning drive.*
>
> *Pieter must have been thinking about better times because he said, "I guess that Dinny is reading," and Jon said, "No, she's buttering the toast." I knew that the tulips were blooming there by now and that it must be quite warm, the birds singing in the trees by the river.*

Milo and Betsy had expected that they would have to drive about 100 miles before having breakfast but were pleasantly surprised about 7:00 a.m. to see a shiny new log cabin in a clearing and a sign that said they served meals at all hours. Breakfast would be just a matter of minutes.

They sat at a table by a "large, sunny, east front window" with window curtains that were "blue and white and yellow check," Betsy wrote, continuing:

> The tables and chairs were of the same colors. . . . It was a
> neat snug cabin on a concrete basement," owned by a Mr. and
> Mrs. Jillson, "who built it when they got fed up with big city
> life in Anchorage. . . . The inside walls were varnished peeled
> logs and it was as clean and bright as possible. . . . One wall
> was covered with wolverine and fox skins ready for market.
> . . . It was the most reasonably priced, best prepared meal of
> the whole trip. We consumed fruit juice, bacon, eggs, wheat
> cakes, toast and I had three cups of coffee—the food so good,
> it made us all feel warmer and in better spirits.

Later that morning, they enjoyed spectacular scenery—"mountains, glaciers, in front and on either side." At a noon stop at Duffy's Tavern in Slana, some 250 miles from Anchorage, they got gas and changed the bad front tire for a better one. "It was quite a job as Milo had to take the wheel off the car and then take the tire off the wheel." They took turns pumping up the replacement tire by hand. Milo was working on the tire and Betsy was chipping a new accumulation of ice from underneath the car when, as Betsy wrote, they heard "a loud shout and a 'gee' and a 'haw'."

> There was my first close-up of a dog team. I took pictures
> and bothered the man with questions. He comes 40 miles
> once a month for his mail. The lead dog was a beauty and
> had been borrowed by the Army for experimental purposes
> in planes and even in a submarine. I watched him unharness
> the dogs and chain them to trees—well apart. They are ugly
> to each other but friendly to people. They never use female
> dogs because of the nuisance. They had been two days on the
> trip, working all the way, breaking trail, and they looked as
> though they had just come from a kennel.

The Fritz's car, however, was in rough shape. They pulled away from Duffy's with "the rear end whining, the transmission groaning, the rear seat loose from its moorings, one bumperette gone and one taillight broken—the whole car dirty and dusty."

They nosed south and west, following the Glenn Highway successfully to Palmer in the fertile Matanuska Valley, the site of the farming colony where Dr. Albrecht had gotten his first taste of Alaska medicine, prior to

World War II. Here, the ground was now free of snow. The air, though still and cold, felt nice and warm in the sunshine. Betsy could picture the little farms being "green and pretty when summer comes." They spent the night at a hotel in Palmer. "The town had grown some since Milo had seen it last and now it boasted three steel-and-concrete buildings."

The next day they covered the last forty miles, finally pulling into Anchorage.

PART IV

Alaska, Again

FROM DREAM TO REALITY

Alaska, where Larry and our wives and I hope to live and grow up with the country. My mad dream of a Medical Air Service to all the settlements seemed not mad at all.

—MILO FRITZ, 1937

"MILO HAD ALWAYS WANTED ME TO get here on one of those lovely clear spring days when you could smell the heather," Betsy wrote about arriving in Anchorage. The reality was different:

> We arrived in a terrific wind which whipped blinding dust two stories high and which did nothing to make me warm up to the place. Fortunately, we found a hotel room and carried our heavy enough baggage—made twice as heavy by the accumulation of dust and mud—upstairs.
>
> Milo a busy boy seeing all of his friends. The whole situation looks mighty discouraging to me. Somebody got us a mailbox which is wonderful. The Post Office is a huge building but already too small for the volume of mail that it handles and the parcel post work is carried on in an old Army

*barracks behind. Long lines of people wait at the General
Delivery window.*

*Heard of a house out in Mountain View, but if we had
had to live in that I would have balked. Dust, dust, dust.
Found a house which we would like to have the first night
we were here. It seemed to be vacant and there was a young
fellow painting inside. Milo went and asked him about it and
he said that he was getting it ready to sell. Milo told him to
hold it for him.*

Milo had his own recollections of Anchorage at the time of their arrival.
"We remembered Anchorage and knew what a tremendous opportunity
was here," Milo told a writer from the *Homer News*. In the interview, occasioned by Milo's retirement from medicine in September 1985, he recalled:

*There were no more than eight doctors in the small town
then, serving a vast Territory with its own special set of medical problems. Villagers, especially, were in bad shape. A kid
would come into town to get his appendix removed and, my
gosh, you'd find he had a club foot, skin problems and fluid
coming out of his ear. There wasn't a kid that didn't need to
see the dentist.*

The date was still etched in his mind. "We arrived in Anchorage on
April 22, 1948," he told me forty-three years later. With Anchorage as his
base and stepping-off point for the rest of Alaska, Milo finally felt set to
live out his dream: "to grow up with the country."

He described those early days:

*There was a doctor up there who I had known during the
war, A. S. Walkowski, whom we called Wally, and he let me
practice in his office. . . . I was busy from the moment I got
there until I could find a place of my own to practice in.*

He and Betsy found a property on the westernmost end of Fourth
Avenue, close to the waters and mudflats of Knik Arm at the northern
edge of Cook Inlet. It seemed ideal at the time. They remodeled the two-
story, wood-frame building so there was space for living quarters as well
as Milo's medical office. Within a few years the property included a grassy
play area for the boys and a small guest cottage for Betsy's parents—all
enclosed by a white picket fence. It would serve their needs for more than
sixteen years—until the Good Friday Earthquake in 1964.

With his medical office located less than half a mile away from Providence Hospital where he did his surgery, Milo was soon commuting by bicycle during warm weather months. In those early years of the 1950s, Betsy said, Anchorage was still such a small town that Milo's cycling habits were noted by an announcer on the local radio station: "Spring must be here—Doc Fritz is back riding his bike today."

Milo described the health conditions he saw upon his return to Alaska:

> Among the white people in Anchorage, you'd find the same conditions there that you'd find any place in a city like New York, or Philadelphia, or San Francisco. But in the villages outside, especially in the Native villages, tuberculosis was a terrible thing. Outside of each town there was a little colony of white-walled tents where they would put the cases that were beyond hope to die. And I remember when I'd go in to see them, I don't think I did any more than wear a mask.
>
> I remember how tragic it was to see these beautiful young girls—their faces were flushed from the TB and their eyes glittering, and how pretty they were, and, my God, within a matter of weeks or months they'd be dead. And the young men the same way. Until the drugs were discovered—the isoniazid and para-aminosalicylic acid, I think they were—tuberculosis was the number one problem. The Territory didn't have the money to build a hospital and the States had their own problems, so those that got well, got well with modest medical attention and those that were overwhelmed just died.

Milo described how tuberculosis was treated then:

> They had various things, pneumothorax, which was pumping air into the space between the lung and the chest wall to collapse the lung. They'd do thoracotomies, they'd remove sections of ribs and collapse the chest on the lung when there was a cavity—brutal operations, but that's all we could do.
>
> . . . And the kids suffered from mastoiditis and a disease called phlyctenular keratoconjunctivitis—call it PKC— which was an allergic response on the part of the cornea of the eye to infection elsewhere in the body, which would be in the tonsils or in the mastoid. The most frequently performed

operation was tonsil and adenoid surgery because of the effect it had on the ears. If we could get them before the ears broke down, we could save the hearing in these cases.

The need was such that Thursdays were soon set aside for Alaska Natives enrolled in the Territory's Department of Health programs. But appointments in Anchorage couldn't begin to fill the tremendous need. Health care throughout rural Alaska was virtually non-existent, distances were great, and most people couldn't afford to come to Anchorage. Doc Fritz began taking his medical skills into the bush, traveling to the remote Native villages and setting up clinics to treat those scattered populations.

"When I was in Alaska, I just carried on the work I'd started in North Carolina."

MID-CENTURY SNAPSHOTS – ANCHORAGE AND ANCHOR POINT

You have crows that go with the black sheep and we have the ever-complaining gulls which are white. So, your crows are the bad guys and our gulls are the good guys. We rather like to hear them complain down there at the river's mouth because when they are there in strength, the fish must be running and that is good for the sport and the economy.

—MILO FRITZ

"UNCLE MILO'S HERE!" I CAN STILL hear my father's voice in the mid-1950s, the announcement of his brother's arrival resonating with affection and excitement as it carried up the stairs. I would have been six, maybe seven years old, the oldest of four children born to Larry Fritz, a commercial photographer and his wife Helen, a home economist.

By then, my parents, brother Karl, baby Lenore and I had moved from the garage apartment at Hillcrest, Gammy's bucolic estate—where my father had routinely taken pot shots at the crows that menaced the songbirds he liked to hear—to nearby Merion, another suburb of Philadelphia. We were now living more or less shoulder-to-shoulder with our suburban neighbors in an old house that could accommodate a growing family as well as a studio and darkroom for their home-based food photography business.

My earliest memories of Uncle Milo are episodic and impressionistic, my imagination fed by the wonderfully impractical Christmas gifts that Uncle Milo and Aunt Betsy sent us: huge white fur mittens that went halfway up our skinny arms, skin moccasins with furry interiors and colorful beaded designs on the toes, necklaces with lockets containing flakes of real gold, fur-trimmed leather pouches that I used for my jacks and ball, a twenty dollar gold coin strung on a gold chain, and a fur piece—a series of soft brown pelts, complete with silky little heads, beady eyes, and dangling paws—that my mother wore circled about her shoulders on the few occasions when my parents took a break from the obligations of family life and running their business.

Uncle Milo's visits were usually brief and appended to some medical event that drew him from Alaska to our suburban Philadelphia home. He would sometimes arrive professionally dressed in a double-breasted trench coat over a tweed jacket, carefully pressed trousers and bow tie. At other times he might arrive wearing a fur-ruffed parka or an Alaska tuxedo on his tall, slender frame. Fit, full of energy, with a faintly military bearing, Uncle Milo always seemed a dashing figure to me, as if Arctic winds swept in the door with the man I had heard called "Alaska's Flying Doctor."

Uncle Milo's visits were always a cause for celebration. We children would assemble in the living room, tentative and as wide-eyed as deer. We would sit on our little wooden stools, or, when we were older, settle into living room chairs or pile onto the sofa, curious and expectant. We were a receptive if often uncomprehending audience as we listened to whatever "Alaska's Flying Doctor" had to say.

With enough notice, my father would order a case of his brother's favorite beer—Priors Double Dark—from the beer distributor. "Been through the horse twice, you know," my father would state with mock seriousness, a favorite line that would get the desired effect from Uncle Milo who would let out a startling roar, slap his thigh and say, "Larry, you slay me!" They would savor the foamy beer in their mugs. We would carefully sip our glasses of ginger ale as the stories and conversation flowed. We watched as these two authoritative figures transformed into the mischievous boys of their youth.

Though separated by three years in age and over 3,000 miles, Milo and his younger brother were very close, writing lengthy typed letters to each other weekly. My father once said that certain events in his life didn't quite feel complete until he wrote his brother about them. Uncle Milo's letters—with his anecdotes about life in Alaska, his observations about current events and the books he was reading—laced with his witticisms, were often posted on the refrigerator. They made for entertaining and instructive reading.

During the mid-1950s, Uncle Milo and Aunt Betsy mailed a photo album to our family, presumably to help us better visualize their lives in Alaska. Larry's and Milo's lives were somewhat parallel: both men were self-employed, both in business partnerships with their wives, both raising children on roughly quarter-acre lots. But in most respects, their worlds could not have been more different.

The photographs from Alaska were secured to pages of heavy black paper by black corner mounts so they could be slipped out to read comments on the back. A few from 1953 and 1954 offer brief explanatory notes, most in Aunt Betsy's handwriting, a few in Uncle Milo's scrawl. The black-and-white snapshots gave us some concrete images of where and how they lived and also rare glimpses of our cousins Jonathan and Pieter.

About half of the photographs were taken in Anchorage at their combined home and office at 1027 Fourth Avenue. Multiple photographs, taken in winter and summer, provide views of a white, clapboard building with a grassy, fenced-in yard and a playhouse. Except for views of Cook Inlet, visible through bare branches in winter photographs, the attractive home could be almost anywhere in the United States. In several photos the boys stand alternately with their mother and father in front of a day-sailer named *Ariadne*, which Milo built from a kit. Jonathan and Pieter are shown with their cats, finches, and friends, and with Betsy's parents, Tom and Margaret ("Dinny" to her grandsons) Berry, who lived with them until Pieter was in his teens. There are several photos of Jonathan, dressed in the red cassock of an altar boy, and of Pieter with the cake he baked for his mother's birthday in September 1954. Photos of the home's interior reflect Betsy's touches of both hominess and formality—kids and pets in the kitchen, comfortable-looking traditional furniture, and a wall of glass-doored cabinets displaying antique silver pieces along with sets of glassware and china.

In a photo from February 1953, nine-year-old Pieter and twelve-year-old Jonathan—each boy cuddling a cat on his lap—flank their father on a sofa. Milo sits between them with his arms folded firmly across his chest.

SNAPSHOTS TAKEN DURING THE SUMMER OF 1953 and in September of 1954 offer scenes of Anchor Point and the extended Fritz family at work and play. Milo's dream of owning the Anchor Point homestead on the Kenai Peninsula had become a reality in 1949 when he and Betsy bought the property with its cluster of rough-hewn structures built by the original Swedish homesteader. The magnificent stretch of land along the shores of Cook Inlet offered the family periodic escapes from their life in Anchorage, which lay more than 200 miles away, up an unpaved road to the north. There are photos of Milo on a ladder, bare-chested and smiling as he turns from tarring the roof of a cabin; using a scythe to cut the waist-high grass growing around the rustic buildings; relaxing in the doorway of the weathered boathouse, a Rolleiflex camera swinging from his neck. On the back of a photo of a two-story log cabin, Betsy wrote, "Lower part of the house that is used to store coal from the beach. Upper part for storing [illegible]. Attached behind is the only outhouse I know with fur doorknobs."

Milo and Betsy, along with her parents, are pictured sitting at the kitchen table, the well-stocked shelves and the wood walls visible behind them, and reading in the sun on chairs set out on the grassy cliff above Cook Inlet. Photographs show Pieter, Jonathan, and a friend in front of a tent they've pitched down on the beach and on a rickety-looking raft they seem to have assembled from flotsam.

A group photo taken on a mild September day in 1954, was one I had previously skipped over, as I did not recognize the two men—one in a light-colored windbreaker, clasping a fedora behind him; the other man distinguished by black-rimmed glasses and bowtie. They are standing near one of the old cabins with Milo and Betsy. On the back of the photo Betsy had written: "Drs. Fritz and Crabtree, Betsy and Dr. Parran (former Surgeon General, U.S. Public Health Services) at Anchor Point this summer."

From my research, I viewed the photo with new eyes. Pictured was *the*

Dr. Thomas Parran of Alaska's groundbreaking *Parran Report* and one of his colleagues, Dr. James A. Crabtree.

Dr. Parran was head of the medical research team that traveled throughout Alaska in the summers of 1953 and 1954 at the request of the Department of the Interior, the Territorial Governor, and the Territorial Legislature. Dr. Parron and his three colleagues were all faculty members at the Graduate School of Public Health of the University of Pittsburgh. Their task was to complete a comprehensive health survey of Alaska.

Never one to mince words, Milo presumably gave Drs. Parran and Crabtree an earful that day during their visit to Anchor Point. Milo must have hoped that perhaps, finally, the range of medical problems that he had been battling since his arrival in Alaska would be trumpeted by someone with the necessary clout in Washington, DC to push for the policies and resources to help solve them. Milo must have awaited the completion of Dr. Parran's survey with great eagerness.

The *Parran Report's* publication in the fall of 1954 did bring nationwide attention to the terrible health conditions in Alaska, especially among the Native populations. It included this compelling passage:

> In tragic contrast [to White Alaska], the Indigenous peoples of Native Alaska are the victims of sickness, crippling conditions and premature death to a degree exceeded in very few parts of the world. Among them, health problems are nearly out of hand. If other Americans could see for themselves the large numbers of the tuberculous, the crippled, the blind, the deaf, the malnourished and the desperately ill among a relatively small population, private generosity would dispatch shiploads of food and clothing for Alaska alongside the cargoes setting out for Korea; doctors and nurses would be mobilized and equipped with the urgency of the great hospital units in wartime; the Alaskan missions would not need to beg for support. Flood victims in Europe and famine victims in India are the prompt beneficiaries of generous United States Government assistance, but our own year-in-year-out victims of hunger, disease and exposure are unpublicized and still "far away."

The 300-plus page document was sweeping in its approach, offering a lucid overview of Alaska at the time. The report included detailed descriptions of Alaska history, geography, demographics, the ethnology of the various primary Native populations as well as their current living conditions, their cultures, and the dreadful medical problems afflicting them. It described the inadequacies of the current medical system, the overlapping efforts of various federal agencies as well as the intrepid heroes of Alaska, the public health nurses—"those magnificent women," in Milo's words.

The outrage generated by the *Parran Report* in the national press and the U. S. Congress resulted in new legislation and increased funding from the federal government that would begin to address the profound medical and administrative problems described in Dr. Parran's report.

Those Fritz snapshots, unexpectedly, captured a bit of Alaska medical history as well as a glimpse of their family life.

FROM ANCHORAGE TO
CLINICS IN THE BUSH

*Here you are, the only eye, ear, nose, and throat man
in Anchorage and yet you go off to the Native villages
and leave us sit. I said, "Well, I feel that that's my job
and that's what I'm going to do."*

—MILO FRITZ

MILO'S EXPERIENCES IN KETCHIKAN, TRAVELING ALASKA during World War II, and work with Dr. C. Earl Albrecht's survey team in 1947, made it clear to him that middle ear disease and mastoiditis were prevalent to a frightening degree throughout the Territory. A report to that effect and Milo's recommendation that tonsils and adenoids be removed, when indicated, were submitted to Dr. Albrecht, who continued to serve as the Territory's first full-time Commissioner of Health until 1956. Earl Albrecht, Milo's friend and colleague from their World War II days at Ft. Richardson, shared Milo's concerns and his sense of urgency. Milo recalled Albrecht's efforts as Commissioner of Health in our 1991 interview:

He did more for the Territory and the State than anybody. He was no trained politician, yet he taught himself to go before the committees and lay down the facts about the medical problems that he was having with the Eskimos and the Indians and the white people away from the cities. He went to Washington and appeared before the subcommittees of the House of Representatives and the Senate and got money out of them. He was absolutely marvelous. And yet, he was still a doctor and he had a trusting nature. A bureaucrat, you know, if there's any way that they can avoid doing something and referring it to higher headquarters, they did it. But not Albrecht, you'd get the answer from him if he knew it, or he'd find out.

One of the nice things he did, we used to have a little book of documents called travel requests, and usually bureaucrats would deal out one at a time in case you'd rush off to San Diego or something like that. But he gave me a whole book of them. He relied on my honesty that I wouldn't abuse the Territory's money and go off on junkets but would use it only for going to Kodiak or going to Ketchikan, Sitka, or Nome.

Milo's clinics were often held in places where there were no doctors at all. Some towns—Well Point, Barrow, Kotzebue—had hospitals, but sometimes there was no doctor or anesthetist there, just a nurse or nurses. In McGrath, his clinic was in a roadhouse. In the tiny villages of Allakaket, Venetie or Rampart they would use the schoolhouse. At times, instruments were sterilized by boiling them on a Yukon stove outdoors. Doc Fritz only did the simplest of surgeries under those conditions—tonsillectomies and adenoidectomies. T&As were under general anesthetics; tonsillectomies were under local anesthetics, generally speaking. He would not do mastoidectomies, brain tumors or anything difficult in these villages, but time and again he would pick up something that was outside his specialty. If he could take care of it, he did, if not, he would wire the Alaska Native Service or the appropriate agency with permission to have the patient sent into a medical facility that could take care of the patient's problem. Commissioner Albrecht helped facilitate the process Milo said:

Well, you see that's another reason why Albrecht was so great. How the hell he ever did it I'll never know. If you were a Native, you were under what was then known as the Alaska

Native Service. It's now called the Alaska Native Health Service. But Albrecht, who was Commissioner of Health for the Territory was in charge of everybody, so you see there was an overlap—if you had a Native kid, he was a ward both of the Native Service and of the Territory. And yet Albrecht had to get along with those guys. They always had to refer everything to Washington.

I quickly learned that these operative permits were a marvelous stumbling block that the bureaucrats could use. Let's say a kid came in to have his tonsils and adenoids out, and in the course of doing a careful physical examination on him, I'd find that he needed to have a hernia repaired. "Oh, you can't do that, we don't have an operative permit." I said, "OK go get your lawyer to draw up a document that will allow the surgeons of the Territory or of the Native Service to do any surgical procedure that they deem necessary."

And the bureaucrats jumped on that and said, "Oh, the people won't know what they're signing for."

And I said, "You mean to tell me that if I ask them for permission to do a cholecystectomy, they'll know more about it if they read about it on a piece of paper?"

It was a constant battle to do nothing or to do as little as possible, versus Albrecht, who tried to do as much as possible with little or nothing.

Betsy managed the office and its small staff of nurses and secretaries and stayed in Anchorage with the children during the early years. She would organize the documentation, the supplies and the equipment required for each one- or two-week clinic and would schedule the patients. In addition, Milo said:

She knew the ferry schedule, she knew the Halibut Point Road was being torn up that day, and so the patient that was scheduled from beyond Halibut Point Road construction site couldn't get in, she knew when the ferries came, she knew the airline schedule. How the hell she ever kept it all in mind I don't know, but she did.

. . . She did all the bookkeeping, and the collection of fees, because in the villages and in the cities where there *were doctors, people paid for their care. In fact, the clinics in Ketchikan—I made money on those. But usually, the clinics were a break-even affair or you'd lose a little money.*

. . . Some Betsy and I financed ourselves. We even got the Episcopal Church to finance one. If you can get anything out of the Episcopalians you've got to be good. Most of them were under the aegis of the Alaska Department of Health under Albrecht, and his successors Elizabeth Bishop and Bob Smith, who were typical bureaucrats. But Albrecht had laid the groundwork and I was used to it, so I knew what could be done and what couldn't be done. Nobody could tell me because I knew and then I'd do it, so they had to go along with what I wanted to do.

With Betsy overseeing the office in Anchorage, Milo relied on the help of public health nurses, who were, he said, "the top of the heap as far as I'm concerned."

By God, when something had to be done, it was done. It wasn't done "if I don't forget" or "if I don't go fishing" or "it was raining that day," it would be carried out. In fact, the tuberculosis program, if it hadn't been for the public health nurses, never would have succeeded. They were marvelous women. And each one of them would have a group of villages in her charge and she knew everything about it, everybody in those villages—who was sleeping with whom, who was about to be divorced, what kids were sick, who was about to have a baby, whose infant was having trouble. And, of course, she'd overwhelm me with the whole works. I tried to stick to eye, ear, nose, and throat, but I had to be a psychiatrist, and orthopedist, and that's where my internships and all those things came in so handy. So, if I'd only learned one damn thing, I would have been a total loss—not a total loss, but I wouldn't have been nearly as useful as I've tried to describe.

Milo explained how he ran the clinics:

The first week, in the mornings, I would do the surgery, because when there are complications in surgery, they usually take place in the first 24 hours. And certainly, by the end of the week, if anything is going to go wrong, it's going to go wrong in that length of time. Two reasons for that—first, you don't want to lose a patient's life, and the second is, no doctors in these communities liked to be cleaning up my messes for me. If I did a T&A on a kid and he bled, well I was there to take care of it.

. . .You could only do so much surgery because they weren't medical centers. We were either working in a hospital or a school or whatever was available. And the most useful people were 15-year-old girls. You could ask them after they scrubbed their hands and put on their gloves to hold their hands folded in front of them. In the painting showing my activities [the mural True Pioneer by Fred Machetanz hangs in the Alaska Native Medical Center in Anchorage], the artist depicted these girls standing there with gloves on and everyone thinks they're praying. . . . I could get them to sit right down next to me there at the head of the table, I'd show them how to use the suction rod and whatnot, and after two or three operations they were experts. . . . You'd never get a boy to help you, "Blood frightens me. I don't want to do that."

And one thing that I did that is being done now to some extent by conventional doctors is having the father go to the delivery room with the mothers and taking them to Lamaze courses and teaching them about pregnancy and all that.

. . . I used to have the clinics open to the public. The first few days I'd be playing to a full house. The whole village would come to watch me do tonsil and adenoid surgery. Towards the end, there'd be only one grandmother that would come every day. And in the clinics where I'd test eyes and see about eyeglasses and hearing aids and all that, people could come and look. I said, "All I ask you to do is that you be quiet. I don't mean to go tiptoeing around, but no unnecessary conversation because the patient deserves that much respect."

But they're all each other's friends and neighbors, so I wasn't violating confidentiality or anything like that. I mean you wouldn't be talking about pregnancies and sexual intercourse and AIDS—we didn't have AIDS in those days—but *in that way the people in the towns and villages that I went to became educated.*

. . . I did a thing I certainly would never do now. There's no way I could get an anesthetist or an anesthesiologist to go with me so I began giving the anesthetics myself and operating at the same time. And thank God, I never lost a case. I was exceedingly careful about a history—did he bruise easily; did he bleed a long time after a tooth came out. Any problems like that, I'd say no we'd have to take him or her into Anchorage or to the nearest hospital, if it weren't in Anchorage. But the others I did there, right in the field.

I'd operate and I'd be at the head of the table doing the tonsils and adenoids or whatever I was doing and we had five air mattresses. We'd blow them up and put them on the floor with a blanket over them and the mother would usually be the nurse, so when the child would still be under the effect of the anesthetic, we put them on the air mattress until they came to. Then we got an army cot and we had an ambulance crew—six Native boys. We'd put the patient on the cot, lift it up and take the patient back to his cabin. Then I'd make the rounds at night and see that everything's all right, and I made it for years. So, I like to think there was more to it than just blind luck. I might have been lucky two or three times, but I just did this over and over again, and was very severely criticized for it. I said, "Well, why the hell don't you guys go out and do some of it and help me out? I don't see any volunteers!"

Milo described the rural villages where he held his clinics:

Well, they were frame houses and . . . dirty. If an outboard motor didn't work, pitch it out the door. If there was a car or a vehicle, a three-wheeler, a four-wheeler, or something like that, that had passed it best days, nobody ever bothered fixing the damn thing, except for the most elementary repairs. They just set it out in the snow! And the rain could rust it away!

. . .But they're very much devoted to their children and have great respect for the elders, or did in those days.

*Remember, I'm speaking now of years ago—20 years ago or
more [1970s or earlier]—and I would hate anybody to read
this and say, "Oh, my God, when you go to Kotzebue now,
the kids demand a dollar for taking a photograph of them,"
things like that. That wasn't true then.*

*Another thing, I respected the people and they, I found
out, appreciated it greatly. I talked to the people about what
I was going to do, what I had planned to do. And I would
say, "In return, I'd like you to be willing to pose for photographs. Let me take pictures of you when you're cleaning fish
or hanging wash on the line, or whatever your daily activities
might be." And they talked it out among themselves and said
you can go ahead and take all the photographs you want.*

By the time Doc Fritz retired after fifty-one years of practicing medicine, he had treated over 58,000 patients. During the years when his practice was based in Anchorage, Doc Fritz spent about a third of his time
doing itinerant medicine elsewhere—about 150 clinics all told, in his es-
timation. As the only EENT specialist in Alaska at first, Milo would hold
clinics not only in remote bush communities, but in larger towns as well,
often three times a year. He explained:

*In civilized places like Kodiak, Sitka, and Ketchikan, the
doctors there would pick the patients out that they wanted
me to consult on and they had enough confidence in me
to realize that I wasn't there to undermine their position.
Sometimes, you know, patients don't all have wings sprout-
ing out of their backs, and they would say, "Oh, you say I
have sinusitis, well doctor so-and-so has been treating me
for something else." And the opening would be for me to say,
"Yes, well he's a pretty dumb doctor." I'd say, "Well, I wasn't
there when he examined you and I find this condition exists
now and let's take care of it." That way the [local] doctors
were never downgraded or spoken of ill by Betsy or me in
these clinics.*

*. . . Where there were hospitals, like in Kodiak and
Ketchikan, I'd do eye surgery too—cataract extractions, to
correct cross-eyed conditions and the opposite of that when
the eye turned out, and then there were various minor plastic*

procedures on the eyelids that would be done. I'd do anything I didn't need a big hospital for. I wouldn't do a mastoidectomy in the field. That's a complex and difficult operation and takes three to four hours to do it in some cases—two-and-a-half hours even if everything goes well—and they require careful postoperative care.

*   ... When the others [EENT specialists] came, they weren't interested in doing itinerant work—it's too much work! Hell, in order to get the stuff ready and down to the air terminal to be sent out by airplane to wherever you were going to go, that took lots of work. And then when you came home you had all the letters to write to the Department of Health and the Native Service and private doctors. It was a backbreaking job, but I loved it!*

Eyes – Tuberculosis and the Scourge of Phlyctenular Keratoconjunctivitis

During the 1930's various individuals noted that the vison of many Alaskan natives was impaired by white scars on the corneas of the eyes. This was variously attributed to snow blindness, cataract, tuberculosis, or nutritional deficiencies. In 1947 it was definitely established that the scarring was caused by repeated attacks of PKC.

—MILO FRITZ AND PHILLIPS THYGESON

So BEGAN A PAPER ABOUT PHLYCTENULAR KERATOCONJUNCTIVITIS that Milo co-authored with Dr. Phillips Thygeson and presented to the Alaskan Science Conference, convened in Washington, DC in 1950.

Prior to 1950, PKC was the principal eye disease in Alaska and, Milo wrote, "Almost never found in absence of TB, chronic middle ear or suppurative mastoid disease or both." Tuberculosis was still ravaging Native populations in 1956 when Milo wrote: "The TB rate in Alaska is greater than any recorded area in the world. Life expectancy of an Eskimo is 34; for a white man in the United States, it is 68."

To help him deal with the PKC epidemic he found upon returning to Alaska, Milo reached out to his friend and colleague Dr. Phillips Thygeson, one of the leading figures in ophthalmology. Phil, as Milo remembered from their many hours of ophthalmology discussions during their World War II service in Florida, had done clinical research on trachoma, an eye infection common among Apache Indians in Arizona when Phil was a resident at the University of Colorado medical school in the early 1930s. In the late 1940s, Milo was particularly interested in Phil's extensive experience with TB and PKC—also called phlyctenulosis—both doctors used the terms interchangeably.

In a 1987 interview with medical historian Sally Smith Hughes, Dr. Thygeson described his early experience with TB at the University of Colorado clinic where the majority of his patients were children:

> At the time, Colorado was full of what were called 'lungers' who had come from the East to recover in the Rocky Mountains. They used to think that the care for tuberculosis was fresh air and sunshine. . . . Our medical school was staffed by 'lungers' from Hopkins and Harvard and so on. . . . The children of 'lungers' would get low-dose tubercle bacilli in their environment—they don't get the full pulmonary disease. They got a tuberculosis infection without the clinical pneumonia. Wherever tuberculosis was rampant, there you had phlyctenulosis. . . . You couldn't possibly remember what tuberculosis was: it was the white plague. Every family had a death from tuberculosis—consumption—in the early days. Even the operas were written around consumption.

In the early 1950s, Dr. Thygeson was part of a group ophthalmic practice in San Jose, California. Previously, in 1947, he had co-founded the Francis I. Proctor Foundation for Research in Ophthalmology at the University of California San Francisco to carry out research in ocular infections and inflammatory eye diseases. The resulting pioneering work on PKC, primarily done by Dr. Thygeson and Dr. Fritz, but also assisted by another old friend and colleague of Milo's, Dr. Davis Durham, would define the nature and extent of the PKC problem among the Indian and

Eskimo populations in Alaska.

As Dr. Thygeson would come to see, tuberculosis was a much bigger problem in mid-twentieth-century Alaska than in the lower forty-eight states. As Phil noted in the interview:

> Eskimos had nine times the mortality rate from tuberculosis. . . . It was terrible. . . . As bad as it was for the Indian population, it was worse for the Eskimos. "[It was] the way they lived. They were cooped up all winter in—they weren't in igloos, but little one-room houses. So, if one had an open tuberculosis, the whole family got it.

"Milo was the one that got the phlyctenular project started in Alaska," Dr. Thygeson told interviewer Sally Hughes:

> He was the spark. . . . The Procter Foundation made a special two years' study of the Eskimos with Milo Fritz in Alaska. He got the [Alaska Department of Health] interested and they financed our trips. . . . At the time, the Eskimos had blinding phlyctenulosis. . . . There had been no effective treatment at all. In fact, the only beneficial effect that I knew of was to improve the nutrition of the child so that the tuberculosis would improve. But we had no topical treatment that was of any value except the use of atropine that cut down the photophobia [sensitivity to light] of the disease.
>
> We did our preliminary work at Sitka, at Mount Edgecumbe, where there's an industrial school for Eskimo children. We used that as the base, and from there we went around to various towns like Haidaberg [sic], and so on. We rented an airplane and went around the Indian villages. Dr. Fritz carried on in between our visits. They discovered that "steroids had a miracle effect, stopping the phlyctenulosis overnight, and only requiring two- or three-days' use, so we didn't get into any complications at all.

Their work resulted in several published papers. Subsequently, "Dr. Fritz got through the Public Health Service that every Eskimo child with a red eye would get forty-eight hours of steroids, without any diagnosis," Dr. Thygeson remembered. "The nurse would use it." He continued:

> That was the main victory for steroids. We could stop phlyctenulosis cold, but we didn't cure the tuberculosis which

> *was in the chest. . . . Isoniazid came along and took care of*
> *the tuberculosis. . . . You can use isoniazid in children safely.*
> *In adults you get into trouble by liver damage, but in children*
> *the isoniazid works very safely.*

By 1970, Milo could report that pulmonary TB, once Alaska's number one health problem, had assumed only a minor role. Corneal scarring from PKC and all its complications had also been dramatically reduced.

"No tuberculosis. That's the greatest single thing," Milo told me with quiet satisfaction in 1991.

In the 1950s, eye problems, other than PKC, continued to plague Alaska Natives. Milo was addressing those as well. He recognized the tremendous need for regular eye examinations, including refractions. In Milo's view, "Providing accurately fabricated, attractive, reasonably priced spectacles within a few days of the examination transcends all other ophthalmological problems in importance." He felt the standard two- to six-month wait for glasses was unacceptable, noting, "In this interval people may move in the course of their occupations, especially many youngsters who move to schools and jobs within and outside of Alaska, vastly decreasing the likelihood of their spectacles ever catching up with them in time to do them any good."

In the early years, when Betsy's role in Milo's itinerant clinics was primarily one of logistics and organization, Milo's clinics were usually solo affairs. Providentially, in the mid-1950s, an optician named John Spahn returned to Alaska.

In the aftermath of World War II, Alaska's civilian population had begun to swell. Many former GIs, intrigued by their first taste of Alaska, decided to stay on. Others left and came back. John Spahn was one of the latter. He had been stationed at the naval base on Kodiak Island during World War II. The beauty, the adventure, and the fishing offered by Alaska appealed to John, so in the early 1950s, he and his wife Alice moved to Anchorage. By 1956 John was working in the optical laboratory of an Anchorage optometrist who soon began touting John's technical and personal virtues to Doc Fritz in hopes the ophthalmologist would send more business his way. Milo decided to give the new man a try.

"This was the beginning of a long and fast friendship," Milo recalled. Within a year of meeting John, Milo asked his new friend if he would be willing to join him on his annual clinic in Kodiak and take over the dispensing of spectacles which Milo had done up until then. John, who by then had established his own optical firm, was glad to do so.

The optometrist was a soft-spoken, congenial man. Milo's junior by eight years, John was physically strong—the pitcher Warren Spahn was his cousin, Betsy said—so could assist Milo with the "heavy lifting." And Milo found him to be a quick learner.

> *Of course, at this first clinic it was necessary for John to see the mechanics of it. I always hired a local nurse to help with the drops, which we use for younger people as cycloplegia [paralysis of eye focusing muscle during examinations]. He had to learn the customs of the town, the peculiarities of its terrain, the influence of rain and snow, as the case might be, according to the season, and he had also to evaluate the intelligence and initiative of the local girl whom I hired on this occasion.*

> *Before the week was over, he had learned to help with the drops, judge the speed of my work and, by observing what was going on in the examining room, he could tell whether I was falling behind in my work, whether I was gaining ground and would soon run out of patients, or whether I was on a state bordering on utter collapse which has become more frequent as the years have gone by.*

One night that first week, while Milo was working on the day's charts in a room at the top of the little frame hotel overlooking Kodiak Harbor, he saw John coming up the main street from the local drugstore bearing a package.

> *I was particularly tired. The day had been long and trying, and my interest in doing paperwork was flagging considerably. John entered and presented me with a milkshake. Never was a gift more gratefully received and it proved to me what I found was important—that he felt that he was part of this effort, not a hired hand or a servant, but a fellow worker in the vineyard.*

"Thus, we undertook the first joint clinic," Milo recalled. It would be the first of many that they would work on and finance together for over two decades.

The two men also soon started a nonprofit organization in Anchorage called the Eye, Ear, Nose and Throat Foundation of Alaska, Inc., with John Spahn its president. Aside from the occasional rummage sale, Milo noted, the Foundation depended "almost entirely for funds from the generous contributions of individuals in Alaska and elsewhere who have heard of the Foundation." Milo described the dynamics of the health problems he and John encountered and their diplomatic solutions:

> In Alaska there are many individuals, and among these we consider the children most important who require hearing aids and spectacles but are unable to afford them. For various technical reasons, many of these individuals, and adults as well in the same economic plight, are unable to qualify for this kind of medical assistance under the various federal and state medical programs. . . . On every private clinic that we hold, such as the ones we have had in Kodiak, there is always one day set aside for the examination of individuals, chiefly children, who are so-called beneficiaries of the Alaska Department of Health or the Alaska Native Health Service.

John Spahn helped with these patients, Milo noted, as well as the private ones in the Kodiak clinic, "dispensing and fitting of spectacles entirely free, and out of the kindness of his heart."

But even so, Milo and John found that there was a certain stigma attached to the wearing of the Berwyn type of gold-filled metal frame being dispensed, as it "brands the wearer a recipient of charity under some governmental scheme." They noted that some children, "even those who are very severely handicapped because they do not do so, absolutely refuse to wear these glasses." They decided to allow the children and others to select among modestly priced frames that were currently fashionable, and then had "no difficulty in having them wear these spectacles." And though this added to the cost of each pair, contributors to the Foundation shouldered it without complaint.

Another innovation was the Plus One Dollar fund in which the dollar added to the price of the glasses, provided at cost by John and his optical company, would cover replacement and repairs for broken frames, lost temples, or screws and all the paperwork, shipping, and handling.

John's big-hearted nature, his willingness to learn new skills and his sensitivity to the variety of cultural situations they encountered on many clinics in the field during the 50s, 60s, and 70s, resulted in a close working relationship and enduring friendship.

Milo taught him to give anesthetics. "John would look at the patient's size and his general condition and got to be very, very good. We were always shaved in the morning and we always had on a white coat, and no matter how poor the people were, we treated them just the same as though they were patients in Anchorage. And, needless to say, that went over well."

Out in the bush, each clinic was different, with its own challenges—"no pushbutton and Esquire-clothing type adventure."

It requires the wearing of durable and warm clothes, the carrying along of survival gear and extra clothing, the lugging of five-gallon gas cans and emptying them into the wing tanks of the plane, stamping out runways in deep snow, servicing the plane surrounded by literally clouds of mosquitoes and other hard-biting insects. In addition, we have had to keep our index of adaptability turned up to full power since in every village we found little differences in the customs of the people. In some places perhaps a trader's wife will be the dominant individual in the community who has taken hold and organized the clinic. In another, the Public Health Nurse will have done the necessary preliminary chores. In the third, a group of citizens will have arranged for the work to be done. In each instance little differences and our acceding to them make for much smoother relationships than an adamant and rigid approach to the problem of ophthalmology and otolaryngology in the bush would bring.

John also became Doc Fritz's dental assistant. At Duke, the nose and throat clinic was across the hall from the dental clinic, and a dentist taught the inquisitive EENT resident how to block the nerves to the teeth, and so Milo learned how to do dental extractions painlessly. A dentist in Anchorage gave Milo some instruments that he didn't use any longer because the plating on them wasn't clear. "When the people in the villages found out that not only did I pull teeth, which they would submit to with no anesthetic at all, but I would give an anesthetic, it was a land office business."

A change from the traditional Native diet had led to their dental problems, Milo explained in an interview.

*If you noticed the skulls that have been exposed by chang-
es when the mountainsides have been caved in or something
on, let's say, St. Lawrence Island, you would find the skulls
of these people with perfect teeth even though the teeth gave
evidence that the people were in their 50 or 60s or even older,
but they were on the Native diet. As soon as the store came
in with its popsicles, ice cream, Kool-Aid, starch and sugar,
there went the teeth. They brought in the white man's food
but didn't bring in the white man's dentist.*

*. . . I did a lot of dental extractions, which used to break
my heart. Here you'd have a handsome young Eskimo boy or
beautiful Eskimo girl and leave her with a handful of teeth
that were rotted out.*

John would assist Milo in the "disagreeable chore" he took on "since
in most of the villages of the hinterland, the dentist is a very rare sight
indeed."

TONSILLECTOMIES AND ADENOIDECTOMIES WERE PROCEDURES that Doc
Fritz commonly performed in treating ear, nose, and throat problems,
particularly middle ear disease and mastoiditis. For decades he worked
to establish recognition of tonsil-adenoid disease as a source of middle
ear-mastoid infection. Doc Fritz found it an uphill battle. In an article
published in *Northwest Medicine* in 1963, he summarized his findings and
skirmishes with Alaska's medical bureaucracies.

*A few months after coming to Alaska, in January
1940, fresh from my graduate training in EENT at Duke
University, it became indisputably clear that the reason for
so much mastoiditis in Southeastern Alaska at that time
was a non-recognition of the indications for doing tonsillectomy and adenoidectomy.*

*By submitting reports to the Territorial Commissioner
of Health and representatives of the federal government
in charge of native health, I hoped to bring attention to
the connection between mastoiditis middle ear disease
and the need for doing tonsillectomy and adenoidectomy, when indicated, to those in authority. But, in the 18
months' time of my stay in private practice in 1940 and*

1941, was unable to gain acceptance for this important concept, recognized by properly trained otolaryngologists since about 1890.

Two-and-one-half years' duty throughout the Territory of Alaska during World War II disclosed that middle ear disease and mastoiditis were not confined to Southeastern Alaska but were prevalent to a frightening degree throughout the Territory. Deaths from meningitis, brain abscess and labyrinthitis, all of otitic origin, were not recognized as such by any of those in charge of public health in the Territory. And, to my knowledge, by only one physician in private practice, namely, Fred M. Langsam of Nome.

In our interview, Milo's had high praise for the doctor he had worked with both in Bethel and Nome:

Among the doctors that I revere in life besides Albrecht, there was a fellow by the name of Fred Langsam. I can't be sure of this, but I suspect that in order to avoid getting into the war, he went to Alaska and ended up in Nome and ran the hospital up there. He was the best all-around doctor that I have ever known, and by all-around, I mean he knew the basics of dermatology, he could put on beautiful casts, he could do a splendid gall bladder operation or appendectomy or hernia repair and he was also a concert-grade pianist, a gourmet cook and he was terribly fat. Somehow or other, he attracted to him all kinds of odd people. One of them, an old lady, was his secretary. She took care of all the unpleasant details of his life for him.

And yet, he wasn't popular among the people of Nome at all. They didn't realize what they had. He wouldn't let them take their sled dogs into the hospital with them. He said, "Dogs don't belong in the hospital." Things like that would irritate them and so they would somehow translate that into the fact that he wasn't a good doctor.

. . . Doctors still are loath to go out on clinics. I'm convinced it takes a certain type of personality. Fred Langsam used to make clinical rounds out of Nome and they nailed him because he lost a patient—an anesthetic death—which

was always hanging over my head, you know. And, gee, he
was brutally criticized for that. Rather let the whole Native
population go deaf rather than take a chance—that was the
philosophy.

. . . I can't think of anybody that could equal Fred Langsam
or Albrecht.

Milo's views for treating the ear diseases running rampant through
the Native population were further supported by what he had observed
as a member of Dr. Albrecht's nutritional survey team under the Alaska
Territorial Department of Health.

On this trip in the spring of 1947 the lethal and alarm-
ing prevalence of suppurative diseases of the middle ear and
mastoid bone with dreadful complications was even further
disclosed. A detailed report of these findings and the rec-
ommendations that tonsils and adenoids be removed, when
indicated, throughout the Territory, was submitted to Dr.
Albrecht.

When Milo returned to Alaska to practice in Anchorage the following
year, he again, took up his crusade for recognition of tonsil-adenoid disease as a source of middle ear-mastoid infection. He brought it to the attention of officials in the Alaska Territorial Department of Health, the Alaska
Native Service, the children's Bureau in Washington, DC, the Bureau of
Indian Affairs, and other federal, territorial, and private agencies, "part of
whose energies were, or should have been," he wrote, "devoted to the erad-
ication of this preventable type of hearing loss, infection and, often, death."

Dr. Albrecht contracted with several Alaska physicians in private practice to hold operative clinics throughout the Territory, "sometimes with
the cooperation of the Alaska Native Service," Milo noted, "and sometimes
without it, sometimes in their hospitals, sometimes not." T&As were the
most frequently performed operation. The physicians who participated
in this effort during the late 1940s and early '50s were Fred Langsam of
Nome, Hugh B. Fate of Fairbanks, Joseph H. Shelton, of Anchorage, and
Milo Fritz.

For a child in the United States in the 1950s and '60s, having your tonsils out because of frequent colds, coughs, laryngitis—or perhaps, even as
a preventative measure—was no big deal, a rite of passage, even. And the
reward, summed up in a phrase that many young patients knew by heart

was: "Ice cream, we're going to have ice cream!"

Medical thinking changed over time. By the end of the twentieth century, routine tonsillectomies came to be seen as outdated as leeches by most of the mainstream medical profession. It was a controversial subject for several decades prior to that, and Doc Fritz felt the heat of that controversy, responding:

The general feeling was that I was "knife happy." I said, "Read the textbooks, I didn't write them all under an assumed name. I'm just doing the things that are conservative and acceptable through the time-honored diagnosis.

Doc Fritz considered T&As to be necessary and effective procedures for the chronic ear and throat infections he encountered in the bush for longer than some of his peers elsewhere did. Drugs were generally playing an increasingly significant role in treatment, but the situation in Alaska was somewhat different, as Doc Fritz described in his 1982 interview with Ken Kastella:

Sulfonamides were discovered when I was at Duke [1930s]. . . . They made a tremendous difference, I can tell you. I reported a case of meningitis of otitic origin with recovery. It was so rare that it made a medical journal, and we used something called Prontosil which was red, one of the first sulfonamides available; patient would have died without it.

. . . You have fellows and women in medicine now [1982] whose only job is to prescribe the proper medication. You get the bacterial sensitivity test; you grow the bacteria until you know all about its mothers and fathers and cousins and aunts and its reaction to various enzymes. Now you have immunosuppressed patients who have had cancer therapy that has knocked out their immunologic responses, and the people who can handle those drugs are specialists in the field of therapy, if you believe a thing like that. Well, in those days we didn't have anything like that. Hell, you did the best you could. But we didn't have immunosuppressed patients either. The life expectancy was 45 years of age, and the people in the bush, the Eskimos and the Indians, there you had people in the prime of life—those that weren't riddled with

tuberculosis—and they were operated on in their own environment, so they had a more or less immunity to their own germs, and the germs, or the bacteria, of their environment. You know yourself, iatrogenic and hospital infections when a person is perfectly immune to all the bugs in his house, but he goes to the hospital and has a staphylococcus there that somebody brought in with a carbuncle or something else and boy, they come down with staph pneumonia because they have absolutely no resistance against it.

Things are so complex now; for me to do now what I was doing then, I realized then that I was taking chances, and all I had to do was lose one case you know. I never lost one; never even had any close calls; because I'd use a certain amount of intelligence. If some kid came to me and I'd say, "Did you ever have any teeth filled? How did he make out?" . . . If he bled like a stuck pig for three weeks, well, by God, I'm not going to take his tonsils out.

FLYING – ANOTHER PASSION

Oh! I have slipped the surly bonds of earth
And danced the skies on laughter-silvered wings;
Sunward I've climbed and joined the tumbling mirth
Of sun-split clouds – and done a hundred things
You have not dreamed of – wheeled and soared and swung
High in the sunlit silence. Hovering there
I've chased the shouting wind along and flung
My eager craft through footless halls of air.
Up, up the long, delirious, burning blue
I've topped the wind-swept heights with easy grace
Where never lark, or even eagle flew -
And, while with silent lifting mind I've trod
The high untrespassed sanctity of space,
Put out my hand and touched the face of God.

—JOHN GILLESPIE MAGEE JR.

AFTER ESTABLISHING HIS PRACTICE IN ANCHORAGE, Milo was able to pursue the long-deferred dream inspired by his childhood hero

Charles Lindbergh: to become a pilot. "Flying an airplane, Milo said, "may not seem like very much to most people but to me it is just as exhilarating and exciting as my surgery was and is always a pleasant experience."

Milo approached flying with the same ferocious intensity and attention to detail as his first love—medicine—and he was eager to combine both passions in his itinerant clinic work. "I decided I would have to learn how to fly because the mail planes would go at certain times and you had to adjust your schedule to that. I found that was pretty inconvenient and pretty expensive."

As far back as 1939, airplanes were "used as casually by Alaskans as are taxis in continental United States," Governor John Troy noted in his introduction to Merle Colby's book, *Alaska: Guide to the Last American Frontier.* Anchorage, central Alaska's aerial hub, was an ideal place for a man like Milo, keen to fly. Both Merrill Field, Anchorage's bustling general aviation airport—already one of the busiest in the country—and nearby Hood Lake, ringed with private floatplanes, were within a ten-minute drive of the Fritz home and medical office. Milo thought Anchorage's setting, with its view of distant Mt. Susitna, "The Sleeping Lady," was beautiful, its weather much more "salubrious" than the cloudy, rainy, foggy conditions routinely encountered in Ketchikan and Southeastern Alaska. In pilot slang: Anchorage was apt to be CAVU—Ceiling And Visibility Unlimited; Ketchikan too often was EBAW—Even Birds Are Walking.

Milo always spoke highly of World War II pilot Glen Coons, who taught Milo how to fly. Glen was "a meticulous and very particular teacher," Milo remembered. "He worked for something called Anchorage Aeromotive. He was an instructor there and drew me—I was the oldest one in the class. I wasn't a very talented flyer, but I was careful."

Glen was "a disciplinarian," Milo recalled.

> He wasn't a popular instructor. If you didn't do what he told you to do, you'd hear about it in plain English. . . . If you followed his precepts, you'd keep out of trouble when you were flying an airplane. I remember thinking a couple of times when I got into a bad situation, if I cracked up my airplane, I hope to God I didn't do something that Glen said not to do!

Milo learned to fly in 1951, then earned his commercial license and bought a second-hand Piper J-3 Cub with the name *Slow Poke* stenciled on it. For the next four years he traversed Alaska on wheels, skis, and then floats at an average cruising speed of 59 mph. "It sure as hell was the slowest airplane in the world," Milo joked.

Doc Fritz became an increasingly skilled bush pilot, practicing flying and medicine as he began holding more medical clinics in rural communities throughout Alaska. "That was how I got around my love for flying," he explained. "They couldn't very well tax me for it, because, hell, I was going out and doing clinical work. That was how I was able to fly, which I dearly love to do. . . . Flying so enriched my life and increased my usefulness to people in remote areas or where they were too poor to afford a trip to Anchorage."

Milo also recalled:

> There was a women's organization that took care of women and children in the field of Alaska—a charitable effort, I've forgotten the name of it—and I got them to buy me a pair of floats for my J-3 Cub, so I could go up and down the Kuskokwim and Yukon Rivers, touch down in the river, haul the airplane up on the bank, pull out my instruments and go to work. The instruments in the case of surgical situations would be sent out by commercial air, and John Spahn and I would go out in the plane.
>
> . . . And then after a while, Betsy bought me a Tri-Pacer, which was more advanced, but still a very simple airplane— fixed landing gear and extra tank under the back seat so you had a little increased range. We just flew it and enjoyed it and we'd stop off and fish at places. John Spahn was a terrific fisherman. Fish wouldn't dare not bite when he was fishing. I enjoyed it too.

Flying seemed to offer Milo a measure of relief from his many cares and pressures, and, from the way he talked about flying, it seemed to carry a spiritual component as well. When aloft over his beloved Alaska— whether as part of his medical work or simply for pleasure—he no doubt felt that he had "slipped the surly bonds of earth" and "danced the skies on laughter-silvered wings," in the words of "High Flight," a poem written by nineteen-year-old Royal Canadian Air Force pilot John Gillespie Magee Jr. a few months before being killed during World War II. The poem seemed much like a prayer to Uncle Milo, who would quote it on occasion when he took me flying.

Nearly twenty years later, I would hear those words again, the poetry instantly familiar, as was the tone of awe and reverence. Senator Barry Goldwater, who had served as a pilot in World War II, recited "High Flight" in the library of our Eastern Shore farm where a dozen or so dinner guests had gathered following a day of goose hunting. Barry's straight-talking, sometimes prickly manner often reminded me of Uncle Milo. There were other parallels: both men served in the Army Air Corps; both flew Piper Cubs; both had a deep-seated passion for flying and aviation; both tended to be blunt and quotable. As Barry Goldwater's distinctive voice resonated off the pine-paneled walls of the hushed room, I again sensed what flying must have meant to Milo and so many other pilots who had in some sense "touched the face of God."

Milo's passion for flying and Alaska often enlivened his "official" correspondence. For five or six years in the 1950s, when he served as Alaska's delegate to the American Medical Association, Milo's newsletters became popular reading back in Alaska, as his recaps of the professional proceedings were entertainingly laced with his personal observations and anecdotes. Milo's final letter back to his Alaska colleagues was a thirteen-page, classically Miloesque account. Dated November 26, 1960, it began with a lyrical description of his flight south:

> Leaving Anchorage on a gold and blue day by propeller-driven Northwest Airlines DC-7C for Seattle was, as always, difficult to do. The sun, reflected from the new snow on the mighty peaks of the Chugach Mountains, was dazzling. The crevasses in the glaciers were of the deepest blue, while the ocean reflecting the blue of the matchless sky was picked out in little whitecaps easily seen from 19,000 feet. The passage of a moose here and there was marked by his hoof prints stitched across the flat unrelieved whiteness of an occasional lake. The red and orange of sunset soon gave way to the purple, gray and blue of dusk, not noticed in detail because of the elegant seven-course dinner served by our hosts, Northwest Airlines, complete from hot towels before, a la Japan, for freshening up, to Crème de Menthe afterwards, which distracted somewhat from the beauties of nature. I had the pleasure of sitting across the aisle from an airline captain with 26,000 hours flying experience, and still learning. In 26,000 hours of flying,

he never dropped a plane through the ice even once. In this I
am his superior.

It's not clear what incident Milo was alluding to in this letter, but in his
oral history he recalled two other memorable flying misadventures:

The first time I landed in snow was in a place called
Snowshoe Lake, and instead of making a racetrack design in
the snow while you're taxiing and then stopping on it because
the snow would be packed down, I just taxied along and cut
the engine. She stopped and, of course, immediately sank down
to the tie-down rings. I learned that because I had snowshoes,
which you always had on the struts, and I had to tramp out a
runway. And I got out that way, but I learned something.

I remember one time Tom Rambo, the great ear surgeon,
came up to visit me. We went to Kenai and I was taxiing up
the river—so I thought. The trouble was I was taxiing at five
miles an hour and the river was running down at seven miles
an hour, and, gee, I crashed into a barge, almost cut it loose
with the prop, banged up my wing. It was just experience. To
do a thing like that now would be ludicrous, but I didn't come
prepared to meet all situations in flying.

"You have to be careful," Milo maintained. "If the weather's bad, don't
go. I remember I had to go back three times for my airplane in Fairbanks
because there were clouds in the pass by the time I got up there. I just
wouldn't do it, because life after life today is lost in Alaska because people
push the weather. You just know, if you can't see and you're not trained,
you're going to get in trouble."

Milo wouldn't fly over to Kodiak Island, he said. "Because I had only
a single-engine airplane and as soon as you run over water with a single-
engine airplane, the engine begins to sound bad. So, I'd go by commercial
air that way. But to go over to Lake Iliamna, or if I had a post-op patient to
see in Fairbanks, I'd fly up and see them."

Milo likened flying to medicine:

You learn as you go along. That's why they call it practic-
ing medicine. There's a lot of routine things in medicine, but
every once in a while, something comes along that you just
have to use your training, your experience, intuition, and in-
telligence to solve.

CUTTING EDGE MEDICINE AND THE LEMPERT INSTITUTE

Having been appalled at the prevalence and incidence of mastoiditis in Alaska, I had found, as soon as I had returned to Alaska for what proved to be the last time in 1948, that the classical attack on the problem of mastoiditis was hopeless.

—MILO FRITZ

A S MILO WAS LEARNING, THE STEEP and hazardous learning curve of an Alaska bush pilot was continuous. When flying, Milo didn't "push the envelope"; he was a cautious, by-the-book pilot. When it came to medicine, however, Milo often questioned the safe path of the status quo. Since his medical school days, Doc Fritz had always strived to keep current with the latest advances in his specialties, reading and contributing to a variety of medical journals. He also sought out other doctors who might help him advance his own skills as well as those of his colleagues. He was a seeker and an innovator.

Mastoiditis, still one of the most prominent and pervasive of the health problems of Alaska Natives in mid-twentieth-century Alaska, was a dis-order caused by unresolved middle ear infection. It required surgery to remove diseased mastoid air cells—cells that sit behind the ear in a hollow space in the skull. Untreated mastoiditis and the resulting hearing prob-lems were of utmost concern to Doc Fritz, which was why the passen-ger aboard his float plane—and eyewitness to the fledgling bush pilot's instructive and nearly disastrous 1958 encounter with the barge on the Kenai River—was otologist Dr. J. H. Thomas Rambo from the Lempert Institute in New York City.

Milo had first heard about the Lempert Institute and its founder Julius Lempert during his EENT residency at Duke in the late 1930s. A fellow EENT resident at the time was Ralph Arnold, a doctor who would later teach at Duke. As Milo remembered, "We both, within an hour, read Julius Lempert's monumental contribution entitled, "Improvement of Hearing in Cases of Otosclerosis" published in July of 1938 in the *Archives of Otolaryngology.*" Both Milo and Ralph were tremendously excited by Lempert's innovative surgical approach for treating otosclerosis, a con-dition where spongy bone grows in the middle ear, later preventing the vibration of small bones (stapes) crucial for hearing. No surgeons in the United States were performing any type of surgery for otosclerosis at the time, so both residents suggested to the senior members of the staff that someone on the house staff should observe this new surgery, and, hope-fully, introduce this advancement to Duke's ENT Department. "This idea," Milo told me, "was not received with enthusiasm." As he characterized the situation back then, "Mastoidectomies in those dim and distant days were done with a set of instruments more calculated to bring joy to the heart of one trying to lead joints between sections of cast iron pipe than to a doctor who was working in one of the anatomically most treacherous areas in the human body."

As it happened, Milo had a break from his responsibilities as an assis-tant resident coming up in October of 1938, during which he and Betsy planned to take a long-awaited trip north to see their families. Milo also seized the opportunity to write Dr. Lempert.

"Clearly outlining that I was, of course, a very low member on the totem pole at a very high-class university," Milo wrote, he asked if he might watch Dr. Lempert do one of these operations during an upcoming visit to New York City. "With graciousness that could hardly have been exceeded had I been the Professor of Otolaryngology himself instead of the merest neophyte," Milo recalled, he was invited by Dr. Lempert to come to his hospital and watch him operate, which the young surgeon eagerly did:

> *I was given a loupe and light combination with which to peer over his shoulder as he methodically and deftly went through his monumental operation that has been so influential, both directly and by the kind of work it subsequently stimulated, in the restoration of hearing to thousands of individuals throughout the world.*

Years later, after his return to Alaska in 1948, Doc Fritz saw the burgeoning problem that untreated cases of mastoiditis represented in the isolated Eskimo, Indian, and Aleut communities and decided to upgrade his knowledge of mastoiditis and its treatment. In May and June of 1950, Milo returned to the Lempert Institute in New York City and took a six-week course in fenestration surgery for the improvement of hearing in cases of otosclerosis. The course was partially financed by the GI Bill, and Milo's round-trip travel from Anchorage was largely paid for by the Alaska Department of Health. Milo purchased a light and loupe. He trained with Julius Lempert and his "brilliant young associate J. H. Thomas Rambo," the doctor Milo would subsequently invite to Alaska. Milo described initial moments of his summer course at the Lempert Institute in 1950:

> *I remember sitting down at the first cadaver head. . . . After making the initial gross maneuvers to uncover the mastoid labyrinth, I put on my light and loupe and there before me, through the endaural approach, lay the mysteries and tortuous anatomy of the temporal bone, clearly delineated and easy to see.*

Once back in Alaska, Milo immediately put his new skills and his new tools—the light and loupe—to work. However, over the next eight years and despite Milo's busy practice in Anchorage and his EENT clinics throughout Alaska, Milo and others in the Alaska medical community found themselves fighting a losing battle. Throughout the Territory—soon to become a state—the number of chronic ear problems was increasing, especially in Alaska Native communities. By 1958, middle ear infection and mastoiditis had surpassed tuberculosis as Alaska's most pressing health problems. According to a United States Public Health Service statistician, in an Indigenous population estimated to be 50,000 at the time, about 3,000 had chronic mastoiditis and were in need of surgery.

Milo called on his former New York City mentor, Dr. Thomas Rambo for help. As a result of Milo's urging, Dr. Rambo made a week-long trip to Alaska in the summer of 1958 to share his expertise and new procedures. These included surgical techniques he had devised that sharply reduced the time needed for post-operative care following a radical mastoidectomy, as well as a newly developed operation to restore hearing in deafness resulting from chronic otitis media.

Milo arranged for Dr. Rambo to perform mastoidectomies in the Public Health Service Alaska Native Hospital and Providence Hospital in Anchorage and then to examine clinic patients who had come to town from all over Alaska. In an article about that event-filled week, reported by the Physicians News Service for *Scope* magazine, Dr. Rambo said, "It must be appreciated that these people are scattered over an immense Territory in which my friend Milo Fritz is the only temporal bone surgeon."

Milo gave Dr. Rambo a sense of the immensity of Alaska and of the health problems ravaging far-flung Alaska Native populations. They flew into the Alaska bush on a trip that included a stop at a tiny medical facility in Kotzebue "where in one day he saw 40 children with chronic discharging ears." At the end of his week-long visit to Alaska, during which Dr. Rambo examined well over 100 children, the New York otologist was "struck by the legendary stoicism of the Eskimo youngsters . . . not one of them had cried during any diagnostic procedure or postsurgical treatment." He was impressed by "the fine professional equipment and personal devotion of the physicians and hospital staffs in Anchorage, and the aching need for more trained men and women, more outlying clinics and more health education to cope with a severity and extent of ear pathology which is almost staggering."

The *Scope* article refers to Dr. Fritz as Dr. Rambo's "sponsor and guide." Milo saw to it that his New York colleague's visit to Alaska was both productive and enjoyable. "Dr. Rambo addressed groups of physicians, was feted at receptions, appeared on a health education television program, and flew with Dr. Fritz in his Piper Tri-Pacer to Lake Iliamna to visit a homestead, examine a patient, and do a little fishing." In the article, Dr. Rambo made no comment about tangling with a barge while he was a passenger in his "sponsor and guide's" floatplane—except perhaps obliquely. Dr. Rambo characterized his Alaska trip as an "unforgettable interlude."

While trying to make headway against mastoiditis and other fundamental ear, nose, and throat problems that were rampant throughout Alaska, Milo's inquisitive mind was also receptive to new ideas and advancements in the other half of his combined specialty—surgical and medical ophthalmology. One day, while performing glaucoma surgery under a standard overhead light, Doc Fritz lamented that he "could not clearly see that portion of the anterior chamber in which I was most interested."

And, as Milo recalled in a 1959 article published by *Alaska Medicine*:

> *The very obvious and brilliant idea entered my brain: why not use the Lempert light and loupe in the performance of ophthalmological surgery?*
>
> *... If one can do better temporal bone surgery by virtue of better light and magnification, would not the same thing hold true with the human eye?*
>
> *Accordingly, I tried this revolutionary idea on a couple of cases involving surgery on the ocular muscles and was immediately rewarded with the unbelievable satisfaction of having the light always fall exactly where I was looking. Also, the details of ocular anatomy became much more easily seen and handled. The only difficulty was that a suture end would sometimes get out of the field of vision and occasionally I would bump a knuckle of my glove against the contaminated head-light and would have to change them. But it was not many days before these little accidents seldom occurred and as soon as I had begun the practice of having my own surgical nurse helping me in these efforts, I had no further difficulty. As a matter of fact, my operating time and the wear on the nervous system of not only myself but those young women who have so faithfully helped me through the years with this type of work became less and less.*
>
> *Eventually the day came when I tried this technique on a cataract operation. I remember with what gratification I was able to place my sutures exactly halfway through the cornea and halfway through the sclera rather than perforating into the anterior chamber.*
>
> *... The name of Julius Lempert is known to almost every physician, and certainly every otologist, throughout the*

world today. It is also known to every Eskimo or other Alaska Native upon whom I have done temporal bone surgery for the suppurative diseases of that structure because I have made it a point to tell these people as they have come and gone in hundreds since 1950, of the great city doctor who taught me how to do this surgery that has often resulted in the restoration of a child's life or the rehabilitation of an individual whose foul aural discharge made him a pariah among his peers, especially if living in a small, crowded cabin.

. . . I have been able to serve my Alaskan patients better and more efficiently since invoking Lempert's great contribution to ophthalmology—Light and Magnification.

Lempert's headlight and loupe were the precursors of the modern-day operating microscope, which Milo was using routinely by the mid-1960s.

ON THE CUSP OF CHANGING TIMES

To me Alaska means all of Alaska. Its people means all of its people, a great land and a great people.

—MILO FRITZ

As HE HAD ENVISIONED, MILO WAS GROWING UP with the country. In the early 1950s, he was elected president of the Alaska Territorial Medical Association. One of Milo's original partners in Ketchikan, Dr. Arthur Wilson, recalled the circumstances in an interview almost thirty years later:

> Somewhere in that period I went up to Juneau to a medical meeting and they put me on the nominating committee. Well, my old friend Walkowski was up there in Anchorage, and I thought, "Gee whiz, Wally ought to be president of this association. He never has. I am going to nominate him."

Dr. A.S. Walkowski was a friend of Milo's, too—the man who offered Milo space in his office when Milo arrived in Anchorage in 1948. Dr.

Walkowski had come to Alaska with his new bride in 1928 to be the doctor on an island-based copper mining camp. Later he was asked by Dr.
Joseph Romig, Alaska's legendary "dog-sled doctor," to work at the Alaska
Railroad Hospital in Anchorage. The two doctors were two of the first
three members of the medical staff when the original Providence Hospital
opened its doors in 1939.

Dr. Wilson described what unfolded following a big cocktail party at
the Juneau conference:

> I guess rumors spread pretty fast there. I had not any
> more than gotten back to my hotel room after this party than
> someone from Anchorage called me up and said they wanted
> to see me. So, they came over and my gosh there were eleven
> doctors from Anchorage in the room and so I laughed and
> they said, "Now Dr. Wilson, we know that you want to put
> Dr. Walkowski's name up for president and we love him. He
> is just a great old guy, which is true. But he does not want to
> be president and we want Milo Fritz." Well, you have got over
> 50% of the votes right here in this room. Gosh, it was one of
> those funny things.

Between 1940 and 1960 Alaska's population more than tripled, to a
population of 226,000. Anchorage, too, was growing apace. Milo's forward
thinking and leadership were being recognized beyond the medical profession. In the mid-1950s Milo Fritz won a commendation from the National
Association for the Advancement of Colored People for "democratic methods of employment of office personnel." Doc Fritz, who described himself
as "color-blind," had hired Helen Gamble, a Black R.N. newly arrived from
Texas, to join his office staff. Personable and no-nonsense, Helen was soon
a mainstay in the Fritz office.

New arrivals like Helen Gamble and John Spahn were part of a huge
increase in Alaska's population after World War II. More and more doctors,
including other EENT specialists were part of the burgeoning numbers.
Milo took to holding regular sessions with other doctors in Anchorage,
not to talk about their successes, but about their problems and failures, so
they might learn from them. Change, though perhaps not at the pace Milo
Fritz was advocating in medical and other matters, was coming to mid-
twentieth-century Alaska.

In the fall of 1958, Milo ventured into politics and was elected to the

Territorial Senate. He never had a chance to serve, however, because in Jan. 1959, Alaska became a state. In 1962 Doc Fritz ran for governor, but later admitted, "I didn't even get the Republican nomination for that, I was so terrible. But I was very much upset at the way the government was going then, and I felt I had something to offer. So, I ran and got flipped, of course."

Throughout the 1950s and '60s, Uncle Milo visited our family in Merion fairly regularly—maybe every year or two—whirlwind visits after an AMA meeting or a medical course. A vivid memory captures his sense of urgency and humor. During one of his visits, when I was about ten, Uncle Milo paused at my bedroom door to scrawl a few words on a construction paper mail pouch I had tacked there: "Dr. Milo H. Fritz, ophthalmologist—tonsils removed while you wait."

Visits and letters from Aunt Betsy were rare. By nature, more self-effacing than Uncle Milo, she was mostly an enigma to her young nieces and nephew. However, Betsy, too, was a catalyst for change. In the early 1950s, Elizabeth Berry Fritz pressed to establish better working conditions for the nurses in Alaska. "Her work on the contract with Providence Hospital in Juneau resulted in better pay and a 40-hour work week," noted the Alaska Nurses' Association, which awarded her its Hall of Fame award in 2004. She helped found the organization in 1950, serving as its first president from 1951-53.

In 1952 Aunt Betsy was a delegate to the Biennial Nurses Association convention that was held in Atlantic City and visited our family at Hillcrest before heading over to New Jersey. Many years later, my mother remembered how "smashing" she looked in her ensemble—probably a product of her own design and seamstress skills. Accessorized with a fur piece on her shoulders, she left no doubt that she represented Alaska.

Betsy had her own skirmishes with the status quo. As president of the newly formed Alaska Nurses Association, she flew down to Juneau in 1953 to shepherd the Nurses Practice Bill through the legislature. "Up until then the Sisters would take in any woman or girl, dress her in a white uniform and say she was a nurse," Betsy wrote. "We licensed (from other states) nurses wanted a law licensing only qualified persons to be nurses." While waiting for the bill to come up for a vote, Betsy wrote nightly letters to Milo back in Anchorage, describing how she "approached Legislators in the corridors, in their offices, in the aisle at church on Sunday, etc.; how one night I had to rewrite the whole Bill over at the suggestion of one of the lawyers. . . . We did win." No longer the shy young doctor's wife she had been in Ketchikan, Betsy, too, was growing up with the country.

*Milo (seated) and his brother Laurens circa 1915, wearing
what the brothers later referred to as their "dingwadddlers."*

Lifeguards for Willson's Woods Pool, Milo, (far left) & Larry (far right) early 1930s.

Milo & New York City – June 24, 1936.

Map of Alaska in Larry's Greenwich Village apartment in NYC.

Between eye clinics, Milo and public health nurse (probably far right), braved the Outer Banks beach road, getting assistance along the way.

Milo at Wright Memorial, Kitty Hawk, NC - 1937.

Major Milo H. Fritz, U. S. Army Air Force.

Milo (holding cat) with Army Air Force medical staff mid-1940s.

Fritz home/office at 4th & L. St. prior to earthquake.

*Milo with sons Piet and John at their house in Anchorage
in front of Ariadne, the boat they built from a kit.*

"Milo tarring roof on the oldest of our cabins." — Betsy, 1954

"Drs. Fritz and Crabtree, Betsy and Dr. Parran (former Surgeon General U.S. Public Health Service) at Anchor Pt. this summer [1954]." — Betsy

Dr. Fritz, Betsy & office staff with Alaska Native children.

Milo Fritz with new 1955 Piper Tri-Pacer, N-808MD.

Dr. Fritz starting Tri-Pacer on floats, 1970.

Photo by Ward Wells, courtesy of Northwest Medicine

Dr. Fritz, about to leave for a Native village in the Interior, 1961.

Dr. Fritz with Native boy in Teller, AK, circa 1969.

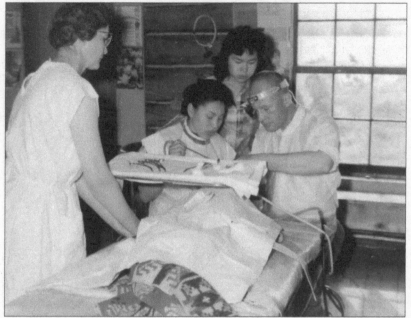

Dr. Fritz, assisted by Betsy and two Native girls, performing surgery in makeshift operating room during summer clinic to eight Yukon villages in 1961.

Stretcher bearers returning a surgical patient home after tonsillectomy during 1961 clinics to Native villages in the Yukon.

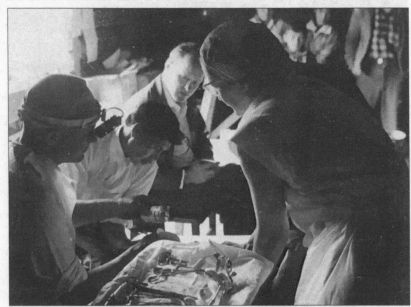

Young man learning to be an anesthetist, pictured with Dr. Fritz,
Betsy & John Spahn as villagers watch the surgery—best show in town.

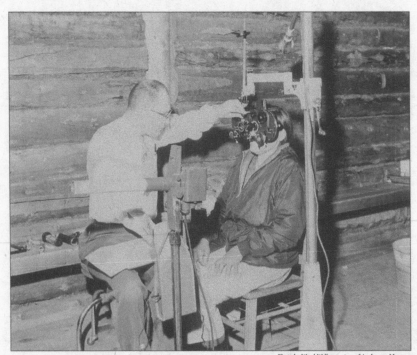

Dr. Fritz and a patient at clinic in Allakaket, 1961.

Betsy Fritz with patients in Allakaket, 1961.

Sixteen-year-old author filing medical charts, 1966.

Cartoon poster characterizing the inadequacies of Health, Education and Welfare in addressing the medical needs of Alaska Natives, signed by Milo Fritz, Willie Hensley, Ted Stevens, Don Young, and other members of the Alaska State House of Representatives, circa 1968.

Ted Stevens and Milo Fritz both served in the 5th Alaska State Legislature, House of Representatives, 1967-69; pictured at Alaska State Republican Convention in Fairbanks, 1978, per Ted Stevens Foundation archives.

Milo operating his Case tractor at Anchor Point, 1977.

True Pioneer, *mural depicting Fritz EENT clinics in rural Alaska by Fred Machetanz.*

Unveiling ceremony of Fred Machetanz's True Pioneer *mural at Southcentral Foundation's Anchorage Native Primary Care Center, 2006. Pictured: Dr. Ted Mala, SCF Director of Tribal Relations and Village Initiatives, Betsy Fritz (center) and former Fritz medical team members (left to right) Helen Gamble, Theresa Thurston, Johnnie Childs.*

PART V

Bush Clinics

KODIAK CLINIC, 1961

*One of the delights of Kodiak is its odor. To me it is
reminiscent of my boyhood days in Maine. The combination
of salt air, tar and the pilings, fish products and rotting
vegetation constitutes a perfume, to my nose at least.*

—MILO FRITZ

BEGINNING IN 1950, MILO HELD ONE OR TWO CLINICS on Kodiak Island
each year. The initial otolaryngology and ophthalmology clinic was
requested by Dr. A. Holmes Johnson, who was the only practicing physician there at the time. It was held in his office, which was then attached to
the Kodiak Hotel, a small frame building and the town's only hotel.

Excerpts from Milo's account about one of his Kodiak clinics, published in *Alaska Medicine* in 1961, offer a sense of how Doc Fritz conducted his clinics and a vivid picture of that large and remote island off
Alaska's southern coast:

> *In the spring it is buffeted by raving storms of unbeliev-
> able ferocity and in the winter blizzards of such severity that
> instrument approaches to its airstrip are not risked even by*

*the veteran commercial and bush pilots of Alaska. In its cen-
ter, largely untrod by the foot of man, are hundreds of this
continent's most formidable carnivore, the Kodiak bear.*

*However inclement the weather both winter and summer
is on this island, it is possessed of a singular beauty and scenic grandeur on its clear days that made its original coloniz-
ers, the Russians, establish the capital of Russian America
first at Three Saints Bay and later, following a devastating
earthquake and tidal wave, at Pavlov, now the site of the city
of Kodiak.*

In February of 1961, Milo and John Spahn were seeing patients on the
main floor of the former downtown school building, which was no longer being used as a school. Assisting them on that clinic was Mrs. Robert
Hall, "wife of the owner of Kodiak Airways," an R.N., Milo noted, "whose
knowledge of the local people and their habits and availability is extremely
important in the smooth running of the clinic."

*These clinics are always oversubscribed and are felt by the
host doctors and Mr. Spahn and myself to be a great thing for
the people of Kodiak and its environs. They are spared the
expense of a trip to Anchorage, plus the doctor's fee, plus hotel and hospital bills and often have only to leave their work
or their responsibilities for an hour or two instead of for days
at a time.*

Patients were largely from Kodiak, a town of 2000 inhabitants, served
by the semi-retired Dr. Johnson, who still did surgery and consults with
the two younger doctors—his son Dr. Bob, as he was called, and his partner Dr. J. Bruce Keers. Other patients came from the nearby naval station
of 3000 people, whose general medical needs were cared for by six naval
medical officers, but to Milo, "the most interesting, most needy and the
group exhibiting the greatest pathology come from places with such fascinating names as Afognak, Larsen Bay, Woody Island, Karluk, Ouzinkie
and Terror Bay."

Milo made it a point to see only patients referred by the local physicians. "This has been my policy in visiting all the towns and settlements
of Alaska where there has been a practicing physician. By this means the
control of the practice of medicine, even on the part of consultants, is kept
in the hands of the practitioners, where, in my opinion, it belongs."

The purpose of these clinics is to supply spectacles to those people in need of them and to see people from Kodiak and its environs who, in the opinion of the three practicing physicians, have difficulties in the eye or ear-nose-throat fields which may be treated locally, by surgery in Kodiak (such as the removal of tonsils and adenoids) or by more complex surgery (such as SMR [submucous resection of the septum], cataract extraction, EOM surgery [extraocular muscle surgery to correct eye alignment] and mastoidectomies), which can be done by me in Anchorage at the Providence Hospital or at the Alaska Native Service Hospital.

The clinics usually are held in late January, early February, or early March. This time is chosen because the children are all at school, air traffic to and from Kodiak is at a minimum and passage easy to get, and excess baggage can always be taken along with us as we go. In the summertime, tourist trade and commercial travel to and from the island are heaviest. It is then difficult to secure passage and, due to multiple flights in bad weather, sometimes the doctor and the optician arrived one day and are held up from doing the necessary work by the delay of equipment which has been put on another flight and held up by the weather.

Ever appreciative of Alaska's beauty, Milo always requested that the room with the best view be reserved for him and John:

Room 43 is up under the eaves of this frame building and looks, more or less, south to Kodiak Harbor, dotted with its lovely islands in blue water and the winking lights of the distant naval station. From the window we can see the ever-changing weather, the ships in the small boat harbor and the arrival and departure of the large planes of the naval air station and the amphibious and float planes in the narrow channel between Near Island and the city of Kodiak.

Milo and John brought with them roughly 300 pounds of equipment, medical instruments, surgical sets, drugs, and administrative supplies. The phoropter, a refractor used in eye examinations, and several other bulky pieces of equipment are sent on a day or two ahead and addressed to Mrs. Hall who would see that they are delivered to the downtown school.

The rest of the equipment, less liquid medicines, are packed into World War II surplus ammunition cases and are brought along as excess baggage, which costs 15 cents a pound between Anchorage and Kodiak. Medicines and solutions of any kind that can freeze are carried with me in a doctor's bag in the cabin of the aircraft because the baggage compartments are not heated and on one occasion all the liquid medicines froze and burst their containers, making a delay in one of the early clinics to Fairbanks of 24 hours until replacements could be sent up from Anchorage.

The trip is made by a propeller-driven DC3 or C-47 of Pacific Northern Airlines and makes stops at Kenai and Homer before beginning the hour-and-10-minute flight across the water to Kodiak.

With excess baggage in the two ammunition cases, Milo and John boarded the 7:00 a.m flight for Kodiak on February 5th. Clear as far as Kenai, it was instrument weather at Homer and at Kodiak, which was why Milo always flew there commercially. "Even though I am a licensed commercial pilot, I've never felt brave enough to transverse the long over-water flight between Homer and Kodiak in my own single-engine Tri-Pacer of 1955 vintage."

Commercial multi-engine operations land at the naval airstrip on Kodiak and the 7-mile trip to town is accomplished by means of a bus, which to quote a local wag, is half a car high and two cars long. Our excess baggage and personal baggage is brought in by the P.N.A truck.

. . . Dressed in the fleece-lined, hooded parkas we wear in Anchorage, we caused much amusement when we got off the plane on the first Sunday, since up to that day, the atmosphere of Kodiak had been rather spring-like. The first four days of our visit were marred by blizzards and extremes of temperature that made many people wish out loud that they had been as sensibly dressed as we were.

Once at the school, they were met by Mrs. Hall, who worked with them every day. Milo wrote:

[She] had arranged to have all the windows of the room in which I was to do my work blacked out with old World

*War II blackout curtains. Mr. Spahn and I took out the start-
ers of the fluorescent lights of all but two of the six ceiling
fixtures and set up the equipment using the usual schoolroom
furniture. It was necessary to borrow a couple of extension
cords in order to have handy all the electrically powered pieces of equipment brought along. In an adjoining office Mrs.
Hall unpacked the case containing the administrative material and envelopes containing the charts of patients who been
seen before and those who would be new patients. All this
had been prepared previously at home by my wife and separated into envelopes representing each of the days the clinic
would be held.*

That Sunday afternoon they saw twelve patients, mostly refractions,
and "then enjoyed a social evening at the home of Dr. and Mrs. A. Holmes
Johnson," Milo wrote. "This was at their lovely log home in a grove of
spruce, appropriately called Spruce Haven, just outside of town which, on
clear days, gives a prospect on one of the grandest seascapes in a country
where grandeur is commonplace."

*On Monday, Tuesday, and Wednesday we saw patients
as quickly as we could, most of them coming from Kodiak
city, a good number from the naval station close by and the
rest from the surrounding villages. . . .Our breakfast and the
noontime meals were taken at the Belmont, which is a combination of restaurant on one side and bar on the other, the
latter inoperative during the day. Here we meet and mingle
with the people of the town, almost all of whom know us either as a physician and optician, are friends of other patients,
or are friends of friends and not above asking for curbstone
consultation for themselves or their loved ones right there at
the restaurant counter.*

*. . . On Wednesday evening before the big push on clinic
day, we were the guests of Dr. and Mrs. Bruce Keers, where
we had a venison dinner, homebrew, and much good conversation before 9 o'clock came and both Mr. Spahn and I were
overcome by the need for sleep.*

*. . . On Thursday we saw 44 children, wards of the Alaska
Department of Health, the Alaska Native Health Service, or*

*of the Kodiak Health & Welfare Council which undertakes
to see the children who, for various technical reasons, cannot
be seen under the aegis of the federal or state health systems.
These constitute the most interesting group, being mostly native or half-native and in the greatest need of dental care,
spectacles, eye surgery, mastoidectomies and the removal
of tonsils and adenoids. . . . Mrs. Dora Kramer, R.N., indefatigable public health nurse with the Alaska Department
of Health, was responsible for 43 of the 44 patients seen.
Shepherding her charges throughout the week was the equally indefatigable school nurse, Mrs. Marion Lynch, R.N.*

By the end of the day Thursday, Milo noted that Mrs. Hall, Mr. Spahn
and he "had got beyond the stage of fatigue and approached the stage of
utter exhaustion."

Milo observed a "remarkable jump in the number of ear, nose, and
throat patients that the doctors had me see."

*I am convinced that submucous resection of the nasal
septum [usually to treat a deviated septum] that I did on Dr.
Bruce a year ago or so gave him and Dr. Bob a new insight
into the importance of the proper examination of the nose
after the use of 10 per cent cocaine swabs in order to properly
be able to visualize its interior. I think the number of cases
that he sent in consultation increased two or three thousand
per cent and included 14 individuals who badly needed a
submucous resection of the nasal septum, including the local
dentist.*

Milo and John got a midday break from medicine on Friday, "a blue-
and-gold day that found the mountain tops, hidden for the previous four
days, resplendent in new mantles of freshly fallen snow." Helen Hall's husband Bob offered to take them on a short ride in a Skimmer, a four-person
amphibious light plane that Milo had become enamored of during a previous clinic to Kodiak in 1960. Milo found it to be "extremely stable, airwor-
thy, seaworthy, rugged, and dependable. In addition, it had characteristics
of stability and resistance against spins and flipping over on its back that
made it a very desirable airplane indeed." But the cost of a new one, "in
the neighborhood of $25,000 without radios," was well beyond what Milo
could afford.

After a day crowded with patients, they had dinner with Dr. Bob and his wife at their large home on the same estate where the senior Dr. Johnson and his wife live. "The high spot of the evening was playing piano duets, two in number, with Dr. Bob, who is as much of an expert as I am a tyro in this particular field."

> On Saturday we were overwhelmed all day with patients, but after the last patient had been seen, the lights turned off, the school locked up, Dr. Bob came by in order to take me in his Volkswagen up to see the new airport, which is in a cleft of hills parallel to the narrow body of water lying between Near Island and Kodiak Island. The mouth of this valley opens on the village and is filled with a housing project. Further north in it is a long lake serving as a seaplane base. Higher still and quite steep is an area which will be used as a ramp between the lake just described and the new airfield which lies just above. This is the field that we went to see and it is already in operation for light planes and small commercial aircraft.

"Sunday dawned gorgeous and clear." They worked hard until 12:30, had lunch at the Belmont and then returned to the school "to dismantle our equipment, pack it up and get the obliging truck driver from Pacific Northern Airlines to carry it to the airplane ticket office where we took it home, not as excess baggage, but as freight, a courtesy and kindness often enjoyed when one goes on clinics throughout this great state."

> We loafed about the waterfront when all this had been attended to, talking to Alf Matson, a world-famous big game guide and a hair-raising pilot of a Piper Tri-Pacer similar to mine in which he performs feats of aerial legerdemain I would not even think of, much less have the temerity to try.

Milo offered a statistical summary of the clinic:

> We worked from noon of Sunday, 5 February to noon the following Sunday, 12 February. There were 190 patients seen, 140 white, 48 native (1/4 or more Aleut), and 2 Negro. Of these 190 patients, 103 were children 87 adults. 106 refractions were done, 26 examinations of the ear, nose, and throat, 53 refractions combined with ear nose and throat examinations, and 5 miscellaneous examinations. 152 of the patients came from Kodiak city, 15 from the naval station, 4 from

Larsen Bay, 4 from Old Harbor, and 1 each from Karluk,
Alitak and Anchorage.

> *146 patients were classified as private, 43 as wards of the*
> *Alaska Department of Health, and one from the Department*
> *of Public Welfare.*

Milo also took the opportunity to take a jab at the tight-fisted ways of
the new bureaucrats:

> *It is worth noting that the 43 patients seen under the*
> *Alaska Department of Health, in former and more equitable*
> *times, were managed quite differently than they are now. Up*
> *until about five years ago the Alaska Department of Health*
> *undertook its fair share of the cost of transportation and per*
> *diem for the consultant. Now the Anchorage representatives*
> *of the Department wait until they learn that a private clinic*
> *is being held someplace and then ask, full well knowing that*
> *it will be done, if the doctor could find time to "squeeze in"*
> *some A.D.H patients!*

> *At 4 PM on that Sunday afternoon with the mountains*
> *pink in the setting sun, Robert and Helen Hall drove us to our*
> *waiting Pacific Northern Airlines DC-3 which took us un-*
> *eventfully home to Anchorage via stops in Homer and Kenai*
> *while enjoying a snack aloft and the pleasant conversation*
> *of a beautiful stewardess, Miss Stevens, who some years ago*
> *had been a patient.*

St. Mary's Clinic and
Bureaucratic Indifference,
1961

*I did this demonstration at St. Mary's and on the
Yukon to show that this work could be done safely, even
without an anesthetist and outside a hospital. . . . The
people were so tremendously grateful. . . . The whole
village would get into the act.*

—Milo Fritz

A LARGE, FRAMED MAP OF ALASKA held a prominent position in Milo's
medical office. The map, updated frequently by Betsy, was studded
with colorful pins that marked the locations of Milo's EENT patients, scattered throughout Alaska; thumbtacks indicated both the major towns and
the bush communities where he held his itinerant clinics. This graphic re-
minder of the scope of Doc Fritz's medical practice is now in the archives
of the University of Alaska in Anchorage. Each community, invariably

shaped by its particular location, had sometimes subtle but significant differences in the customs of its people. Each clinic presented its own challenges, requiring a measure of flexibility, resourcefulness, and collaborative care.

"I love itinerant medicine," Milo told an interviewer, "because you get to see things and do things, and meet the people and, above all, you feel useful. You go to a place where there hadn't been anybody who did this kind of work at all; it builds up your ego or something: I don't know what it is. . . . Whenever I went, whether it was Valdez, Cordova or someplace else, somebody would say, 'Hey gee, I didn't know you were coming down, Doc, I'm glad to see you.'"

During the eight years after his return to Alaska in 1948 Milo continued to have a productive working relationship with Dr. Albrecht, Alaska's Commissioner of Health. Dr. Albrecht summarized his administrative approach in an interview: "It's my hard job to make it easy for them [medical providers, educators, and other health experts] to do their job. Get the money, take the heat off of them, so they can really work and operate. That was my credo."

In 1956 Dr. Albrecht resigned to take a job in Ohio and, after his departure, Milo became increasingly frustrated by the bureaucratic foot dragging and red tape he began to encounter. "The ENT program fell upon evil days," Milo wrote in Alaska medical journal *Northwest Medicine* in 1963:

> *Those following Dr. Albrecht in his important post had little imagination, less courage, and virtually no knowledge of otolaryngology, even though many of them were physicians and all of them had access to the reports submitted by others, as well as myself. . . . Eventually, incompetence succeeded in terminating all ENT work except sporadic and so-called crash efforts on the part of imported ENT men who occasionally held unscheduled and very inefficient mass operative clinics here and there throughout Alaska.*

When the Bureau of Indian Affairs was taken out of the medical business in Alaska in 1956 and ceded the Territory's medical problems to the United States Public Health Service, Milo had been optimistic:

> *With this change in administrative responsibilities for native health, those of us interested in the problem of mastoiditis, middle ear disease, deafness and a tonsil-adenoid*

*program hoped that a better day was at hand. For two or
three years this appeared not to be the case. For instance,
it was necessary for me, at my own expense, to go to the
Mission of St. Mary's and do seventy-one operations in five
days, administering my own anesthetics.*

*Throughout these years, until the Clinic to St. Mary's and
the Yukon Clinic [both in 1961] proved otherwise, the officials in charge of the native hospitals throughout the state
repeatedly claimed that doing tonsillectomies and adenoidectomies in their small hospitals was dangerous and not in
the public interest. I did this demonstration at St. Mary's and
on the Yukon to show that this work could be done safely,
even without an anesthetist and outside a hospital.*

Ultimately, however, Milo found his suggestions for improving medical care for the Native population were disregarded or ignored. By 1961,
he found the situation intolerable. Fed up, he took action that he hoped
would jolt the bureaucrats from their complacency.

Doc Fritz had worked with the United States Public Health Service as a
medical consultant for years, but in May 1961 he resigned, opting to take
matters into his own hands. That June, Milo wrote an editorial, "A Clinic
to St. Mary's," also published by *Northwest Medicine*. He wrote the editorial
to illustrate "some of the reasons why enlightened doctors are adamant in
their opposition to further socialistic federal encroachment on the private
practice of medicine." Doc Fritz offered this account both to detail government failings and to demonstrate what was possible:

*Last year [1960] at Easter time, John Spahn, an opti-
cian friend, and I flew to St. Mary's Mission on the lower
Yukon to examine the 250 schoolchildren from an EENT
viewpoint. This mission school was established by the Jesuits
to educate intellectually superior Eskimo children. The students are there because they are orphans or from broken
homes. The Order has taken in these children to give them
some sort of home and education until a proper niche can
be found for them.*

*On that visit we had bad flying weather all the way
and instead of spending five days at the mission as we had
planned, Mr. Spahn and I were only able to work there three*

days. In that time, we examined over 100 children and prescribed 66 pairs of eyeglasses. Some of these spectacles were
paid for by the Jesuit Fathers themselves, others were provided by New Eyes for the Needy, Inc. of Short Hills, New Jersey.
The remainder was furnished to the children by the Ear, Nose
and Throat Foundation of Alaska, Inc. [the nonprofit founded and run on a shoestring by Milo and John Spahn].

Among the children examined there were 40 who had ir-
refutable and clearly visible indications for the removal of
tonsils and adenoids. This evidence consisted of six cases
with mastoiditis on one side, one patient with bilateral mastoiditis, and the remaining cases with either dry perforations
or badly scarred and retracted eardrums.

The 1960 St. Mary's clinic was undertaken at no cost to
the government, but the results of our findings were forwarded to the Public Health Service Area Medical Director as is
our regular practice. Soon after this report was submitted,
the Father in charge of the Mission received a letter from the
Area Medical Director saying that the 40 children recommended for tonsillectomies or tonsillectomies and adenoidectomies would be airlifted for surgery at the nearest satellite hospital operated by the Alaska Native Health Service at
Bethel, 100 miles away.

This year Mr. Spahn and I intended visiting St. Mary's
Mission again at Easter in order to complete the work we had
begun the year before. About three weeks before our planned
departure, we were appalled at finding that of the 40 children
reported as being badly in need of T&A's, only two had been
operated upon! Accordingly, we wired the Father, asking if he
would be interested in having us remove the children's tonsils
and adenoids instead of continuing with the general work
we had started. He answered immediately that he would be
very happy to have this work done as apparently the Alaska
Native Health Service was unable or unwilling to do anything other than what has been indicated above.

With the tireless devotion of my wife, who is my partner
in these enterprises, and with the assistance of a fine office

staff, it was possible to sterilize and wrap disposable drapes and other materials for the removal of 40 sets of tonsils and adenoids. We placed a rush order for a case of ether and a case of Vinethene and purchased a $240 suction and pressure machine for administering ether by insufflation and for removal of secretions during surgery. In addition, we shipped twelve sets of tonsil and adenoid instruments from my own office to the Mission. All this was undertaken on a rush basis through the good offices of Northern Consolidated Airlines, who gave our medical supplies priority in spite of a backlog of three weeks freight to the Yukon. It was necessary to carry the 45-pound suction and pressure device in my small airplane, which already had a staggering load to carry across the snow-covered tundra.

Upon arriving at St. Mary's, we were greeted with the usual enthusiasm and warmth which is in such contrast to the lethargic, disinterested greeting one often receives at the U.S.P.H.S. [United States Public Health Service] hospital here in Anchorage.

It developed that a lay apostle who is a full-time public health nurse in Colorado was in residence at the Mission for one year, giving her time and talent for the glory of God by serving children along the lines of her training. She indicated that there were 20 more individuals who needed their tonsils and adenoids removed and asked if we would undertake it.

We had only five days in which to accomplish all this. Nevertheless, we started to work at once, stopping only to wire back to Anchorage for additional supplies. There was no one to handle anesthesia so I doubled as anesthetist and surgeon for 34 of the cases. Once the child was asleep the insufflation device and the suction-pressure machine were turned on and Mr. Spahn either increased or decreased the amount of ether according to the vital signs upon which I kept an eagle eye while operating.

Three lay Sisters assisted me. One reassured the children, another acted as instrument nurse, while the third washed instruments. Some of the larger and stronger boys acted as stretcher bearers and the Reverend Mother Superior was our circulating nurse. The Colorado public health nurse handled the logistics—the difficult task of administering the hypodermic and intramuscular injections of Thorazine, Demerol and atropine that were ordered before surgery, and also the roster and meeting place where physical examinations of the next day's patients would be performed.

Because of permafrost and the surface water situation at this particular time of the year, the water supply at the Mission was very critical. We ran out of water on every day except the last one and had to wash our hands under a pitcher of flowing water and then rinse them in alcohol. We ran completely out of clean laundry. Children gave their beds to others from the village and they themselves slept in their sleeping bags on the floor. Postoperative nursing care was provided by a parent (if the child was from the nearby village) or by a volunteer adult. The patients slept overnight in our makeshift infirmary and walked out the following morning as the new day's contingent arrived for their operations. Everyone turned to with a willingness that made it a pleasure and an inspiration to give one's best.

All the patients did well. Three had to be re-sutured. One had what seemed like an epileptic grand mal seizure in the early period of recovery from the anesthesia. Because the Fathers had made available a tank of oxygen from their welding shop, we met this emergency with no difficulty whatsoever.

On Friday, the fifth and last day of the clinic, we found that we had performed 71 operations. Thirty-four tonsils and adenoids had been removed under general anesthesia and the remaining of the tonsils or tonsils and adenoids were removed under local anesthesia. Surely if one otolaryngologist with the help of an able and willing lay crew can perform such a prodigious feat, a government hospital such as the U.S.P.H.S. operates in Anchorage with an annual budget of twelve million dollars should be able to do at least half as well. It should be able to do it continuously and relentlessly, *thereby matching the continuity and relentlessness of suppurative middle ear disease and mastoiditis in Alaska.*

Lack of water, lack of a nurse-anesthetist, improper bed space, inadequate nursing personnel—each one of these stumbling blocks would have been sufficient for the Alaska Native Health Service to have canceled out such an effort. Their philosophy, through my experience at least, has been that whenever something can be discovered that prevents a perfect project, the defect, no matter how insignificant, can be blown up and presented as reason enough for canceling an entire program.

Let anybody who approves of the practice of medicine by the government read and ponder on what has been written here.

The reader may wonder why we suddenly decided to undertake this seemingly impossible task with inadequate facilities and personnel. The reason was pure anger and disgust. It was also felt that if this thing could be brought off successfully, perhaps there would be enough feeling and anger generated among physicians and laymen so that the Public Health Service would be awakened (even if rudely) and their status changed from that of ruling servants to medical servants who actually accomplish what they are being paid for.

Before concluding I would like to present an example of the inefficiency of government medicine, as practiced in this part of the country at least. The reader should feel indignant and incensed.

Of the 71 patients operated upon, 14 had been seen in 1949, 1953 in 1959 and had been recommended for the removal of tonsils and adenoids. The faithful and indefatigable public health nurses who made these recommendations and forwarded them to the representatives of the Alaska Department of Health and the Alaska Native Health Service saw their efforts come to naught.

Of these 71 patients, four had actually been in the Alaska Native Health Service Hospital in Anchorage for other reasons, but because they had not been brought to the attention

of the EENT department, they had returned to the bush coun-
try with their tonsils and adenoids uncomfortably in place!

At this point it might occur to the reader that the au-
thor of this contribution is middle ear or mastoid happy. Let
him search the record and in it he will find that, within the
past three years, mastoiditis and middle ear disease consti-
tute the leading public health problem among the natives of
Alaska since tuberculosis in its protean manifestations has
been more or less laid low with new medications and surgi-
cal techniques. Various officials of the Alaska Native Health
Service at public medical meetings have acknowledged this
to be the case. What has been described above is the method
of medical bureaucracy in attacking this profoundly impor-
tant problem.

The issue now lies before the public of whether or not it
wishes medicine to be practiced by the doctors of its choice or
through physicians whom the bureaucrats, in their wisdom,
choose for them. If in the light of this the public chooses fed-
eralized medicine, it will indeed get what it deserves.

Milo wasn't finished. He saw that copies of "A Clinic to St. Mary's"
were distributed by the editor to newspapers throughout the country. In
addition, a copy of the editorial was sent to each member of the House
of Delegates of the American Medical Association, each member of the
United States Congress in Washington, D.C., and to each member of the
legislature of the state of Alaska. Milo described the response to his editorial in a subsequent article:

At first there was no reaction at all from the United States
Public Health Service. Eventually the Service categorically
denied that any of its officers had promised the removal
of the tonsils and adenoids of the 40 children at St. Mary's
Mission. A thermofax copy of the letter regarding this prom-
ise was forwarded to the editor of the Washington Report on
Medical Sciences *in which the United States Public Health*
Service refutation appeared. Next, in this same publication, a
faceless and unidentified "official" of the United States Public
Health Service said that in the fiscal year 1961 the Alaska
Native Health Service had done 600 T&A's. I would like to

underscore the total inadequacy of this effort by pointing out that forty medical officers with six hospitals in one year and an $11,000,000 budget were able to do 611 operations where thousands needed to be performed, while one individual in five weeks with no hospital, giving his own anesthesia and spending his own money—somewhere in the neighborhood of $6000—was able to do 227 operations.

... Many letters from all sorts of individuals throughout our nation were received as a result of the editorial, "A Clinic to St. Mary's." It was very comforting to find that our citizens are indeed concerned over the plight of the native people of Alaska. I would respectfully suggest to the interested readers of this contribution that they write, not to me, but to the representatives in the Senate and House of Representatives in Washington, urging that this simple program be undertaken at once and prosecuted with vigor for as many years as it takes to eradicate this easily preventable affliction from crippling or killing more of our fellow citizens. Let all who read consider: "A nation that neglects its children has forgotten God."

Doc Fritz, relentless, was in full cry that year. In June 1961, intent on remedying the continuing problems caused by disease and neglect in remote Native villages, Doc Fritz was back out in the bush again.

CLINIC ON THE YUKON AND ITS TRIBUTARIES, 1961

The clinic motto was, "Education, Participation and Responsibility." The clinic was conducted, as the bureaucrats have it, "at no expense to the government."

—MILO FRITZ

MILO, A PROLIFIC WRITER, WAS A FREQUENT CONTRIBUTOR to a variety of medical journals and other publications. What follows is drawn primarily from accounts written by Milo, detailing his month-long clinic in villages that were further upriver from St. Mary's. Much of this narrative was published in December 1961 in *The Alaskan Churchman*, an Episcopalian publication, founded in 1906 and published quarterly. More personal and frankly spiritual in tone than his articles for medical journals, it provides a sense of the tremendous collaborative effort and the significant role that various religious organizations played in these rural outposts throughout Alaska:

In thirty providentially sunny days from 3 June through

3 July 1961, my wife, a nurse, and Mr. John Spahn, a Guild Optician, and I, held an itinerant eye, ear, nose and throat and dental clinic in the Yukon Valley of Alaska. We were accompanied on the safari by Nancy Sydnam, a general practitioner of Anchorage. Almost human and very much a part of the voyage was my old well-worn, and reliable Piper Tri-pacer airplane, N-808MD, which has traversed the bush country and hinterland of Alaska since 1955.

Dr. Sydnam's expenses, Milo noted, were underwritten by the Alaska Chapter of the American Cancer Society. Remaining expenses were financed by "generous Episcopalians in the other states as well as ourselves. A check for over $300 for spectacles was donated by Father James Poole, S. J., director of St. Mary's Mission on the Yukon where we had held a clinic earlier this year." Milo continued:

We chose to follow the admonition found in Galatians VI:10, "While we have time, let us do good unto all men; and especially unto them that are of the household of the faith." This year, instead of attending two medical conventions, each a fortnight in duration, my wife and I thought it would be a fine thing during the month of June, when flying weather is best and daylight never ceasing, to hold a month-long clinic visiting villages in which our own Episcopal faith has held sway for many years. The purpose was to test eyes and supply eyeglasses, test hearing and supply hearing aids (generously supplied gratis by the Zenith Corporation), extract painful and decayed teeth and, finally, remove tonsils under local anesthesia and tonsils and adenoids in the case of children under general anesthesia in six to eight villages under the aegis of our beloved bishop, William J. Gordon, Jr.

With his blessing therefore, we by letter contacted 26 of the villages where our church is well entrenched, explaining our purposes and asking that certain forms be executed in order that we could undertake the important logistics.

... It was interesting to find that from some of the villages we received no response at all. From others we received the suggestion that we should contact the Alaska Department of Health, the Alaska Native Health Service or the itinerant

Public Health nurse of the district for the information that
we sought. However, from eight settlements we received an
enthusiastic welcome and a complete and wholehearted sup-
port of the whole idea. These villages included Holikachuk,
and Shageluk on the Innoko under the local religious guid-
ance of Mrs. Jean Dementi, nurse-evangelist for those two
settlements. From the Reverend Patterson Keller we received
a simple form executed on every member of the village. From
the Reverend Randall Mendelsohn at Allakaket also on the
Koyukuk, we received many requests that guided us in what
to expect. Fr. Mendelsohn also asked if we could see a few
people from the satellite village of Hughes, eighty miles to the
south of Allakaket. From the Reverend Alfred H. Smith, new-
ly ordained and responsible for the spiritual life of Steven's
Village and Beaver, we also received a helpful response and
well and promptly executed forms. From the most primi-
tive village of all, Venetie, the nurse evangelist, Miss Susan
Carter, we also received an enthusiastic response.

Accordingly, we ordered disposable paper drapes, the nec-
essary medications, and had the Orah D. Clark Junior High
School Medical Society and the Future Nurses Association of
Anchorage High School help us with the folding of sponges
and the packaging of supplies.

These supplies, which also included ether, "trade goods" (lollipops), disposable paper drapes and towels, gauze, tonsil sponges, and adenoid tam-
pons with strings attached, had been sent by air freight from Anchorage to
the bush villages, scattered across a 500-mile stretch in which they planned
to do surgery. These villages were small, with populations generally of one
hundred or so.

Dr. Sydnam and Betsy Fritz, using commercial transportation, arrived in
Shageluk on June 3 about 2:00 in the afternoon. John Spahn and Doc Fritz,
flying in his heavily loaded Piper Tri-Pacer, on floats, landed on the Innoko
River soon afterwards. In addition to their survival gear and personal effects,
the men brought a heavy ether pump and suction machine for the adminis-
tration of ether anesthetics and the aspiration of secretions from the throat
and mouth. Between the four of them, they also brought dental instruments
and seven sets of tonsil and adenoid instruments from Anchorage. They

had determined earlier that electricity was available at each of the proposed stops. Milo described their work at these Yukon villages:

> The clinic motto was, "Education, Participation and Responsibility." We permitted any interested villager to watch everything we did from dental extractions and refractions to ether anesthesia and T&A cases and tonsillectomies done under local anesthesia. This was the education.
>
> In each village from eager volunteers, we chose one girl to be my surgical assistant, one to scrub instruments, one to change scrub basins and keep alcohol rinse basins full, one to sit with the post-operative patients and six boys to be ambulance crew. This constituted participation. None of these eager volunteers had passed the sixth grade in formal education, but all made up by eagerness, willingness, and heroic ability their formal education deficiencies.
>
> In each village we had a collapsible Army cot supplied by a native family and this was used as the ambulance to carry the post-operative patients back to their cabins after recovery from the anesthesia. Supplying the cot was the responsibility of the ambulance crew along with promptness in appearing for duty. The responsibility of each parent or foster parent was for the appearance of his children at the proper time with a blanket and without having anything by mouth after midnight of the evening before or after breakfast at eight o'clock, if the child was scheduled for operation in the afternoon. We used our four air mattresses on the floor for the patients; the ambulance cot was bed number five.
>
> . . . Dr. Sydnam did the pre-operative general physicals. Mr. Spahn did the optical dispensing and ran the ether suction pressure machine. My wife trained the surgical assistants, did the logistics of briefing patients, urging promptness, and explaining the importance of having nothing to eat for six hours prior to surgery. She also administered the two-hour pre-operative intramuscular Thorazine and the one-hour pre-operative hypodermic injection of atropine sulfate and Demerol. We boiled the instruments and set them up for use during the two hours between injections and the start

of operations. We used either the cook stove of a neighboring cabin or a Yukon stove outdoors for the boiling of water and of instruments, depending on which was convenient. The people supplied the wood.

On the days for surgery, we did five T&As or tonsillectomies between 10:00 AM and noon and five more between 2:00 and 4:00 in the afternoon. The rest of the day we pulled teeth, looked over the next day's patients or did general examinations, refractions and, of course, washed the instruments we had used and cleaned up the "hospital."

My job was to give the anesthesia and operate, calling on John to increase or decrease the amount of ether as the occasion demanded. I also did the flying and shared photographic chores with the others. Also, the plane had to be watched over in case of rising or falling water levels in the rivers, change in the strength and direction of the wind, or the appearance of logs floating down the rivers and acting as battering rams against everything that they touched. Also, screws had to be tightened or replaced, and constant tinkering had to be indulged in to keep the plane in tiptop flying condition. Constant vigilance (and tinkering) is a price not only of liberty but also of trouble-free aviation.

... We were in Shageluk (St. Luke's) on the Innoko 3 through 10 June. We lived in a log mission house and held our clinics in the parish hall, also of log construction. We did twenty-one tonsillectomies and adenoidectomies (T&As), two tonsillectomies under local anesthesia, extracted a few teeth prescribed fifteen pairs of glasses, as well as four hearing aids. At mealtimes we enjoyed the gut-busting viands of Jean Dementi, who we firmly believe, knows how to look after the physical as well as the spiritual needs of not only those in her village, but also visiting physicians and their wives and associates.

Almost all of the people of Holikachuk (St. Paul's) also on the Innoko came down by boat to Shageluk. Among these people we did nine T&As, four tonsillectomies, extracted many teeth and prescribed fourteen pairs of glasses and one hearing aid.

On 10 through 15 June, we were at Huslia (Good Shepard) on the Koyukuk, living in the schoolteacher's quarters operating in the school room. In Huslia three audiograms were made, three hearing aids and thirteen pairs of spectacles were prescribed, twenty-three T&As, one adenoidectomy and two tonsillectomies were performed. Many teeth were extracted.

Here we were the house guests during mealtimes of the Patterson Kellers. When one realizes that these villages all had less than 125 people in them, the gastronomic logistics as well as the housing problems represented a burden on the communities at best. It also should be realized that our advent, however well-intentioned and useful it might be, interfered to some degree with the usual village chores.

In Allakaket we operated in a log community hall and slept in the schoolteacher's quarters. We had stupendous meals with the Mendelsohns and staggered away from the table well fortified for the chores of that day or the following day. In this village we did twenty-two T&As, five tonsillectomies, extracted a few teeth and prescribed two pairs of glasses. Five of the patients had come up from the Koyukuk from Hughes and were boarded in the village.

We took one "night off." Nancy Sydnam, John Spahn, and I in my airplane went off into the wilderness to a heavenly spot called Selby Lake where we fished for grayling and lake trout amid majestic surroundings that were as simple, beautiful, and unspoiled as they must have been on the Seventh Day. We were in Allakaket 15 through 20 of June.

At Steven's Village (St. Andrew's) on the Yukon we worked 20 through 23 June. Many teeth were extracted, fourteen T&As were done, fourteen pairs of spectacles were prescribed. At Steven's Village we lived and worked in the schoolhouse, striking our air mattresses and sleeping bags early in the morning in order to clear the large room for the operative or eye clinic to be held the rest of the day. Here we had the assistance of the Reverend Alfred H. Smith and his lovely young bride, Stevie, who for all her youth turned out satisfying artistically prepared meals that compared well with those veteran purveyors to hungry medicos, Jean Dementi, Connie Keller, and Dorothy Mendelsohn.

When we had finished at Steven's Village, I took Fr. and Mrs. Smith to their home at Beaver (St. Matthews). John and Nancy stayed with the schoolteachers, Mr. and Mrs. Charles Richmond, and we did our surgical and clinical work in the schoolhouse. My wife and I slept upstairs in the Smith's little log quarters behind the church. At Beaver we did twenty-one T&As, seven tonsillectomies and extracted many teeth. We stayed in this village 23 through 27 of June.

Finally, at Venetie we were under the charge of Miss Susan Carter who fed us in what we now regard is truly Episcopalian fashion. We slept in the log quarters of the schoolteachers who were absent and operated in the log schoolhouse. This was by far the most abject village of the lot. Its wealth can be surmised by the presence of only one outboard motor and three kerosene powered refrigerators. There was virtually nothing for the children to do and there was no evidence of the usual activity seen in other villages at this time of the year, namely fishing, or the gathering in of wood against the coming of a long, hard winter. Many of the log houses had packed earthen floors.

We had inquired about and established the presence of 110-volt alternating current . . .but, at Venetie we found two diesel plants, neither of which would run, and with their starting batteries completely depleted. With the help of a Wien Alaska Airlines employee, Mr. Botts, who was clearing a strip for that company's larger airplanes, we were able to diagnose and cure the difficulties of one of the diesel plants. However, there still remained a problem of a starting battery since it was beyond the strength of any of us, or anyone in the village, to crank it into life.

Fortunately, my venerable airplane carries within it a 12-volt battery that was well charged from the trip we had so far taken. With this hooked up to the plant we were able to have electricity for our time there which was from 27 to 30 of June. Here we did seven T&As, four tonsillectomies, and extracted *innumerable teeth and prescribed nine pairs of glasses.*

From there we went to Fort Yukon, staying a few hours on the eve of the centennial celebration in that historical outpost of our church. From there the ladies proceeded home by commercial air and John Spahn and I struggled home in our plane, being forced to stay overnight at Nenana because of poor weather.

No surgical or anesthetic deaths marred the perfection of our medical effort. Neither did we have the slightest damage to our airplane. God in His infinite wisdom supplied us with thirty days in a row of sunshine, something which almost never happens in this area of Alaska. True, we had a few rain showers on several days, but these served to lay the dust, fill the rain barrels and scatter the clouds of mosquitoes and other stinging and buzzing insects that gathered in clouds as soon as the breeze stopped blowing.

. . . Each individual in the village who required spectacles was asked to pay six dollars for single vision glasses and eight dollars for multifocals. These are the state rates and where the individual was deemed to be in hardship, as judged by those in his village, a lesser price was charged. But in every instance the odious quality of a free gift was avoided by as low payment as twenty-five cents. The difference between the six- and eight-dollar fees and the actual cost of the glasses, as fabricated here in Anchorage at cost plus one dollar, was made up by the Eye, Ear, Nose and Throat Foundation of Alaska, Incorporated, and those generous people throughout the country who support it, a charitable institution.

. . . That this was an exhausting trip, there is no doubt. The mental hazards of operating in other than hospital surroundings and doing anesthesia as well as surgical operation simultaneously, while at the same time being responsible for the maintenance of an airplane, as well as flying it, were considerable. Nevertheless, the outcome was satisfactory and we hope that what we have tried to do and what we have accomplished are pleasing in the sight of God.

NOME CLINIC, 1965

*I landed on the shorter of the two runways in the teeth of a
steady 30 knot wind which cut my landing ground speed to
what seem like a fast canter.*

—MILO FRITZ

IN THE SPRING OF 1965 DOC Fritz was asked by the Alaska Native Health
Service if he would be willing to hold a T&A clinic at the Maynard
McDougall Memorial Hospital in Nome. It was run by the Methodist
Church and Milo had been there many times in years past when his col-
league Fred Langsam was the doctor in charge. He hadn't been back since
Dr. Langsam's departure, so Doc Fritz was eager to accept the offer. His
colorful account of his visit to Nome that June was published in *Alaska
Medicine* the following March.

Milo took off at 8:00 a.m. on June 12, with hopes of making it to Nome
by that night:

*As usual, I went through the Rainy Pass area, never being
quite sure whether I was over the Pass. It is the kind of pass
where if you are not in it, you are in something else that ends*

up in a blind canyon. Therefore, if the day is poor and the ceiling 3000 feet or less, the cautious and the safest way to go is through Ptarmigan Pass and down a fork of the Kuskokwim River where you can pick up the Farewell beam. And from Farewell it is no trick at all to find your way to McGrath.

At McGrath I found that the Northern Commercial Company's supply of 100 octane gas had been accidently diluted with diesel fuel. But fortunately, I obtained a full load from Alaska Airlines and so continued on my way. I reached Unalakleet, crossing the mighty Yukon River and the Unalakleet Mountains. I followed the Unalakleet River with no difficulty and landed on the strip, tying up the plane and walking into the still quaint village of Unalakleet, built on the sand spit between the Bering Sea and a lagoon into which the Unalakleet River empties.

The houses are mostly frame but many log houses persist. The gardens which used to surround every habitation up to 10 or 15 years ago have almost completely disappeared. They were a unique feature of this little town and had been started by a Swedish Covenant Missionary many years ago.

I ate my lunch on a barge drawn up on the lagoon beach and enjoyed the brilliant sunshine and blue skies of that particular day. A group of little Eskimo kids played the games of childhood on the beach and talked to me in a friendly fashion as I regretfully walked back toward the airstrip and climbed aboard once more, after the usual consultation with the FAA crew on duty.

I decided I would land at Moses Point which I had passed and spoken to many times on my trips in this part of the world but at which I had never landed. Accordingly, I landed on the shorter of the two runways in the teeth of a steady 30 knot wind which cut my landing ground speed to what seem like a fast canter. A brief consultation with the FAA controller revealed that Nome was clear all right but that the weather between Rocky Point and Cape Darby was dubious according to a pilot report.

But the day was bright, the sky blue and the sea sparkling,

and the wraiths of fog that could be seen far ahead after I got airborne seemed a remote menace indeed.

But eventually I got into it and as it menacingly ebbed and receded toward the rocky coast, I was forced down lower and lower until I was flying just 50 feet off the surface, nervously listening to the reports from Nome which showed everything to be easy there if I could just get around these two rock capes. Finally, Solomon appeared under my wings and eventually I could clearly hear Nome and be understood by them as I bleated into the microphone telling them of my position. In a brief time, the ceiling lifted, the sun shone once more, the sky became a pristine blue, dappled with fat little clouds. All the anxieties of the fog just past seemed to disappear as I touched down at Marks Field. I tied the airplane down, forgetting of course to turn off the main switch due to my fatigue and relief at making my landfall safely.

A former patient, Mr. Galliher, took me into town. He returned and told me about the main switch the evidence of which appeared in the navigation lights which were still turned on. He returned me to the field, I unlocked the plane, turned off the switch and then went back to the North Star Motel, crowded to the rafters with construction men. I crawled into bed in the reserved room overlooking the sea wall, the social center of the younger set of Nome (when it isn't raining.)

The next day was Sunday and I walked around the dilapidated moldering little town. I was amazed at the heaps of broken-down equipment and automobiles that festooned every vacant lot. There was ceaseless activity of construction equipment going to and returning from a long road that is being built along the coast to Teller. I went to morning service at the Methodist Church and was far more interested in the cute little Eskimo kids crawling around and under the pews than I was in what was going on in the pulpit. I checked in at the hospital and then went down to the "old town" where I saw an old timer doing a little placer mining on the beach. He was Andy Anderson, 70 odd years of age. Before long I was busily digging sand from the beach while *he ran it through the sluice box on the bottom of which were several silver plates covered with mercury. On these mercury-covered plates a coarse meshed screen rested.*

After a while he warmed up telling me stories of the olden days. He then showed me how they used to clean up, as the saying went, by scraping the mercury with its imprisoned gold flakes off the silver plates with an old rubber heal and then burning the mercury off in an iron pot leaving the gold residue in the bottom of the pot. For all my years in Alaska I have never done any mining, and even though I now scarcely qualify as a miner, I had a good time. The amount of gold that I recovered is not apt to upset the balance of payment or the International Gold Market but it was fun.

While I was there and Andy was across the street in his house preparing coffee and cake, a load of tourists came by from Wien's Hotel. One of the passengers, a stout man with a New England accent, asked me what I was doing. I replied that I was doing a little placer work for gold. He was obviously impressed and undoubtably thought that I had come up there in '98. He then asked how long I had been working at it and I told him 10 minutes. He thought I was giving him a sassy answer and huffily turned away, climbed in the bus and took off for safety, far to the east.

In the evening I went back to the hospital and with the help of Miss Betty Shamlin, the chief nurse, I examined the 8 youngsters that we were to do in the morning. They were the usual cute Eskimo kids and every one of them came from St. Lawrence Island. Most of them had been referred by one of the itinerant physicians (name unknown) from the Alaska Native Health Service as being in need of T & A's. The age old but, to far too many physicians, ever new criteria of greatly enlarged tonsils and nasal obstruction from adenoid hypertrophy and perforated or scarred drum were present among others. The greatest number had one or other eardrums damaged or perforated, three cases being bilateral. Many ears were draining.

As day succeeded day, the patients came and went in an orderly fashion, boarded outside the hospital by an Eskimo lady who had, what in Nome, would be considered a large home.

On the second day in Nome, a young man who had completed his second year of medical school at the University of Tennessee in Memphis, arrived. He was Austin Carr and soon became the backbone of our effort there. He made the whole trip unusual and stimulating. He evinced a real interest in the problems of these Eskimo children and the wealth of clinical material, however tragic, they represented.

In the evenings I always walked along the seawall or breakwater and took a different way through town between the hospital and the North Star Hotel.

Since I was there three or four years ago, the seawall had been completed to protect the town against storms from the Bering Sea. A new Federal Building has been erected of concrete and steel to replace the one across the street that is disappearing into the tundra at interesting angles. A new hotel had been built by the airlines for the care of their crews and tourists. A sewer and waterline was being built down one of the streets close to the hospital. But on the whole, Nome is, I am afraid, a depressing sight, living in the glories of the past and dreaming of a future when gold will again be free and can be mined at a profit.

One evening, Betty Shamlin, the chief nurse, and Jamie Umbarger, the lab technician, invited several of us to attend a showing of Kodachrome slides of historical photographs collected over the years in Nome by Mrs. Carey McLain. This was a fascinating collection of photographs. I hope they will find their way to the University of Alaska Museum before they are lost in the inevitable fire that seems to destroy everything in the wooden town. These slides showed the city of Nome packed with elegant wooden buildings and long wooden streets crowded with people like Wall Street at noon. The beaches were covered with tents before each of which was a "Long Tom" beach box by means of which the stampeders extracted the gold from the sands along the sea, an area now deserted except for rusting machinery and youngsters playing.

There were slides of the great fire in the 1930's, a blow from which Nome has never recovered and will not recover until gold is freed once more.

Even today there are several rusting great dredges sinking into the primordial ooze of the tundra completely out of operation.

On another sparkling clear evening, the girls took me in the Jeep out to Port Safety to the east of town where great floes of ice had beached themselves and were slowly disintegrating in the brilliant sun.

Outside the dismal town the treeless hills were a beautiful green and yellow and the little streams sparkled and twinkled on their way to the lagoons along the sea.

Eventually, Barbee gave the last anesthetic; Betty Shamlin took care of all the details of admission and discharging and the work in the surgery; Austin Carr, the two student nurses, the two Eskimo nurses that helped us, and I finished the 44th case and it was time to take off for home. I went out to the field and cranked up the faithful Tri-Pacer. Austin Carr helped me across the runway by hanging on to the upwind wing and I was off for home.

The trip was lovely in the evening with the sun behind me as I sped along the coast past Moses' Point, Solomon, Golovin and finally Unalakleet, across the great Yukon River, over the plains to McGrath where, in the setting sun, I landed. In spite of the lateness of the hour I was able to purchase a fresh supply of gas from Alaska Airlines and continue on my way.

The trip above the north fork of the Kuskokwim into the mountain fastness was ominous because of the turbulence and the gray cloud layer at about 7000 feet, but I finally threaded my way along Ptarmigan Pass, past Puntilla Lake and the Branham's Hunting Lodge, down past Alexander Lake and past sleeping Mt. Susitna where I was first able to see the lights of Anchorage. Finally, dog tired and exactly 2 minutes after 12:00, I dropped the tired airplane with its even more tired pilot, safely onto the runway at Merrill Field, happy in the sense of accomplishment that every itinerant clinic leaves in me.

PART VI

Times of Change

Milo's Earthquake Letter

*That was something that I will never forget, even if I live to be
a lot older than I suspect will be the case. I remember going
home; we were wiped out; we lost three buildings; everything.
That night Betsy was planning on our taking a trip to Hawaii.
Well, I have never financially recovered from that.*

—Milo Fritz

The Good Friday earthquake, the second largest recorded in North
America, struck near Anchorage on March 27, 1964. Milo chronicled
his experiences in a letter he wrote to family and friends on July 2, 1964:

> Dear Folks,
>
> Very few among you are geologists. However, I am sure
> that on a Sunday drive or a trip through a national or state
> park, you have noticed areas bare of earth where the forma-
> tions of quartz, sandstone and other kinds of rock have been
> in a position other than horizontal and sometimes almost
> vertical in their direction. These, of course, represent major
> upheavals in the earth's surface eons ago when there were no

seismographs to record the events and nobody felt any pain unless it was the trilobites or other pre-Cambrian inhabitants of this earth.

These manifestations represented major disruptions of the earth's crust at some remote time. Here on Good Friday of 1964, a minor footnote in the geologic history of this earth was written. Had the great quake occurred at Mt. McKinley Park or in the great mountain fastnesses with which the State abounds, the phenomenon would have been of interest only to seismologists, a few trappers, hunters, or prospectors that might have been in the area and perhaps to the foxes and bears especially the latter who were just then emerging from hibernation after a long and severe winter on the usual short rations.

Good Friday came at the end of a particularly difficult week. I had had surgery every morning. One of the cases was a difficult cataract, two of the others involved handsome young women who needed extensive nasal surgery and the rest of the cases were, as the saying goes, routine (for everyone except the patients themselves).

So it was that when I left Betsy in the old, combined house and office at 1027 Fourth Avenue to make my evening rounds at the Providence Hospital, I did so with a light heart since our month-long reorganization of our practice promised to give us more time in the immediate future. Besides, a three-day holiday over Easter was eagerly anticipated by both of us.

I arrived at the hospital a little bit before five, having outsmarted the workers at the bases who converge on our pitifully inadequate road net about five o'clock. As is my custom, I started on the fifth floor intending to work my way down, looking after the patients upon whom I had operated who were looking forward to being discharged from the hospital and going home for Easter.

While talking to the two young women upon whom I had operated, the building gave a lurch. Neither they nor I were much impressed since we have felt this phenomenon over many years. However, a second or two later the building shuddered. This too seemed quite routine but then began about four minutes of the most terrifying, lurching and careening that ever a building endured. Amid the crash of solutions as they pitched from the shelves and the screams of the few psychiatric patients that were on the floor, was a grinding, wrenching sound that was probably caused by the steel from which the building had been honestly constructed. The steel window frames seemed to be trying to rotate in the walls and as I looked out the window, there indeed I saw a dance of death.

All the trees seemed to be motivated by a great string tied to their tops and some invisible giant hand was jerking the string back and forth. The trees would bow their tops to the north and south alternately in a very deep obeisance. This, of course shook off the snow and while the north and southward bowing went on in ever increasing tempo, the twisting motion that I felt in the building was transmitted to the trees which, as they alternately bowed deeply north and south also twisted around their long axes. The concrete covered steel light poles bordering the hospital parking area also went through this kind of gyration until a couple of them snapped off but the others remained miraculously standing.

While looking out the window I pushed the patients' beds toward the wall because I felt it would be safer there and had I not been holding on to something I could not have kept my footing. There was a television set attached to the wall and ceiling above the door behind me. Had it come loose and hit any of us it would have done considerable damage. Everything was on the floor; pieces of plaster fell from the walls but none from the ceiling and everything from the bedside tables was strewn on the beds and on the floor including the water pitchers, the supper trays and everything else in one grand mess. Finally, with one grand shudder, the whole thing stopped and except for the sobbing and moaning of the unstable patients on the floor, there was a deathly silence. I went out into the hall and for lack of anything better to do I began helping the nurses and others on their feet to pick up the mess of solutions, bottles and other destroyed things placing them in the garbage cans which are in the kitchen area. I tried to phone home because right away I wondered what had happened to Betsy but of course, the lines were dead. In a few minutes, the hospital diesel plant started up and so we had light almost at once.

After discharging one of the young women whose boyfriend was with her and because I saw no further reason for having her stay there, I checked on my other patients and went down to the emergency ward where one other doctor, Fred Hillman, happened to be also for his evening rounds. We were the only ones there and we figured out that pretty soon the casualties would be coming in. I was extremely anxious about Betsy but figured that my place of duty was the hospital and that running around on roads that were undoubtedly torn up might result in my being of use to nobody and even in my getting killed. Of course, the radios were dead and nobody knew anything about anything. However, looking from the fifth floor, there were no flames or smoke so we believed that anyone who had not been directly under something that was falling might have fared quite well.

In a few minutes, the casualties began coming in. One woman had been crushed from mid pelvis down when she and her husband fled their house in what is known as the Turnagain area where the greatest destruction was wrought. He had suffered a traumatic amputation of his right leg at the mid-thigh and had a compound fracture of his left ankle. The orthopedic fellows got on him and his life was spared. Another middle-aged man came in exsanguinated with a complete crush of his right leg. Before anything could be done for him, he died. Minor cuts and bruises and simple fractures completed the first wave of casualties and at about 9:30, I decided that I would try to thread my way home and see what had happened. I found the car intact with the dog safely inside. When I go to the hospital to make rounds, he airs himself and gets into the car. I leave the back door open. It was closed this time when I came out.

My own feelings as I recall them were those of having been stunned, bewildered, and absolutely unbelieving of what my senses told me. Here was Lake Otis Road with a tremendous gap in it, wide but not quite wide enough to stop the flow of traffic. Of course, ice and snow were still on the ground and the constant grind of traffic had covered the whole road with a glare of ice. I realized that if I got into any kind of trouble, I would have to extricate myself since there was no help available others having troubles of their own.

Suddenly, the radio came on in the car and the first announcement I remember was "Anchorage destroyed, Fairbanks in flames." This did nothing to help my spirits and as I probed around the periphery of downtown Anchorage mounting panic filled my heart because inflammatory, almost hysterical and, I might add, ungrammatical announcements of the radio announcers made me feel certain that our old house had collapsed and Betsy had surely been killed. Finally, I found a road that was passable but was promptly halted by a sergeant of the Alaska National Guard. He was a young Eskimo and I rolled down the window and said, "I'm Dr. Fritz and I am trying to get down to my house at 1027 Fourth Avenue." And he said "Oh, you, Fritz, you took off my tonsils in Unalakleet that time you visit Grandma Degnan." He let me through and this story repeated itself over and over again as I got closer and closer to our place at Fourth and L. All these youngsters had either been patients of mine or were relatives or friends of people upon whom I had worked on one way or another since coming here so many years ago. So, you see, as the saying goes, bread cast upon the waters sometimes comes back not only wet, but brings with it on occasion, things of incalculable good.

As I finally approached Fourth and L, I was appalled to see the Inlet Hotel draped like a Dali watch over the edge of a deep crevasse on the bottom of which rested the Australaska's just recently completed building in all its white majesty apparently unharmed and as my headlight swept across the space between the cabin behind the building and the old house I

*could see the pale faces of Betsy and Mary [housekeeper] who
had been attracted by the lights of the car as they threw their
erratic beams over the buildings as I slowly approached the
area over uneven ground.*

*I took time to kiss Betsy and to assure myself that she and
Mary were safe and had a place to stay in the little house
on L Street. The cabin was obviously destroyed and the big
house which looked so sound and majestic standing there
all by itself proved to be tipping slightly to the east since the
foundation on that side had been badly smashed. I noted
that the Jeep was in the garage four feet above the alley which
had dropped.*

*Then I turned the car around and carefully threaded my
way back through a new set of Eskimo sentries who only let
me through because they knew who I was and what I was
doing and what I had done for them, their relatives, and
friends.*

*By the time I got back to the hospital it was almost mid-
night and the second wave of casualties had begun coming
in. They were relatively minor except one young woman who
was literally a mass of bruises, lacerations, and fractures but
who miraculously had some life in her still. A young urolo-
gist and I patched up her scalp, which was half off, sewed
up the lacerations that she had here and there, took care of
the fractures, managed to pull her through the night with the
help of others of course. It seems that she had rushed out of
the Anchorage Glass, Sash, and Door just in time to meet
a collapsing wall, some of which landed on her head and
the rest had crushed her chest and bruised and skinned her
literally from top to toe. She had a fractured skull, a facial
paralysis on one side, paralysis of the movements of her eye
on the same side and blood coming from the ear, all of which,
of course was quite ominous. However, she made it and has
almost completely recovered at this writing from what was
almost a fatal set of injuries.*

*A young soldier was brought in unconscious. A wall had
collapsed on him and fractured his skull. All of us, doctors*

and nurses alike, did what we could for this young man including packing him in ice to keep his temperature down but after four days of round the clock work, he also died.

As all of you have no doubt read in the news reports we did suffer surprisingly few deaths somewhere around twenty-six. Many people were injured but not many seriously.

As the doctors reported to the hospital, I was relieved to count them off, one by one and find out how they fared.

By midnight, the true picture of our disaster had begun to come clear. Telephones, electricity, water, and sewer systems in downtown Anchorage were apparently completely disrupted. The periphery of the town had either all the usual utilities or perhaps were minus the telephones. The hardest hit area was the most plush residential Turnagain section where it appears thirty or forty homes had slid into Cook Inlet and many others were tottering on the brink of newly formed cliffs where the sand and gravel had fallen away leaving wave-like escarpments as though some giant hand with a rake had crushed a clod of sand and clay and made one or two rough passes through it with the tines. The houses were scattered about like children's toys.

Our neurosurgeon, Perry Mead, lost two of his children whose exact fate was not known at that time but who were found together at the house at the bottom of a deep crevasse. The older had gone back for the baby and had so given up his life for his brother. In spite of this their father, though completely unnerved for doing surgery himself, stuck around the hospital as we all did in the first forty-eight hours giving life-saving advice to those of us who were able to do the surgery having suffered lesser loss.

After forty-eight hours, I had time to consider my own affairs. Betsy said that at the first shock she had fled downstairs half-dressed out the front door, through the gate and to a loading zone sign that was a few feet west of the big house. She heard the splintering of glass as the earth to the east of her sank down and the Inlet Hotel draped itself over the edge of the crevasse. The Australaska building contained a bar called the Memo Pad. As the glass in the front of it splintered, the door burst open and the customers rushed out screaming. They found themselves in the bottom of a hole with their cars parked neatly at the curb, the only trouble being that it was twelve feet down from the rest of the road and they could not get out. A good many teetotalers were made that night.

While this was going on Betsy said she felt an uneasy rocking and twisting motion of the earth beneath her feet and the chimney separated from the house so that she could see the sky between and then slammed back against the building with a terrific thump. This was repeated three times. She felt herself whirled around the post to which she was clinging a few times and was unable to stop nor was she able to move away from the building which she wished to do in order to be out of the way in case it should collapse. Her big regret was that Kelly our ancient half-moon parrot was left in the house. The cat with the concrete cracking, trunks, cans, and bottles falling about him, had to take care of himself since he had been put down in the cellar after the office was closed. Had she not taken flight at the first jolt, Betsy would undoubtedly, not have been able to keep her feet and could have suffered severe injury or perhaps even death had she stayed in the pitching and plunging, twisting, old wooden building.

As soon as she felt sure that the earthquake was over, she gingerly went into the house prying open a window and climbing in, climbed up the stairs. She found Kelly on the floor in his upside-down cage in a mixture of books, furniture, magazines, glass wear and the television set and the first thing that he said was Merry Christmas!

She picked the bird up and then she and Mary went into the L Street house which was also a shambles. They entered by a window, the door here too, being jammed. They picked up what they could and made the place habitable. They did not dare light the floor furnace not knowing whether the chimney was intact or whether oil was all over the basement. She had no desire to start a fire where by the grace of God, none had broken out.

We found that the Presbyterian Hospital was out of commission, the old Providence was evacuated of its old folks and so all medical attention had to be centered around the new Providence Hospital wrecked as it was. Almost that very night, large cargo planes brought irrigating pipes from Arizona and New Mexico and these were strung on the surface with faucets every few feet to which we could attach hoses and thus be supplied with water. In twenty-four hours, working around the clock, repair crews of the city of Anchorage had power for us and light. The telephone didn't come for three or four days. The commanding officers of our bases had troops posted immediately so that the small amount of looting and stealing that had begun was stopped. Troops were posted about downtown Anchorage and around the Turnagain area where our great friend John Spahn and his wife, Alice, lived. Within hours of the quake our houses were placarded as being unfit for habitation and we were prevented by law from occupying them. However, I again satisfied the Eskimo sergeant who was on duty on our block that I did indeed own the house and I wanted to go in and get something that was very important. So, I rushed upstairs feeling like a guy crossing no man's land during the World War I to pick up a small Easter present I had for Betsy, feeling that she would need a little boost to her morale as I certainly did. I got down safely feeling as though I had cheated death another time. All these feelings of being a hero of course were totally unnecessary since the building did not collapse and had to be knocked over under the city demolition program on the sixth of June.

On Saturday they still would not let us go into the house but on Easter Sunday we decided to go in anyway and save the medical equipment and whatever else we could salvage before it collapsed which we were absolutely convinced it would do. Through the good offices of a friend, we were able to get a mover on Easter Sunday and move most of the vital medical equipment to the top unfinished floor of the Presbyterian Hospital. While working away at the medical equipment, Betsy was in the front of the office and all of a

sudden let out a shriek. My nerves, not in very good shape
had taken just about all they could and I had visions of her
being crushed by something or having fallen, anyway some
sort of new crisis to keep things going between aftershocks. I
shot out of the office on to the front porch of the old house to
find that all the excitement had been caused by the arrival
of our son, Piet, who instead of writing letters, trying to telephone, or sending telegrams, managed to wangle a passage
from Iowa here in order to give us a hand. He and my two
ninety-pound secretaries and Helen Gamble who has been
our nurse's aide for the past eight years and Betsy and two
young friends of Jonathan, Bill Smith, and Dick Unruh,
slaved away clearing the house of everything that we could
salvage. We made great heaps of household goods on palettes
of plywood and other lumber and doors that we put out on
the snow and then covered it with plastic. We piled clothes
and books and the essentials of life and practice into the L
Street, frame house until we thought it would collapse from
the weight of the stuff we put in it.

As we worked in the big house, we got braver and braver
until finally we were running up and down stairs clear to the
attic, tearing up rugs, carrying out books, furniture, clothes
and all of the accumulated flotsam and jetsam of sixteen
years of life and practice. It was an unbelievable effort and
went on for days.

Our household goods we put in storage and the medical stuff remained at the top of the Presbyterian Hospital.
Then Betsy had the brilliant idea on Sunday of using the
surgical wing of the old Providence Hospital for an office.
Agreeing that it was a great idea I immediately called the
Sister Superior and she said that if she were not transgressing
the fiats of the City and Federal tax people we could move
in anytime. We also arranged that John Spahn, our optician
friend, whose business had also been completely destroyed,
could move in also.

The day of the quake, it became obvious that we could
not stay for very long in the L Street house. So, after spending

Friday night in it, Saturday we moved over to the Spahns' place which was also without sewer, water, telephone, or electricity but was intact otherwise, very comfortable and a welcome refuge from the desolate and depressing spectacle of downtown Anchorage. We worked all day and went over there at night using the greenhouse as an outdoor privy, carrying water in from the Providence Hospital in plastic buckets and otherwise doing the best we could. Betsy, Piet, and I ate at the Providence or Presbyterian Hospitals and used their bathroom facilities.

I had been scheduled to go to a clinic in Kodiak on the Saturday before Easter. Kodiak, as you know, was terribly devastated by floods and tidal waves and so, of course, that was cancelled, but we still had a clinic beginning the next Tuesday in Fairbanks. Since everything practically that we could move had been retrieved from the big house even though it was for the most part piled outside in the weather and since there was much renovating to be done in the surgical wing before it could be used as an office, Betsy and I decided it would be best for me to go and hold my two weeks clinic in Fairbanks, already oversubscribed by 160 patients. And so, I flew my plane and John took the jet on Tuesday afternoon, April 7, along with my usual tons of gear and spent two weeks in Fairbanks coming home each weekend in my own little plane in order to help Betsy and keep myself cheered up.

As the weeks fled by from that tragic day until the 27th of May, Betsy and I worked at least 18 hours a day, lifting, sorting, moving, and trying to practice medicine for a week in Joe Shelton's office. When I got back from Fairbanks, twice my own place not being ready in the surgical wing, finally I moved in. For a week or so we had competition from the various renovators but were able to carry on the work. Throughout this I did real prodigies of surgery that had been scheduled before the quake. All the patients with two exceptions went right ahead with their surgery in spite of their having been upset in their way as all of us were to a greater or lesser degree ranging from death itself to minor inconvenience caused by detours and cracks in the roads.

We left John and Alice's sumptuous place after a week and moved into the L Street house. It was very shaky on its foundation but we could use the chimney and floor furnace so we were warm. We had water piped in from the irrigating pipes through the garden hose into the garden hose outlet. We had to have two hoses because every night one would freeze and, in the morning, I would take that off and put another one on which we kept in the house overnight and so had water once more for a few days. We had the only outside privy on Fourth Avenue in downtown Anchorage.

It so happened that the wife of one of the City Engineers had been a patient in the early mastoid days and had finally recovered completely from that dread affliction under my care. It was entirely owing to his friendship that we got some kind of a sewer connection although we are not certain exactly as to where the waste went. So, all liquid wastes we disposed of in the usual fashion holding our breaths so to speak so that we could go to the hospital for showers and major disposal problems early in the morning and late at night. At these sessions we learned about the fires in Seward, the loss of 26 people at Chenega including 2 entire families, exchanged earthquake rumors and stories of miraculous escapes.

It is hard for me to express the extraordinary cooperation, patience, helpfulness, and common decency showed by everyone throughout this difficult time. It is the fashion I know to berate government whether federal, state, or municipal. But I would say now, as I did while it was going on, that never have the police, the military, the city officials and others shone greater forbearance and understanding of the difficulties of others in which they, of course, were involved.

In Fairbanks John and I worked around the clock every day except Saturday and Sunday when we flew home to help with the chores that could not be delegated to painters, carpenters, carpet layers, and other artisans that we had working for us in establishing our new place of business in the old

Providence Hospital. I know very well that activity makes time go faster but every time there was the least bit of a shock in Fairbanks I would shoot out of the office onto the porch of the Traveler's Inn and then sheepishly go back inside and continue what I was doing.

During the days that we lived in the L Street house, Betsy had her own seismograph, which was a lamp suspended on a heavy, thick, silken cord which also contained the electric wires. It had the shape of those wide, peasant, straw hats that the Chinese coolies wear when they work in the field. As soon as this device rocked or pitched the least bit, Betsy would shout "earthquake" and out the door in the street she would go followed by the dog and then by me. It took us many days before we calmed down enough not to rush outside during these repeated aftershocks which became less severe and less frequent as time went on to disappear altogether for the past four or five weeks. We had over 350 aftershocks.

Another thing we noticed was the general appearance of being scatter-brained. Both of us fancy ourselves fairly well-disciplined people and yet we would start one job, see something on the way, take that up and see a third job that needed doing, start that and in other words just keep moving but accomplishing nothing. After a while we diagnosed this ailment and resolutely went after each task until it was completed or brought to as near completion as possible before being beguiled by something else along the way.

My secretary and another youngster I have as a general office girl worked like field hands and are still doing it actually all through these upsetting days. They lifted boxes and books and medical gear along with the men and boys and without them I don't think we would be back in business yet. Their loyalty and devotion as well as that of Helen Gamble, who has been with me eight years, can never be repaid.

Soon Betsy and I found that living in the L Street house was frightfully depressing since it could never be kept clean and was either hot enough to raise orchids or as cold as the inside of a deepfreeze.

*We had our deepfreeze on the porch along with the refrig-
erator and I didn't enjoy going out and getting things from
the latter in the morning and at night while exposed to the
traffic which thundered by on L Street at that time, bouncing
over the surface water pipe that was covered by a mound of
earth so that the cars could get by.*

*Until those who used the road got used to this heap of
gravel enclosing the pipe it sounded as though there were an
automobile accident every five minutes and that didn't help
our nervous systems either. But we got used to that also.*

*The problem of where to live now arose. We found that
our insurance companies were not about to pay their obligations to us. Since it probably would come to a lawsuit,
many months and perhaps a year or even longer might be
used up before some settlement could be wrung from them.
Accordingly, we decided that we could occupy a daylight
basement apartment in the old Providence Hospital and
once again be in the same building for living and working as
we had had for so many years.*

*While we were in Sitka on the 26th of May until the 14th
of June, we had the apartment painted and when we arrived
back here on Sunday, the 14th, we found it fresh and clean.
It will be a cheerful and warm place for us during the winter.*

*Betsy and I both felt pretty well exhausted from years of
work with very little respite on Friday afternoon, the 27th of
March. But after the prodigies of physical work and the nervous strain entailed, of what I have accounted above, we felt
absolutely and completely done in when we staggered onto
the plane for Sitka on the 26th of May. We were pleased that
the city demolition crews took down the big house and the
small cabin behind while we were gone since watching it being
done or even being in the city while we knew it was going on
would have been more than we could have stood. When we
shot around the corner, Sunday afternoon upon returning
from Southeastern Alaska, we saw the trees that surround
the house but nothing other than a hole to represent where
it had been. Even the foundation had been taken out and so*

absolutely nothing was left except in the minds and hearts of the thousands of people who went there as patients and in our own, and those of our boys, the most significant part of whose lives was spent within those wooden walls.

For me surgery has always been fun and an exciting way of serving one's fellow man. But the strain of doing it continuously in spite of the other tasks enumerated above was extremely debilitating until we left for Sitka. Actually, I lost 23 pounds in weight and outside of being nervous, discovered a certain amount of forgetfulness that was almost embarrassing. I would put something down and for the life of me could not remember where I had put it. I would have to write down the things that I went downtown to do, for instance, otherwise I would come back having accomplished nothing. I would no longer trust myself with keys at all since I would lose them every day making it impossible to get into various buildings and offices that we had to visit every day. Betsy carried all the keys in her tremendous purse and so we got along. I also noticed that my handwriting, abominable at best, became absolutely undecipherable even by me and by Betsy. Both of us tended to be unsteady on our feet like sailors after a long voyage. But happily, these things have changed and while we did not exactly rest in Sitka, I did have five days at the medical meeting in Ketchikan which were warm and sunny and without any responsibilities whatsoever.

I have gained back about five pounds and feel pretty well at this writing.

Throughout the most dismal period of recovery from the quake, the most heartening thing Betsy and I feel were the letters and telegrams and offers of financial help and actual checks that generous friends and relatives enclosed with expressions of deep sympathy and understanding.... Because of the magnitude of this event in our lives, and because it would be impossible to write a missive of this length to each of you, I hope that those of you who feel as I about circular letters and cocktail parties will perhaps forgive Betsy and me on this occasion for using this means of telling you what went

on in our minds and hearts and what happened to us as a
result of the Good Friday earthquake.

   Realize that while all these things of extraordinary nature
were going on Betsy and I were carrying the full surgical,
medical, and administrative load of an extremely busy prac-
tice and managed to fulfill two out of three commitments
for itinerant clinics. Our equanimity was upset mostly by
the apparent necessity of suing two insurance companies for
the earthquake damage that we have received. Also, a mal-
practice suit based on a flimsy complaint is also hanging fire
while one of the lawyers is on a delayed honeymoon. Since
our property, our entire nest egg for the future is in the so-
called danger area we do not know whether it will ever be
worth anything, whether we will be able to rebuild on it,
should that be our desire, or whether it will be taken over by
urban renewal, a federal scheme for acquiring land for resale
to municipalities under situations such as we now face.

Not knowing if they would get it or not, Milo and Betsy applied for a
small business loan under the disaster title. It felt like they were starting
over. His letter continues:

   The sorting, throwing away and rearranging of our house-
hold and medical goods will go on for many weeks. Our next
clinic is scheduled at St. Mary's for the Labor Day weekend.
Meanwhile the problems of our insurance companies, Urban
Renewal, SBA and the problems of medical and surgical oph-
thalmology and otolaryngology will go on and somehow, I
suppose will be solved in time. Meanwhile we are both well
and optimistic. The atmosphere of hope in the future seems
to pervade the state.

   . . . The downtown area has been almost cleared of its
wrecked buildings, office, and residences. The demolition and
clearing is moving towards the periphery of Anchorage right
now. Valdez is going to be moved to another site altogether.
Seward is recovering and federal funds have been allotted
for rebuilding the highway to Seward and also the Alaska
Railroad which took a 19 million dollar battering as a result
of the earthquake. The people of Turnagain, whose houses

lie like a child's discarded toys on the furrowed earth that has been so greatly disturbed, are receiving federal assistance through various agencies already established.

. . . We are all hopeful and optimistic about the future. I no longer forget where I park my car, why I drove downtown in the first place nor do I lose my keys, gloves, overcoats, hats, tools, and appointment slips nearly as often as I did in the first weeks following Good Friday.

If this letter has in some way sketched out to you what we endured and how we survived it will have accomplished its purpose. Betsy's left forearm, in a cast for three weeks following a mild fracture incurred while moving things about in the office, is now off and she is under full steam once more. We look forward, as always, to our mail which links us so closely to our beloved friends and relatives throughout the world. Barring another totally unforeseen calamity, I am sure that Betsy and I will be on an even keel once more and be able to take a very badly needed rest by October.

Sincerely,
Milo H. Fritz, M.D.

CALL TO ADVENTURE: SUMMER
IN ALASKA, 1966

It is those we live with and love and should know who elude
us. Now nearly all those I loved and did not understand
when I was young are dead, but I still reach out to them.

—NORMAN MACLEAN, A RIVER RUNS THROUGH IT

WITHIN TWO YEARS OF THAT CATASTROPHIC EARTHQUAKE, Milo and Betsy offered me, their sixteen-year-old niece, a summer job in Alaska. It was a generous offer—round-trip air fare between Philadelphia and Anchorage, full-time summer employment, room and board provided by my aunt and uncle, plus travels with them around Alaska on itinerant medical clinics.

Uncle Milo had three requirements: I must learn to drive a stick shift so I could drive their four-wheel-drive Jeep, I must pass my Pennsylvania driver's license test, and I must wear only skirts and dresses during my stay—no pants—which seemed like an odd stipulation, especially for Alaska. However, despite the black humor that punctuated his letters, I rightly sensed that Uncle Milo was a man even more old-fashioned than my disciplinarian father. No matter. Primed for adventure, I jumped at the opportunity to dip into my aunt and uncle's colorful life.

Aunt Betsy outlined summer plans in a letter (and diplomatically let me know it would be OK to pack one or two pairs of casual pants to wear when we were traveling in the bush):

You will arrive here on the 21st.

June 24 we will drive to Homer which will give you an opportunity to see a glacier close by and a spectacular mountain pass, quaint Russian fishing villages and Homer where the scenery on a good day is marvelous.

June 25th you and Uncle Milo will take the ferry to Kodiak where the two of you will be working for five days. I believe that some fun with young people is planned for that time.

July 1 you will return to Anchorage by plane.

July 2nd we will all leave for the Valley of 10,000 Smokes. Going by large plane to King Salmon and then into Katmai by Grumman Goose or Mallard. This is fisherman's paradise and also a National Park. (pants on this trip.) We will stay three days and then return to Anchorage.

July 16th we will go to Fairbanks via train. We shall be working there for two weeks. On the 23rd and 24th we will drive to Circle Hot Springs and spend the weekend with a short trip to Circle so that you can see the mighty Yukon. (bring bathing suit—not for the Yukon but for the Hot Springs)

July 30th we will return to Anchorage, probably you and I will get off at Mt. McKinley National Park so that we can stay overnight and take the bus trip into Wonder Lake and see the mountain (an all-day trip). Then back on the train the next day for Anchorage.

August 18th we will fly to Juneau and spend the remainder of the day sight-seeing and take the ferry early the next A.M. for Sitka. (pray the weather is clear so that you can see more) Arriving Sitka that night. Where we will work for two weeks.

During the time in Anchorage, we can take short motor

trips to nearby places of interest.
I have just spent the weekend making the arrangements
and reservations.
        A nut Betsy
"A nut Betsy"?!—I never dared mention my aunt's typo to her.

BRILLIANT SUNSHINE HAD WARMED THE AIR to a balmy sixty-two degrees—Anchorage's warmest day so far that year—the afternoon that Aunt
Betsy and Uncle Milo greeted me at the airport. They took a Polaroid of
me—a coltish teenager with long blond hair, wearing a pastel spring coat,
unflattering cat-eye glasses and a shy smile—and immediately mailed the
photo to my parents in Pennsylvania to document my safe arrival.

We drove directly to the old Providence Hospital in downtown
Anchorage. There, in the otherwise deserted wing where Uncle Milo's
medical offices were located, they introduced me to my future co-workers.
At the time they were packing medical equipment and supplies into cases
that would be air-freighted to Kodiak, the next clinic, scheduled to begin
the following Monday.

Uncle Milo, fifty-six, was in his prime then, robust and energetic, with
a shaved head and a countenance that often seemed severe, but, to me,
invariably held the hint of a smile playing at the corners of his mouth.
He had a commanding presence, high standards, and strict rules. The fact
that I was young and had absolutely no nursing experience didn't seem to
concern him. He had faced such situations before in his bush clinics where
he routinely offered rudimentary nursing training to volunteer teenage
Native girls, who became "experts" after two or three operations. Uncle
Milo expected much less of me—I just had to know how to drive a Jeep.

The old green Jeep I was to drive had survived the earthquake by mere
inches, and my aunt and uncle's circumstances had shifted as abruptly
as the ground beneath their feet that evening. Two years later, they were
still living and working in "temporary space" in the original Providence
Hospital at 9th and L. "Home" for Aunt Betsy, Uncle Milo, and now for
me, was still the former priest apartment on the ground floor. Dr. Fritz's
medical office was on an upper floor; John Spahn's optical office was on
another floor.

Of course, I must have read the "Earthquake Letter" that Uncle Milo
sent to family and friends describing the earthquake and its repercussions,

but my blasé teenage mind was not attuned to tragedy. Focused on the moment at hand, I simply unpacked my bags in their attractive apartment in the old hospital and settled in, eager for whatever experiences awaited me that summer. Soon I was outfitted with two white nurse uniforms, slips, stockings, and shoes. And also—this being Alaska—a fishing license, hip boots, suspenders, and thick socks.

At the end of the workday that first afternoon, Uncle Milo drove me to the new Providence Hospital, some five miles out of town near Goose Lake. With a population of over 100,000, the former town of Anchorage had grown into a city; the hospital no longer a convenient bike ride away for Doc Fritz. The new Providence Hospital had opened in 1962, replacing the 1930s-era facility in the heart of Anchorage, still up for sale. My uncle wanted to show me around the modern surgical ward, as my daily duties—in addition to opening and closing patient examination rooms, administering eye drops, filing charts, and running errands in downtown Anchorage—would soon include washing and sterilizing surgical instruments and transporting them by Jeep to this new hospital. Before returning to the apartment, Uncle Milo drove me back through Anchorage, passing by their Fourth and L property. The site of their former home and office was now an empty lot.

"BOURBON RENEWAL," WAS WHAT MY TWENTY-FIVE-YEAR-OLD cousin Jonathan called what Anchorage was going through when he came to dinner that week. I hadn't seen him since I was about eight. The tall, well-spoken Alaskan had piercing blue eyes and a sharp nose, giving him a somewhat eagle-like mien, and a jocular, but quick-triggered intensity. I knew a few years back he had been a student at Yale for a semester—allegedly devoting more time to poker-playing and partying than classwork. "Busted out of the best schools in the East," was Uncle Milo's sardonic assessment of Jonathan's college experience.

After a stint in the Army, Jonathan became a pilot and now was flying freight and working as a flight instructor at Merrill Field, the buzzing general aviation airport just a mile or so east of town, the third busiest airport in the country—after O'Hare and Kennedy—my cousin boasted. Independently, Jonathan and his father were working on getting their "instrument tickets" that summer—which would qualify them to fly by relying on instruments alone when weather conditions reduced visibility.

On the occasions when Jonathan and his pilot buddies came to dinner, talk usually gravitated to discussions about flying and airplanes—subjects nearly as dear to Uncle Milo's heart as medicine.

There was much to do and learn during my first week, but the days were lengthy. The day after my arrival was the summer solstice and the sun didn't set until well after 10:00 p.m. "Alaskans go around all summer with deep circles under their eyes," Uncle Milo told me. "It stays light so late they never know when to go to bed."

On my first day of work as a nurse's aide, despite being attired head-to-toe in all-white, as dictated by Aunt Betsy, I must have looked tentative. To buck me up, Uncle Milo offered some memorable first-day-on-the-job advice: "There's no need to announce you're new at this. If I'd done that, my first surgery patient would have wrapped himself in his sheet and gone screaming into the night."

Uncle Milo soon found time to refract my eyes. Taking me downstairs to meet John Spahn to be fitted for contacts, he assured me, "You'll have the boys melting down into their Keds." Uncle Milo warned that I might find his friend somewhat gruff and standoffish at first, though that turned out not to be the case. John, a powerfully built man with thinning hair, had a very kindly, can-do manner. He measured my eyes, taught me how to properly insert and remove a contact lens, and briefly dipped into his store of funny stories. It soon became apparent why my uncle was so fond of this big, teddy bear of a man and his puckish sense of humor.

Within a couple of days, Uncle Milo checked out my driving skills in the Jeep and declared me a competent driver. I began to learn my way around Anchorage—the bank, Penny's, the stationery story, the new hospital, Merrill Field—observing in a letter that "everyone drives so slowly here. The speed limit is mostly 30. They also have four-way stop signs and flashing four-way red lights for which everyone stops." At the time, Anchorage had the feel of a big, small town, with few tall buildings to mar the impressive view of the Chugach Mountains silhouetted against the sky to the east.

Aunt Betsy and Uncle Milo had taken great pains to plan out a summer of work and travel that would introduce me to the Alaska that they knew and loved so well. By the end of the week, we were on the move.

The journey to Kodiak Island consisted of two legs, the first by road, the second via the Alaska ferry system. On Friday, Aunt Betsy and I set off in the Jeep for Homer, which lay some 200 miles south at the far end of the Kenai Peninsula. We were to meet Uncle Milo who was flying to Homer in a leased Cessna, accompanied by a flight instructor. My uncle was using every opportunity to advance his flying skills in preparation for his instrument test. He would forego the gorgeous Alaska scenery and pilot the plane while wearing a black plastic tube strapped to his head to confine his view to the Cessna's instrument panel. He supplemented these training flights with many hours of instrument "flying" in a Link Trainer, an early flight simulator that had been used to train pilots during World War II.

Near the end of a long day of spectacular sight-seeing that included stops at Portage Glacier and the tiny village of Ninilchik, Aunt Betsy and I drove on to their homestead. Still twenty miles north of Homer, we turned west at Anchor Point, the Jeep sashaying along their homestead's mile-long stretch of overgrown tire tracks to their outpost above Cook Inlet. My aunt and I picnicked near their weathered cabin, barn, and outhouse on a high cliff overlooking the tidal waters, a restorative place of wild beauty where their family used to fish, shoot, play on the beach, and unwind when Jonathan and Pieter were boys and the rustic buildings were still livable. The outhouse, Aunt Betsy told me, had the best view in Alaska. It was a spectacular expanse of water, mountains, clouds, and sunlight on a scale unlike anything I'd seen back East—all impressively pristine and remote.

It felt even more remote when, only half-way back to the main road afterwards, Aunt Betsy realized that our slowing progress along the bumpy path was due to a flat tire. At that point I saw a side of my aunt that I hadn't seen before. Gone was the starchy nurse in spotless whites who had kept a sharp eye on me in recent days as I tried to learn the basics of being a nurse's aide. At their homestead, I saw an Aunt Betsy who could assemble a jack, crank up a Jeep, and change a tire—with scant help from me. Her matter-of-fact competence was impressive, my first inkling of what it took to be an Alaska woman.

The Fritz clinics that were scheduled throughout that summer—Kodiak, Fairbanks, and Sitka—were not in bush villages, but in sizeable communities with modern facilities. In such places, hotel or motel rooms served as the exam rooms and office/patient waiting areas. Surgeries were performed in the local hospital. My clinic responsibilities were much the same as in the Anchorage office: putting drops in patients' eyes, running errands, and in Kodiak, helping Mrs. Hall, the nurse in charge, with clerical work, answering the phones, and patient flow.

AUNT BETSY WAS ON HER WAY BACK UP TO ANCHORAGE by the time Uncle Milo and I were walking around the ferry terminal on the Homer Spit in the full sun of very early morning. We watched the nearly 300-foot blue-and-white *Tustumena* ferry arrive and disgorge passengers and cars before we boarded, leaving Homer in our wake at 6:00 a.m. An hour later we made the most of the hour-and-a-half stop at the picturesque little town of Seldovia, taking what we assured each other were "prize-winning photographs,"—Uncle Milo with his Twin Lens Reflex Rolleiflex camera and me with my point-and-shoot Instamatic. We promised to split the prize money. Back on board, we enjoyed a "real good breakfast," and all was well until mid-lunch when rough waters began to roll the ship. Terribly seasick, I spent the rest of the voyage in the state room that Uncle Milo had thankfully reserved, missing a major stretch of Alaska scenery on the eleven-hour ferry ride from Homer to Kodiak.

John Spahn flew in the next day, a Sunday, and after lunch the three of us went down to the docks to admire the small fishing boats moving about the harbor and to take pictures. John had the same model Rolleiflex as Uncle Milo. All grins, they had great fun comparing f-stops and exposure times on their twin cameras while lining up more prize-winning shots.

"How about F11 at 1/60?" Uncle Milo or John would call to the other, eyes downcast, looking down through the viewfinder. "Fine!" the other would reply, often not lifting his own eyes from his own camera. Sometimes they actually checked. It was like being with two little boys on an afternoon lark.

The docks were busy. Boats were being readied for king crab season which opened on Friday, July 1. Members of Helen and Bob Hall's family were aboard their boat the *Sea Comber* and asked if we would like a tour. More fun as we were shown around the fifty-foot, diesel-powered fishing vessel.

Bob Hall, founder of Kodiak Airways, drove us out to see his new office and new hanger—both moved to higher ground—next to the new airstrip. The company's motto in the 1960s was, "A Shower of Spray and We're Away." His fleet of amphibious airplanes, formerly located close to the water, was nearly swept away by the massive 1964 tidal wave that followed the Good Friday Earthquake. Kodiak had been devastated as well as Anchorage. Bob's company was all but destroyed. He, like his friend Milo and many others Alaskans were still struggling to rebuild their livelihoods in the wake of the natural disaster.

That evening, still in broad daylight, I drove Uncle Milo and John south to the naval base where John had been stationed during the war. Other evenings, during cocktails, they listened as I played the guitar and sang a few folk songs. I had brought a copy of *In His Own Write*, John Lennon's recently published little book of playful, quirky drawings, and poems on the hunch that they might appeal to Uncle Milo, a huge fan of P.G. Wodehouse. Uncle Milo said he loved them!

FOR INDEPENDENCE DAY WEEKEND, Uncle Milo, Aunt Betsy, John Spahn, his wife Alice, and I flew from Anchorage to King Salmon and then landed on Lake Naknek before rolling up onto the beach in the "Katmai Queen," an amphibious Grumman Mallard. We had arrived at the Katmai National Monument, over 4,200 square miles of preserved wilderness in Southwest Alaska, 100 miles or so northwest and across the Shelikof Strait from Kodiak Island. We stayed in rustic but comfortable cabins at the Brooks River Camp for a weekend of fishing and exploring the nearby Valley of Ten Thousand Smokes. There, in 1912, one of the world's biggest volcanic eruptions in history devastated a forty-square-mile area, leaving it so moon-like that the Apollo astronauts trained there in 1965 and in 1966—though not when we were there.

The first afternoon I set out bundled up for fishing in a whaler and hip boots, with rod, reel, and camera. I stepped onto what looked like a pebble beach but turned out to be a swath of floating pumice stones—lingering fallout from the massive volcanic eruption. I lost my balance and stumbled into the Brooks River, my hip boots immediately filling up with water. Uncle Milo and the others quickly fished me out.

The next day a handsome park ranger led Uncle Milo, Aunt Betsy and me down the mile-long trail to the Valley of 10,000 Smokes. Aunt Betsy, in high spirits, walked with her hands in her pockets. "I have to have somewhere to put my prehensile arms, she remarked, in one of her rare whimsical asides, "otherwise it's uncomfortable when the backs of my hands drag along the ground." Uncle Milo's standing joke that day was an offer to carry us "when we get halfway."

We walked along a path of hardened ash and pumice, through the eerie moon-like surroundings, with the ranger offering us a summary of the area's geologic and natural history, pointing out wildlife along the way, especially the birds, which were his particular interest. A fascinating day for us.

John and Alice could not be lured away from a day of fishing the pristine waters—the primary reason the fortunate few journeyed to the remote Brooks River Camp.

FLYING TO BIG LAKE
AND TRAIN RIDE TO FAIRBANKS –
SUMMER OF 1966

God, how I'd love to have a Super Cub
before I pass in my dinner pail.

—MILO FRITZ

UNCLE MILO'S LOVE OF FLYING WAS ALMOST AS INFECTIOUS as his love of Alaska and he seemed eager to share both with me, along with sailing, an activity we both loved. The weekend after our return from Mt. Katmai, Uncle Milo offered to fly me out to Big Lake, twenty-some miles north of Anchorage, for an evening sail on waters he often touted for their beauty and serenity.

Before taking off into the Alaska wilderness from Merrill Field, Uncle Milo walked around the single-engine Cessna 150, rented for the evening. Milo had given up ownership of his Piper Tri-Pacer soon after the earthquake, but he lived in hope of buying another airplane someday.

His methodical inspection of a plane before flying it left a lasting impression on me, as did his pronouncement: "There are old pilots and bold pilots, but no old, bold pilots." As a man approaching sixty, my uncle seemed well qualified to offer living proof of that old adage; he flew airplanes like he practiced medicine—with great passion, precision, and care.

During his preflight check, Uncle Milo sought out anything amiss. His eyes, intent behind no-nonsense eyeglasses, were shaded by a well-worn red baseball cap, a rakish touch that was at odds with his otherwise pressed, polished, and slightly austere air. Aunt Betsy disapproved of the baseball cap, he told me. On several occasions, he had barely thwarted her efforts to wash it or throw it away.

Uncle Milo's versatile hands were also part of the inspection process—opening, feeling, probing, testing. Combined in them were the easy strength of the farm laborer and lifeguard he had been in his youth, and the grace and dexterity of the skilled surgeon, the still-aspiring pianist, and the craftsman he still was. *Ariadne*, the boat we would be sailing that evening, was an eleven-foot Penguin that Uncle Milo built from a kit when sons Jonathan and Pieter were youngsters. His hands also served as impromptu notepads. During the course of a day, the doctor would jot cryptic notes on the back of his hands, reminding him to do something before he scrubbed them again.

Once buckled in, Uncle Milo checked radio, flaps, tail rudder, ailerons, and fuel levels. He had filed a flight plan, as he always did—improving the odds of searchers finding a plane in case it didn't show up, he said. Once satisfied with his preflight check—even if there wasn't a soul within earshot—Uncle Milo shouted out, "Clear!" After a brief roll down the runway, the plane was airborne.

"Cruising at 110 mph," according to my journal, "it took a half-hour to get to Big Lake." We landed on a dirt airstrip a short distance from the lake. Uncle Milo introduced me to his elderly friends Oscar and Beta Anderson, who stored his Penguin at their house. Oscar F. Anderson, born in Sweden, was one of Anchorage's original residents, having arrived with a wave of other Scandinavians in 1915 when Anchorage was still a "tent city." That same year, Oscar built a wooden house in what would become downtown Anchorage. In 1948, when Doc Fritz moved nearby, they became friends. The "Oscar Anderson House," unlike the Fritz house, *did* survive the Good Friday Earthquake and has since become a historic landmark.

That evening my uncle and I rigged *Ariadne* and, once under sail, explored the wide, placid waters of the lake, riffled by a gentle breeze. There must have been other cabins tucked back in the trees around Big Lake—roughly two miles across and five miles long—but it felt wonderfully peaceful and desolate.

THAT WAS THE FIRST OF SEVERAL WEEKENDS OF SAILING at Big Lake. The rest of the summer I sailed by myself. Often, Uncle Milo would fly out with an instrument instructor, dropping me off with the Andersons, who would see me off and greet me upon my return; my sole contact in case of emergency. I would take a lunch and sail contentedly for hours, through sunlit and rain-speckled afternoons that melded into bright evenings, until Uncle Milo flew back, sometimes with Aunt Betsy or Jonathan, to retrieve me.

One evening, my aunt and uncle flew by in a float plane, tipping their wings before circling back to land. I watched as they taxied to shore where I was securing the boat—Aunt Betsy, with a brightly flowered headscarf fluttering about her face, waving gaily. Uncle Milo was beaming under his red baseball cap. To look at them at that moment, you wouldn't think they had a care in the world.

Jonathan, age twenty-five and bursting with swagger and machismo, shared his father's passion for flying, but my cousin's flying style, like his personality was markedly different from his father's. On my first flight alone with Jon, his announced goal was to get his young cousin to throw up. Once aloft and away from Anchorage, he did a series of increasingly stomach-churning maneuvers—going from stalls and rolls to something he called a "chandelle"—simultaneously climbing and turning. In another move, he aligned the tip of a wing with a point on the ground and flew in a dizzying circle around and around it, with the plane banked at what to me was an alarming angle. I was able to control my queasiness—just barely—until he let up.

My aunt and uncle enjoyed the camaraderie of Jonathan and his young pilot friends who came to dinner several times over the summer. Their lively banter and stories enlivened our otherwise quiet dinners and gave Uncle Milo a chance to get their feedback about another plane he was cautiously enamored with, the Lake Amphibian, designed with its single engine mounted atop the hull. That word got around Merrill Flight and one Sunday the owner of a Lake Amphibian, hearing of Doc Fritz's interest, offered to take him and me for a ride. The pilot flew us over to Big Lake where he made two landings. "The pilot was terrible" and "the brakes failed on landing," I noted. We made it back safely, but the brief excursion tempered Uncle Milo's enthusiasm for the Lake Amphibian.

Uncle Milo made a point of acquainting me with Alaskans he particularly admired. Often, they were pilots, such as his esteemed flight instructor Glen Coons and James "Andy" Anderson, another former World War II pilot. "Glen Coons and Andy Anderson came in for lunch and made it a happy day," Uncle Milo noted about our mid-summer lunch with the veteran pilots and Jonathan at Peggy's Airport Café, a favorite pilot haunt near Merrill Field. Andy became a storied Arctic bush pilot from the Koyukuk region after the War, turning the remote Bettles Field into an airplane hub for Wien Alaska Airlines, and probably, on occasion, hauling freight for Doc Fritz's Yukon clinics.

In addition to giving me opportunities to hear some of the freely flowing stories from Alaska's colorful flying community, Uncle Milo saw to it that I had numerous opportunities to experience the thrill of flying that so enchanted him and to view the beauty of Alaska from a variety of airplanes. Cessna 150s, 172s, and 180s were the most common ones, but we also flew in less common ones—the World War II seaplanes still being used commercially for routes to King Salmon (Grumman Mallard) and Sitka (PBY). Our near-calamitous flight in the Lake Amphibian was an unplanned thrill.

Uncle Milo's face lit up whenever the talk turned to flying, airplanes, pilots, and the Alaska terrain they traversed. For Uncle Milo, flying was much more than a basic means of transport around the huge state, it was a passion that he shared with other Alaska pilots—flying echoed the very spirit of Alaska. Doc Fritz had a pilot's frame of mind. Even if he was going to spend the bulk of his morning in a windowless operating room, he habitually began his journal entries with a brief note about that day's weather—flying conditions.

IN MID-JULY, UNCLE MILO, AUNT BETSY, AND I traveled by train to Fairbanks for a two-week clinic. It was a spectacularly scenic twelve-hour train ride north from Anchorage to Fairbanks that took us through country so remote and rugged, I wondered how the Alaska Railroad was able to build those tracks through miles of wilderness, some sections on road-beds carved out of cliffs. Occasionally the train would stop in the middle of glorious nowhere to pick up a passenger, usually heavily laden with gear, or let one off to continue on foot to some remote spot or homestead. Onboard, Uncle Milo introduced me to Kathy, a patient from Fairbanks about my age, who was returning home. Uncle Milo thought she might be a pal for me during our two-week clinic there.

We arrived as Fairbanks was preparing for Golden Days, its annual high-spirited commemoration of the discovery of gold in Fairbanks. On the streets of Fairbanks, a much smaller city than Anchorage, everyone seemed very friendly and caught up in the old-timey fun. Some people were already dressed in old-fashioned clothes—women in long dresses with bustles and big hats, men in fancy vests, string ties, and bowler hats. Men were encouraged to grow beards. Those without beards or costumes ran the chance of being put in a roving jail or fined a dollar. To quote a local wag at the time: "We've had clear Golden Days, but never dry ones."

Uncle Milo must have picked up on the high-jinx atmosphere as we were setting up for the clinic in the "Presidential Suite"—supposedly named in honor of President Nixon, although he never stayed there—at the Traveler's Inn motel in downtown Fairbanks. Uncle Milo was unpacking cases on the concrete walkway outside the suite when a matronly woman emerged from her room. Eyeing all the medical gear with suspicion, she asked the casually dressed man in the baseball cap who he was and what all this medical equipment was for. My uncle looked up at her, taking in her censorious gaze and tone. He stood and tipped his hat. "Dr. Milo Fritz," he said with a mischievous smile, "your friendly abortionist!" The woman quickly retreated to her room and checked out the next morning. Aunt Betsy was aghast. "Milo!" was all she mustered at the time.

John Spahn flew in a few days after our arrival and patients flowed through the rooms at the Travelers Inn that were now set up for ophthalmic and ENT examinations and procedures. Workdays settled into a routine much like that in Kodiak. Additionally, in Fairbanks I was asked to assist "The Doctor" by holding the heads of two patients while he vacuumed their ears.

Fairbanks, centrally located in Alaska's Interior region, also served as a base for several excursions during that two-week clinic. Aunt Betsy and Uncle Milo arranged for my new Fairbanks pal Kathy and me to go on a paddle boat tour of the Chena River, which flows through the heart of Fairbanks. At the beginning of our three-hour voyage, aboard the *Discovery*, a historic stern-wheeler, the guide drew our attention to an airplane flying overhead that was piloted by septuagenarian Sam White, formerly the chief pilot for Wien Alaska Airlines and, before that, Alaska's first flying game warden. Near the end of our trip, we would spot Sam White's plane again as, unannounced this time, the legendary bush pilot flew over us, homeward bound to Fairbanks.

In the hours between, we paddled by an Athabaskan settlement, hearing from the guide that Athabascans had lived in the area for 10,000 years and still relied on dog teams for winter transportation. Farther downriver, we marveled at the dramatic confluence of two rivers—the clear waters of the Chena meeting the cloudy waters of the Tanana River, aswirl with glacial flour.

Uncle Milo and Aunt Betsy went to great lengths to introduce me to the wonders of Alaska, and that sunny, festive summer was an optimum time to do it. A year later, Fairbanks would be hit by one of the worst disasters in Alaska history—the Great Flood of August 1967. Weeks of excessive rainfall, capped by torrential rains from a tropical storm, would cause the Chena River to overflow its banks, flooding downtown Fairbanks. Pilot Sam White reportedly posted a sign on his front door, "Through this house runs the deepest river in the world."

Other Alaska wonders that Uncle Milo and Aunt Betsy wanted me to experience were the natural hot springs at Circle Hot Springs and to see the Yukon River. That weekend, a five-hour drive northeast on a two-lane dirt and gravel road brought us to the town and its historic Circle Hot Springs Hotel, built in 1930—"quite old, but nice," I noted. There were two pools fed by the natural hot springs—the inside one was too hot to stay in long, but the outside one was just right—except for clouds of Alaska's legendary mosquitoes. To swim, we dashed down to the pool, swam a while and tried to outrun the mosquitoes on the way back to the hotel.

Despite the mosquitoes, which abated somewhat the next day, it was a quiet, relaxing weekend for all three of us. Besides frequent soaks in the outdoor hot pool—especially inviting in the long evenings of sunlight after dinner—we took walks, picking berries and wildflowers, and drove out to Circle to see the broad expanse of the mighty Yukon River, its waters coursing northwest in a great arc. Over 1,000 miles downriver, after flowing past the communities of Beaver and Stevens Village, and on past St. Mary's Mission—where Milo had held clinics in 1961—the mighty Yukon eventually empties into the Bering Sea.

Bethel and tiny Yup'ik settlements scattered throughout the Yukon-Kuskokwim Delta in Alaska's Southwest region were other places that had benefitted from Doc Fritz's medical care; he, in turn, had long been fascinated by the distinct Native cultures he had encountered on his travels. With an eye and ear for detail, Doc Fritz had also been sensitive to the cultural changes underway, as he wrote Betsy from Bethel in 1947:

> Eskimos have no swear words. The nearest thing to it being something that means, "oh, how hateful," which seems inadequate when the dogs get tangled in their harnesses or they break through the ice. Their wonderful delicacy and tact is seen in their word for bald which means a man is all fore-head. And they never say goodbye; they say something which means, "The end is not yet"—which is very nice. They have trouble with their s and sh sounds, saying bassful and fiss for bashful and fish—not always, of course. One old chap brought his lead dog for Fred [Langsam] to see last winter and said proudly, "He likesh to be called Nishe Dog."
> ... It is no small tribute to the Eskimo character that they preserve their politeness and sweet quiet ways (though somewhat unsanitary at times) in spite of white teachers and missionaries and their atrocious ways and general ineptitude.

ON THE BANKS OF THE YUKON RIVER AT CIRCLE, we were within fifty miles of the Arctic Circle and as close as I thought I would get to the Arctic that summer . . . or ever. The weekend before, shortly after our arrival in Fairbanks, the three of us had toured an aviation exhibit at the University of Alaska, with Uncle Milo offering his own commentary about some of the bush pilots whose pictures were on display. He and I lingered in front of a striking and somber painting of the Wiley Post-Will Rogers Memorial being viewed by a lone figure, bundled in a traditional Eskimo parka, with his back to the wind-driven snow. Uncle Milo said that the site of the memorial was near Point Barrow, in Arctic Alaska, the farthest point north on the continent of North America. It was there that Wiley Post, the first pilot to fly solo around the world, and Will Rogers, the popular American humorist, crashed in 1935, a tragic end to a bold pilot—not yet thirty-seven—and his close friend Will, then fifty-five, at the peak of his career as a columnist and Hollywood star.

Barrow (now Utqiaġvik)—the largest Inupiaq village in Alaska with a population of 2,000 in 1966—would become a reality to me during the second week of the Fairbanks clinic. Uncle Milo and Aunt Betsy surprised me with a trip that would take me 300 miles north of the Arctic Circle.

Hazardous weather had been a factor in Wiley Post's and Will Rogers's doomed flight in 1935. Four years previously, in August 1931, Charles and Anne Lindbergh had also been drawn to this northernmost point, their flights in and out of Barrow also dogged by Arctic mist, rain, and fog. Outbound, and halfway from Barrow to Nome, Anne had written, "We are at the famous Point of No Return, not enough fuel to turn around and go back, and the mountains were ahead, and the darkness, fog was surrounding the aircraft."

THE WEATHER WAS FAIR FOR MY MID-JULY FLIGHT from Fairbanks. Upon landing after slightly over three hours of flying, the temperature on the ground was about thirty-five degrees. Though nearly freezing in mid-July, there was no snow. A lumbering "box bus" brought us into a low-profile town through streets of mud and gravel. Vestiges of World War II were still much in evidence as a number of Barrow's small buildings were constructed from huge repurposed wooden packing crates that once contained airplane engines and other war materiel.

Home base was The Top of the World Hotel—a two-story wood frame hotel with rooms measuring 8 x 8 x 8 feet. Outfitted with a parka, boots, and gloves at the hotel, I walked through the chilly air and puddle-strewn streets of Barrow, now and then greeted with smiles from clusters of Eskimo children, parka-clad but sometimes bare-footed, who seemingly roamed the village at all hours. An Eskimo woman, demonstrating how to skin a seal and cut up and divide the meat, seemed as oblivious to the cold as the children who waded in puddles that came over the tops of their boots; their tolerance for the cold mirrored that of their elders. After being taken for a dog sled ride on a wheeled cart, I walked around admiring the luxurious coats and sweet faces of the huskies and malamutes that were staked outside houses all over town. When I got back to Fairbanks,

I would ask Uncle Milo which breed might make a better pet. Neither he told me—"They howl!"

The visit to the old Eskimo cemetery was particularly memorable. There, as the guide explained, the ancient Eskimo tradition of leaving the dead to the natural forces of the Arctic had given way to Christian burial practice, introduced by the tide of missionaries who began arriving in the late 1800s. Since then, he noted, shifting ice and permafrost continuously push buried caskets to the surface, and, continuously, they need to be reburied.

On occasion, Uncle Milo would allude to the cultural changes brought by Christianity and modern society in general. Barrow (changed back to Utqiaġvik—its traditional Inupiaq name—in 2006) presented a vivid picture of a Native community in transition—the old trying to accommodate the new. Even in 1966—pre-pipeline days—the challenges of change were evident. The villagers, while continuing to pursue their traditional whaling, hunting, and fishing practices, seemed to also take quiet pride in sharing their traditional activities, performing their dances, and selling their handicrafts—moccasins, dolls, masks, ivory jewelry, and other products of their resourceful creativity. As a child, I had delighted in the finely crafted fur objects that Uncle Milo and Aunt Betsy sent us from Alaska. As a teenager, I was taken by the spare beauty of other gifts they sent—four framed drawings by Inupiat Eskimo artist George Ahgupuk on animal skins—reindeer, seal, caribou, moose. His distinctive pen and ink drawings depicted scenes of Eskimos kayaking, hunting, driving dog sleds and of various Arctic wildlife in a vast, stark land. Some of Ahgupuk's artistic renderings moved into the realm of reality for me that summer. From the edge of the Chukchi Sea, I looked out across the water to the floating ice pack just offshore and, in the bright evening twilight, watched the midnight sun skim the horizon.

By good fortune, my brief introduction to Eskimo life in Barrow was put to use almost immediately. During our twelve-hour return train trip to Anchorage, I met Robert Nick, a twenty-three-year-old Yup'ik Eskimo from a village near Bethel, who had been in Fairbanks for a summer course at the University of Alaska. Although initially perhaps more reticent than I was, we conversed at length about his life and my recent experiences in Barrow, which had given me some context and appreciation for what Robert told me about his life. "He was very interesting," I wrote in my journal, "and told me about his sled dog team that he races, his home life, and that he was planning to be a teacher. He spoke so softly though," I admitted, "I missed quite a few things he said."

Soft-spoken, maybe, but not shy—at least in later years. Robert Nick would become a highly respected leader in education, health care, business, and the Alaska Federation of Natives. The audience for Robert's knowledgeable discourse on Native culture and traditional subsistence hunting and fishing would greatly expand from one rapt fellow passenger on a train to larger groups in more consequential venues, including testimony in district court in 2013 that fishing and other subsistence practices are deeply rooted in the religious beliefs of the Yup'ik culture.

Such cultural tensions between Alaska's Indigenous populations and those who had arrived from the outside world—explorers, fur traders, whalers, miners, World War II military personnel—had been playing out for generations. By the mid-1960s, the juxtaposition between the traditional and the modern in a place like Barrow was striking. Within two years, the discovery of oil two hundred miles east at Prudhoe Bay would bring with it an explosion of change.

Alaska was growing up.

A FEW DAYS BEFORE WE LEFT FAIRBANKS, Uncle Milo surprised me with a possibility: Did I want to consider staying on with them into the school year and completing my last two years of high school in Anchorage? Intrigued, I began investigating the details after our return to Anchorage, but my parents' firm "no" squelched the idea, so my Alaska sojourn ended with a few more weeks in Anchorage and one last clinic in Sitka.

After a flight to Juneau, followed by a tour of the Mendenhall Glacier, Aunt Betsy, Uncle Milo, and I took a ferry to Sitka. On the Sunday before the clinic began, we took the two-minute ferry from Sitka to the island of Mount Edgecumbe where we walked around, revisiting some of Uncle Milo's personal and professional history.

Following World War II, the former Naval base on the island had been transferred to the Alaska Native Service for use as an educational and medical center—a boarding school for Alaska Native students, a sanitarium for children with tuberculosis, and a children's orthopedic hospital for treatment of bone TB. Soon after Milo's return to Alaska in 1948, Mount Edgecumbe had served as a base for his and Dr. Thygeson's research efforts to find a treatment for the blinding effects of phlyctenular keratoconjunctivitis.

Mount Edgecumbe had changed considerably since then. By 1966, with TB a malady of the past, the boarding school had become a high school run by the Bureau of Indian Affairs, drawing hundreds of Alaska Native teenagers from all over the state. The entire community, Milo noted, had grown substantially. The teachers, as well as the administrators and medical people who staffed the new Alaska Department of Health hospital, were all now living on the island.

In Sitka, back on the mainland, the Fritz clinic was held in the Potlatch Motel. Our rooms there had a grand view of the airport and the World War II-surplus amphibians, since converted to commercial use, that powered up the sloping ramp from the water to emerge dripping on its little turnaround. One of these seaplanes operated by Coastal Ellis Airlines was a PBY bomber with glass, bug-eye-like windows—former machine gunner stations—that bulged out from both sides of the aircraft. As at Mount Edgecumbe, Barrow, and elsewhere, such repurposed leftovers from World War II were reminders of the war's huge impact on Alaska.

Notable among the vintage airplanes that intrigued me that summer was the legendary *Pink Lady*, a P-51 Mustang bomber—painted a bright pink—which was used by the Bureau of Land Management for spotting forest fires and coordinating firefighting in the Interior during the mid-1960s. I was fortunate to encounter and take pictures of the WWII warbird after meeting her pilot, Jerry Chisum, one of Jonathan's buddies, who often flew the *Pink Lady* to Merrill Field during breaks from fire patrol. Jerry demonstrated his legion pilot skills to me during a couple of exciting sorties, which included wing turns over Anchorage Airport, in a Cessna 180 and a Beechcraft Bonanza—not, alas, in the storied *Pink Lady*, since immortalized in rapturous accounts by flying enthusiasts.

My journey home at summer's end commenced with the thrill of an Alaska-style exit from Sitka in a PBY bomber—a roll down the ramp followed by a noisy, spray-filled take-off from the water. It was the last in the long string of once-in-a-lifetime experiences that summer that had opened an illuminating portal to my uncle's extraordinary life in Alaska.

FALL USHERED IN A PERIOD OF CHANGE AND CHALLENGE for Doc Fritz. For him, the summer of 1966 was bookended by a renewed interest in government service. After a four-year hiatus from Alaska politics after a fruitless run for governor, Uncle Milo decided to make a bid to become a member of the Alaska State House of Representatives—a part-time position in Alaska. A few days after my arrival in June, Uncle Milo had taken me to a Republican luncheon in Anchorage to hear two candidates speak. At the end of August, just days before my PBY departure from the Sitka clinic, Doc Fritz learned that he had made it through the primaries. As I wrote home from Sitka:

> Uncle Milo didn't just squeak by either; he came in sixth. Considering he didn't make one speech or give out one bumper sticker and went just on his name alone, that is really terrific. 16 Republicans are running for the top 14. These 14 will run against 14 Democrats to become the 14 representatives allowed the Anchorage area.

That was a banner fall for Doc Fritz. After being pleased and somewhat surprised by his primary results, he also received his instrument rating, which I acknowledged with a bit of whimsy—a fake news article I concocted for his amusement that reflected back at him some of his recurrent witticisms from the summer:

Dr. Milo H. Fritz Passes Test with Flying Colors
Special to the New York Times

> In a delayed report from Anchorage, Alaska it was learned that Dr. Milo H. Fritz, the noted eye, ear, nose, and throat specialist finally earned his instrument ticket, which he has been working on for more than 20 years. Dr. Fritz, a resident of Anchorage, who works on clinics all over the State, has been reported as having turned the Bering Sea red with his tonsillectomies. Finding time out from his medical profession for flight instruction, he spent so many hours in a Link trainer that he was thought to be trying for his Commercial Link rating also. When Dr. Fritz was told of his victory over the instruments, but that he couldn't receive his Commercial Link ticket, too, the doctor replied, "You can't have everything!"

Uncle Milo wrote me back in similar light-hearted fashion on New Year's Day:

> It had been brought to my attention that my having been issued an instrument ticket made radio and television coast to coast, but I did not realize that it had displaced Russia

*and China on the front page of the New York Times. Thank
you very much for sending me the original reporter copy. My
biographers will find this a priceless addition to the other
events in my long drawn-out and humdrum life.*

In November, Doc Fritz also won what would be the first of three terms
as a member of the Alaska State House of Representatives. His reason for
running for public office, as he explained: "I just thought that I had a close
knowledge of the people's wants and needs as you only get by being in private enterprise, and I thought I had something to contribute."

THE CHALLENGES OF CHANGE
AND MORTALITY

Politician: a person who can keep both ears
to the ground while straddling the fence.
—Milo Fritz

MILO EMBRACED THE CHALLENGES OF SERVING as a state legislator. At age fifty-eight, Doc Fritz joined other citizen-legislators who were taking time away from their livelihoods—small business owners, contractors, fishermen, lawyers—to serve in the normal ninety-day sessions in Juneau. "I am the only physician in the Legislature and so do a lot of curbstone consultations and help with legislation that has to do with health."

The 1960s was a decade of accelerating changes and challenges for Alaska as well as Doc Fritz. A month before the 1966 election, the Alaska Federation of Natives was founded to address the long unresolved aboriginal claims to ancestral lands that stretched back to the "Seward's Folly" days when Alaska was bought from Russia in 1867. With the discovery of oil in Prudhoe Bay in the late 1960s, this controversy over land rights took on new urgency and had to be resolved before any oil development on the North Slope could proceed. Discussions ensued between the Alaska Natives, the oil industry, the state of Alaska, and environmental groups, including rounds of hearings at the national level. The civil rights movement, which had long been making headlines in the Lower '48, influenced the negotiations of what would become known as the Alaska Native Claims Settlement Act.

MILO, THE "COLOR-BLIND" OPHTHALMOLOGIST, had long been a proponent of equal rights. As one might expect, Dr. Martin Luther King, Jr. was a man that Milo greatly admired. In the early 1960s, on a visit with us in Merion, Uncle Milo learned that Dr. King was to speak at a Baptist church in Philadelphia and proposed a drive into the inner city to hear the civil rights crusader speak in person. Did anyone else want to go, too? Spurred by Uncle Milo's enthusiasm, I, barely a teenager, and my brother Karl, a couple years younger, trailed in our uncle's wake, as we joined the throng of churchgoers in their Sunday best, flowing into the church. Uncle Milo let it be known that he was a doctor who had come all the way from Alaska to hear Dr. King speak. This had the desired effect: we were graciously seated—a trio of white faces in a sea of black faces—and were soon caught up in the rolling cadences of the pastor's voice, the answering "Yes, Lord's," and the fluttering of white handkerchiefs wet with tears. That day we witnessed a memorable slice of history; that day also offered me a greater sense of my uncle's deep-seated belief in equality. Dr. King's philosophy and passion were in strong alignment with Milo's words and deeds in Alaska:

> *People told me I had racial prejudice in reverse be-*
> *cause I'm more interested in taking care of the native folks,*
> *who weren't people then you see, before the Native Land*
> *Settlement Claims were passed into law.*

During his first term in the State House as a representative from Anchorage, Doc Fritz offered his testimony on behalf of the Native population at the legislative hearings prior to the passage of the Alaska Native Claims Settlement Act. He was for the proposed legislation and strongly opposed to a continued policy of segregated medical care:

> *I hope that there will be a subsection in Senate bill 2906*
> *that will do something that will alleviate the health problems*
> *of the Alaskan natives, without which they will not be able to*

enjoy the things that will be granted them if this bill passes as
modified and as I hope it does. I hope in this subsection that
it will be mandatory that over a year's time the health activities of the Alaska Native Health Service will be transferred to
the Alaska Department of Health, including the personnel, of
course, and including the millions of dollars—upwards of 16
million that are used now to carry on the present activities.
. . . This, gentlemen, as you probably know, is the only
State out of the entire 50 where segregation in education and
medical care is a fact of life and attempts to be preserved.
Not only that, but there are two agencies trying to do the
same thing, the Alaska Department of Health and the Alaska
Native Health Service.
. . . For many years I have tried to hold a clinic in Kotzebue.
The only place that I can get is a Quonset hut, the abandoned
portion of some store, or some other building which is difficult to use. Yet in that same town is a magnificent hospital
which can be used for surgery and which has outpatient facilities where I am not allowed, even though I pay taxes to
use this, not for my own benefit or in the improvement of
my situation, but for the benefit of the people who my special
expertise is supposed to help.
. . . I just want to have some room in that hospital, given
adequate warning and all the rest of it so I can take care of the
people in Alaska. We do not believe in segregation anymore.

Milo had had many occasions to critique the territorial, state, and federal bureaucracies when he found them inadequate or unresponsive to
the health needs of Alaskans, especially Native populations. He gave voice
to their problems and frustrations in letters, professional articles, testimony, and eventually in legislative proposals after he was elected to the
State House of Representatives. Even on this serious topic, Milo's wit sur-
faced in his efforts to get his message across. A relic in the Fritz archives—
undoubtably a brainstorm from his legislative days—offers a graphic
example of Milo's humor: a large poster, framed by red tape, depicting
a colorful, cartoonish drawing of a doctor and an Eskimo, divided by a
stone wall. Atop the wall, labeled "HEW" [referring to the Department
of Health Education & Welfare], is a typewriter spewing sheets of white

paper and more red tape. Captioned, "Nihil Agas Ne Alquid Erroneous Erit"—bastardized Latin that warns: "Do nothing for something might go wrong." Signatures along the left hand include those of Ted Stevens, Don Young, Willie Hensley, and other members of the 5th State Legislature. Milo's "John Hancock" tops the list.

DURING MILO'S FIRST TERM IN THE STATE HOUSE, he and Ted Stevens represented the same district in Anchorage for two years until Ted was appointed, then elected to the U. S. Senate. The two men had met previously in a very different setting and circumstance. According to my uncle's oft-told story, they had first encountered each other some years before at a public swimming pool in Anchorage when Ted's young son Benny had slipped and gashed his head. Hearing a call for a doctor, Doc Fritz waded through the commotion to find a shouting father and a crying child with a bloody but minor flesh wound. Milo's response: "Get this hysterical father out of here." In Ted's telling of the story, he's merely "nervous."

Despite having personalities that others sometimes deemed "prickly," Milo and Ted became friends, bonding over their shared love and concern for Alaska and its people. During their early days together in Juneau, their work on legislative issues furthered their professional ties. Each was committed to crafting legislation that would serve their constituents' needs, though in markedly differing ways. Pressing the flesh and schmoozing were not Doc Fritz's style. Ted, the seasoned politician, used to complain good-naturedly about Milo's approach—spending evenings in Juneau in his room reading "every goddam bill," so that Milo was prepared for proceedings the next day. When recalling his colleague's modus operandi in later years, Ted's critique was invariably delivered with a twinkle in his eye.

Tragedy would bring them still closer in 1978 following a horrific Lear Jet crash at Anchorage airport that killed Ted's wife Ann and four others. Ted, by then a U. S. Senator, and another passenger survived, but Ted suffered significant injuries, including to his head and eyes. Doc Fritz accompanied his friend on a trip to California, helping to secure and oversee the medical care that would lead to the Senator's remarkable recovery.

MILO HAD ALREADY FACED HIS OWN CLOSE BRUSH with mortality seven years earlier. By then, Milo and Betsy were living in a house on Vanderbilt Circle out near the new hospital. For a time, they had been foster parents to two teenage sisters, Rebecca and Ravenna. There was a sense that the girls were the daughters that Milo and Betsy never had. During another period, Jonathan and his new wife Maxey, an Anchorage school teacher, lived with them. Then, in the summer of 1971, in another act of generosity, Aunt Betsy and Uncle Milo invited my brother Karl, nineteen, and my seventeen-year-old sister Lenore to live with them and experience Alaska, with Lenore assisting in the office as a nurse's aide and Karl working at an Anchorage automotive service center.

It was an unusually busy household that summer. Ravenna, Jonathan, and Maxey were in and out frequently; soon Pieter, then twenty-seven, showed up for an extended stay. Pieter had never been much more than a name to his cousins. We vaguely understood he was a social worker in New York City. Quite different from Jonathan, Pieter was quiet and serious, and though friendly enough—Lenore remembered him taking her on a tour of Anchorage—generally distanced himself from the day-to-day activities of the teenage cousins he hardly knew.

Mid-summer, Uncle Milo started having terrific abdominal pain and was hospitalized with what turned out to be mesenteric thrombosis—a decrease in blood flow to the small intestine—and "nearly passed in his dinner pail," as he later put it. It was a stark about-face for a man who just a few months earlier had completed a rigorous cross-country flying trip with Lenore serving as navigator during her spring break from high school. They had "puddle jumped" across the United States to deliver a Piper Cub from the Lockhaven factory in Pennsylvania to a friend of Milo's in Alaska. Lenore had eagerly signed on to that novel adventure— skimming above the treetops, navigating their way northward through the countryside—sometimes relying on water towers to confirm the names of the small towns beneath their wings.

But a just a few months later, Uncle Milo was stricken with life-threatening mesenteric thrombosis, and suddenly Pieter, too, was hospitalized. Since our childhood, we understood that Pieter had considerable health issues. Since he was a boy, he suffered from seizures that he controlled with medication. The nature of his ailment that summer, apparently something infectious, was never explained to Karl and Lenore.

With Uncle Milo incapacitated, Lenore's employment ended abruptly. Karl stayed on longer as his job was unrelated to Uncle Milo's practice. When Lenore went to the hospital to bid Uncle Milo and Pieter goodbye before her hurried departure, Pieter was in an isolation room. My sister had to don a hospital gown and tell him goodbye through a mask.

BOTH FATHER AND SON RECOVERED from their immediate health problems that summer. The following year, Doc Fritz made another run for the House and was again elected to represent Anchorage in the state legislature beginning in 1973. By then however, it was his financial health that increasingly weighed on Doc Fritz, as he explained later in an interview: "It cost me so much going down there [Juneau] because I had an extensive staff. I couldn't let them go, because when I got home, you just can't pull them off the street. I had to keep paying them, so I was wiped out the two times I represented the people of Anchorage."

In 1974, Doc Fritz moved his medical practice 200 miles south of Anchorage to the Kenai Peninsula where he and Betsy had recently completed their "dream home." The low-profile clapboard structure—residence on one level, medical office below—nestled into the hillside of their homestead property at Anchor Point. Building the substantial structure—over a mile from the main road—was a monumental effort. The "venture or nightmare," as Betsy called it, tested the Fritzes physically and emotionally, as well as financially.

THE ANCHOR POINT HOMESTEAD
BECOMES A HOME –
A RETURN VISIT, 1977

We shall not cease from exploration, and the end
of all our exploring will be to arrive where we started
and know the place for the first time.
—*T.S. Eliot*

IN AUGUST OF 1977, WHEN MY FATHER AND I ARRIVED at Anchor Point to celebrate Uncle Milo's sixty-eighth birthday at their newly built house and office, he and Betsy were nearing the end of their settling-in period, which had taken every bit of three years. The road had been graded and graveled by the state. Patients no longer had to leave their vehicles on the highway and make the rest of the way on foot when spring thaw or periods of rain turned the dirt road into a tire- and boot-sucking sea of mud.

A string of lesser projects remained. Milo wanted to add a greenhouse for Betsy onto the south end of the house and he had numerous landscaping projects afoot that required use of his Case 350 crawler tractor, which he enjoyed demonstrating for us. He had the hang of it now but learning how to operate it and doing some of the landscaping himself had nearly killed him. Milo once backed the tractor too close to the edge of the cliff and they both went over. Calamity was averted by a lone tree that had fortuitously snagged his descent to the beach below.

On "a day to remember," as he called it in his diary, Uncle Milo took my father and me on a daylong boat excursion from Homer to Halibut Cove on the far side of Kachemak Bay. The picturesque community was home to the Tillion family, friends of Milo and Betsy, who were long-time residents there. Clem Tillion, the patriarch, was a commercial fisherman and a noted authority on fishing issues. He and Milo had served together in the State Legislature where they had become friends. Clem's wife Diana, a renowned Alaska artist, had a studio and gallery there that my uncle thought we should see. Milo was also eager for us to meet Marian, their twenty-three-year-old daughter who was the captain of the *Danny J*, a traditional wooden fishing boat that served as a combination sightseeing boat and ferry to Halibut Cove. Marian had recently distinguished herself by becoming a licensed maritime captain of 100-ton vessels, one of the few women—if not the first—to do so.

Uncle Milo was all smiles as he introduced us to Marian, a striking young woman with long red hair secured in a ponytail. She was chatty, personable, and obviously in her element as she welcomed us and the rest of the dozen or so other passengers aboard the *Danny J* on that overcast but mild day. Marian proved to be an expert tour guide as well as captain, pointing out and commenting on the birds, otters, sea lions, and the other sea life we encountered on our hour-long ride out to Halibut Cove and during our return in the afternoon.

Out on the grey waters of Kachemak Bay, we enjoyed a 360-degree view of spectacular snow-tipped mountains and abundant wildlife. We later explored the serene beauty of Halibut Cove, walking around the hamlet, talking with Diana, and viewing her artwork. It was a grand day for all the three of us. Uncle Milo, who always loved showcasing the glories of his beloved Alaska, was pleased with how everything went, and seemingly as proud of Marian as if she were his own daughter. "He was my champion," Marian would recall many years later.

Milo, fit and full of energy, seemed to thrive on the minor hoopla surrounding his birthday. On August 25, Jonathan came to Milo's birthday dinner, bearing the gift of a boom box so his father could listen to his classical music while working around the homestead. Jonathan had functioned as the general manager of the fraught construction project while his father was mostly away in Juneau serving in the House. I had seen the sweet side of Jonathan's nature in his many kindnesses to me during the summer of 1966, as well as his bluster. I had also sensed the tension between son and father, which the many stresses of building such a large structure in the wilds had exacerbated. The uneasy truce held that evening, but it was tested. The thoughtfulness of Jonathan's gift was undercut by his barbed presentation, "Happy birthday, you old fart."

Milo's ongoing antipathy toward Jonathan was occasionally relieved by hard-won praise, however. Two stand out: My uncle's high regard for Jonathan's flying abilities when he was a flight instructor, and Milo's acknowledgement of Jonathan's skills as a carpenter, which he would express in an interview sixteen years later, when Jonathan was in his forties and living in Colorado:

He's a restorer of old houses. You know, now-a-days, instead of taking a D-8 Cat to everything, we stop and think a minute and say, "Now wait a minute; this was an example of architecture that was fashionable in the 1920s, or the late part of the last century, and it requires a little work to make these beautiful windows, or this lovely brick work, attractive again. We chip off all the paint that people have thrown at it and we get back to what it originally was." Well, that's the sort of thing he does. He's in Denver now, finishing up a house. . . . He's very good at it.

Late in the evening of Uncle Milo's birthday dinner, after the others had retired, Jonathan unrolled a plat of the homestead to show me his grand plans for an airstrip and related development on a section of his parents' homestead. His enthusiasm was palpable, but the more he talked, the less sense he made, the disjointed half-sentences eventually fading into a muddled silence. The effects of alcohol, I wondered as the two of us sat there. In time, that notion would be confirmed. It was a disquieting glimpse of Jonathan at the tail end of Uncle Milo's otherwise successful birthday dinner.

The years since I had last seen Jonathan had taken their toll. He had been married and then divorced by the time the basic construction of the house was finished in 1974. A couple of years later his ex-wife Maxey had died—the victim of a murder-suicide. It sent shock waves through the family, as Milo and especially Betsy were very fond of Maxey who, with Jonathan, had lived with them for a time.

Another tragedy had added to the family's woes just two months before my father and I journeyed to Anchor Point. Milo, talking to Jon who was preparing to go salmon fishing, was outside the house on a gorgeous summer day at the end of June, when an Alaska State Trooper pulled in the drive. As Milo wrote in his diary the officer "tactfully and kindly told us that Piet had died last night in a fire in his house [in Anchorage] at 9 pm. Mattress fire, smoking in bed." Pieter was just a few days shy of his 33rd birthday. Pieter's memorial service was held in Anchorage a few days later, "a lovely, deep and sympathetic service," Milo wrote in his diary. In a previous entry he had noted, "Jon went fishing so he won't be at the service."

Pieter's death was a blow from which Milo and Betsy never fully recovered. They grappled with the sorrow as best they could. Betsy would make frequent trips to Anchorage over the next two years getting Pieter's affairs in order. In the meantime, a mix of patient care and prodigious work on homestead improvements provided Milo with a measure of distraction and solace throughout the summer. Our visit was another.

"Betsy, bless her heart, had arranged for Larry & Linda to be here as a birthday gift," Milo wrote in his diary, "and there could be none finer."

PART VII

End of an Era

PART VII

End of an Era

IDYLLS OF THE KING

When these tragedies—every person has had who has lived
a few years—have struck, medicine has been my salvation;
I can get involved in somebody else's troubles. So, my own
became easier to bear. It sounds corny, but never-the-less
what I'm telling you is true in my experience. Some awful
things have happened to me, and my sanity or my ability to
carry on, has been occasioned by my . . . there's an office full
of patients to see that day. You get involved in operating on
somebody's eyes; everything goes away. That's your problem
right there now.

—MILO FRITZ

FOR SIX YEARS AFTER MOVING HIS PRACTICE to Anchor Point, Doc Fritz had a tremendous surgical practice at the hospital in Soldotna three or four mornings a week. "I'd have to leave by 5:30 to get there by 7:00 to work up the patients by 8:00, and start operating at 8:00, not one minute or five minutes after, but 8:00."

The rigors of surgery helped Milo cope during the bleak period following Pieter's death and the bouts of depression that followed—what he and Larry referred to as "Idylls of the King," Alfred, Lord Tennyson's epic poem that concludes with an aging King Arthur despairing that he had not accomplished all he might have. As Milo wrote Larry in that regard:

> I am happiest when practicing medicine. I know this, for on the days when we see patients the hours flee by and at other times the days seem 48 hours long.

Future days would seem even longer. Doc Fritz would continue his office practice for five more years, but in December of 1980, he decided it was time to give up surgery, "a decision that shook me to my very foundations, but certainly I would never have ceased regretting an error that could have been attributed to my failing powers."

Later, Milo recalled that major decision and the aftermath:

> I said, "Look, Milo, the time is coming, you're 71 years old, time to quit." I did a tremendously complicated sinus and nasal case, hung up my knife. . . . My presurgical nurses [in Soldotna] would tell me, "Doctor, you look worse than the patient when you get through operating." Well, you know when you get a few hints like that. They are very outspoken girls. . . . Without those nurses it would look as though I hadn't gotten more than 6 in a correspondence course.

The following year, Milo happened to encounter a nurse who was an operating room supervisor at the Soldotna hospital, who said she and the other nurses still miss him. "You missing me, is nothing compared with how I miss you," he told her.

Four years after Milo was fully retired from medicine, a nurse from Anchorage would make the four-hundred-mile trek to Anchor Point from Glennallen, Alaska to pay Doc Fritz a visit. "Johnny" Childs was his own "private, special, honest-to-to God surgical nurse" for sixteen years in Anchorage. "We looked terrific together," Milo recalled. "She knew the operations" and Johnny made it a point to teach one or two other nurses about eye, ear, nose, and throat operations so there were always backup nurses for the ambidextrous surgeon. Milo remembered Johnny's instructions to a surgical assistant she was coaching, "Don't give him what he asks for, give him what he needs." Milo had high praise for his surgical nurses:

They had to have tremendous imaginations because they couldn't see. "Looking into a nose or ear, it's a very restrictive field. You can't look over the side because there are attachments that you have to have. I never had them. They were not developed then as they are now.

Without surgery to keep him from dwelling on his woes, Christmas ceased being a happy day. However, a bright spot in that holiday season in 1980 was Ted Stevens's marriage to Catherine Bittner, a comely and accomplished attorney from a longtime-Anchorage family who Milo and Betsy knew well. Even then, despite his fondness for Ted's bride and his hearty approval of the match, Milo's emotions at the wedding ceremony skewed bittersweet, as he wrote Larry:

I did not know whether the tears were because of Ted's happiness, my memories of Maxey who meant so much to me and more to Betsy, Jon's alienation, Piet's death or just what, but they were there I can assure you.

And a month later:

I am surviving a bloodless life. We have referred over 6 patients to other surgeons in spite of importunities of doing 'just one more case before you retire.' It was tough to do but I done it.

. . . I still miss that scalpel.

IN 1981, SHORTLY AFTER GIVING UP HIS SCALPEL, Milo dove into a new venture. In January, instead of driving north to Soldotna to perform surgery, Milo began driving south to Homer for a class in welding, writing Larry:

No ancient relative, the welding is not a hoax. I have a scar on my wrist to prove it—where I touched a hot piece of steel while thinking of something else of course, but it got my attention, I can tell you. . . . Giving up the surgery was, as you surmised, very traumatic. But I did not take up welding to ease the transition from surgeon to non-surgeon. I took the course because I wish to build a plane from a kit.

Among his dozen or so classmates, mostly thirty-five- to forty-five-year-old men, was one teenage boy.

The 18-year-old, a very nice kid, asked me why I was taking the class. I replied in return, "I'm going to build an

*airplane." He broke into a sort of sickly smile and carefully
backed away from me and then ran for a bench 6 seats down
the aisle. I guess I should have said, "I have some pipe welding to do?"*

Soon, it became apparent that neither Milo's build-his-own-plane plan,
nor his "ideal dream" of buying a decent Super Cub or Citabria, financed
from the sale of his surgical instruments, was going to pan out. March
brought a spate of health issues—including prostate surgery and a diagnosis of diabetes—that intensified Milo's "Idylls of the King."

*My depression [after prostate surgery] was caused by an
unusual reaction to Darvon which I took for joint pains since
my previously happily ingested aspirin cannot be taken because it prolongs bleeding time and interferes with clotting.
Well, it's over now and for me sex is now a wind that nobody
blows good. Ah well one has one's memories and regrets!!!*

A hip replacement the year before had preceded these ailments. The
infirmities of old age were piling up. Milo often turned to a dose of humor
at bedtime, as he wrote Larry:

*I was first introduced to E.B. White by you at 217 [our
house number in Merion]. I have been a devoted reader ever
since and have a copy of his LETTERS at my bedside and I
read a little every night, as good an antidote against the cares
of this world as P.G. Wodehouse.*

Milo's chickens arrived in April. As a fan of E. B. White, Milo enjoyed
Points of My Compass and, by then, had read *The Letters of E. B. White* at
least twice, undoubtably taking note of White's many anecdotes about raising chickens and geese. White wrote about ordering "fifty-day-old Silver
Cross chicks" for his farm in Maine and found "nothing more delightful than the details surrounding a hatch of goose eggs." Once again, simi-
larities between the Maine writer and small-scale farmer and his Alaska
counterpart are hard to ignore. Milo wrote his brother about his aviary,
which throughout that summer and fall, provided Milo with a source of
entertainment, distraction, and eggs.

*We now have aboard 12-day-old Rhode Island Reds.
They are not a baseball team but day-old chicks which in
a few weex will begin laying eggs for us—the 2 mutts, the
2 cats and ourselves using about 2 dozen a week. You can*

easily appreciate the J.P. Morgagnian profitability of this: cost of chix 28 bux, feed so far, 8 bux, insulated hen house with perches and nesting boxes $1000. So, our eggs will cost about a dollar apiece and in 14 years the entire enterprise will be sounder than Chrysler and Penn Central combined. But the eggs will be fresh, large, and tasty and they actually do cost a buck fifty a dozen and they just aint fresh.

. . . Nex tweak 50 Cornish Cross day-olds will arrive to join the layers. They go from 0 to 6 pounds dressed or undressed, surgically that is, in 8 weex. For the actual slaughter I will have a bloodthirsty neighbor in because I can't do it: too squeamish or cowardly.

Two goslings completed the menagerie, as he wrote his brother:

Shit through a goose is not just one of those idle poetic expressions of St. Luke or another famous individual. It's true. Our two geese, cleverly named by me, Poop and Repoop eat tons of grass which seems to appear at the back door in amazingly short time. Still much must be metabolized else they would not be growing at the impressive rate that astonish us every day. . . . We don't know whether Poop or Repoop is goose or gander but Poop is taller by 2 inches so I think he is a male. We shall see. . . . One of the cutest things is their parading from garage to cage outdoors and back again following me or Betsy. They really do a goose step and their little feet go slap, slap, slap on the concrete floor of the garage.

. . . As the days race by I find it easier and easier to stay here on the homestead and commune with the geese, the chix, the eagles and the gulls. I had not realized how reduced I had become owning to the life I chose to lead and the chores I chose to do.

E. B. White stated: "I think nothing of sending half a dozen broilers to the guillotine. Come June, heads will be rolling behind my barn." However, Milo was more somber, lamenting to Larry in July:

This coming Saturday we have to kill and dress 40 white Cornish Cross chix that have grown to resemble rocs in size. I dread the job being rather chicken hearted. Executing the geese will be even worse because they are so beautiful and trusting. I will feel much like the late Judas Priest (or is it Iscariot) must have felt that night when he betrayed Jesus. These lovely birds come rushing up to me when I appear at the gate and eat cracked laying feed or snake weed that I always take with me. They honk and croon and poop ecstatically and let me pick them up all trusting while every day the time of their demise creeps inexorably closer and closer. I don't know how I'll ever eat them but maybe Time, the great healer, will have made it possible by Thanksgiving and Christmas.

Milo's thoughts in August:

... The Cornish Crosses are in heaven and butchering them was very traumatic for me to say nothing about how they must have felt. And there is nothing so reproachful as the look you get from a head that is separated from its body, believe me. Never again. And I sort of have the idea that Poop and Repoop will die of old age. The Reds are good for 3 years and then must make the Great Change. Well, I may have made it myself by that time. So. I am not going to worry.

LAST HURRAH

*For Issues "Too Hot to Handle" Vote for Milo H. Fritz,
Republican House, District 5, Seat B*

—CAMPAIGN MESSAGE ON POTHOLDERS

IN 1982, DOC FRITZ DECIDED TO MAKE A THIRD RUN for the House of
Representatives from the Kenai Peninsula. Two previous tries from
his new home base had been unsuccessful—the last time he lost by thirteen votes. The narrow defeat, new health issues—including a knee replacement that brought an end to his years as a private pilot—had further sapped his spirits. With a renewed interest in politics providing a
reprieve from "Idylls of the King," life was once again on the upswing, as
he wrote Larry in March:

> Yesterday, crutches and all, I made my first social essay
> at the 5th District Republican party convention. I almost had
> to throw in the towel early in the day but persisted and was
> rewarded with some strength from heaven and Betsy's care
> and I not only got through the long day, but also attended the
> banquet at 8 p.m. complete with a live act of local girls doing

belly dances which would arouse St. Paul at prayer. In one of the acts the girls put cherries between the lips of some in the audience. I guess I was one of the chosen lucky ones because my tongue was hanging out the farthest. Ah, Me!

In June:

> *. . . One of my well-wishers—a Democrat who gave me 500 of the crispest—also asked me to listen to 12 tapes on the subject of salesmanship. On a recent trip to Anchorage, I listened to them all as I tooled along and listened to them twice more as I stamped the post cards of which you will, in due course, receive 24. I found the tapes fascinating and they have helped me in putting across my message as I visit folks in their town homes, on their homesteads, and at their businesses. The series of tapes is called KISS: Keep It Simple, Salesperson!*

Though no longer a pilot, the opportunities to fly as a passenger were always a thrill, as Milo wrote in July:

> *Today I went to a Candidates' Day at the Seldovia C of C. What made it fun was having my own private airplane and pilot. Ruth Jacobs, my neighbor's wife, has a nifty Cessna 170 (Doyne Conversion) and she did a masterful job of getting on and off Seldovia strip, which is 2500 feet long, and Fritz International, which is 800 feet long.*
>
> *. . . There were 2 Senate candidates and one other House candidate besides myself. We each had 3 minutes to tell how we would save the world and then the members of the C of C asked us questions. Fortunately, they asked me one I could answer. But I forget what it was!*
>
> *. . . The knee is better, thank you, but I can't walk very far. And after a day of campaigning, I am done in. But what the hell can one expect at 72?*
>
> *. . . I am appalled at the great number of folks who are not registered to vote. In one day on the campaign trail Ruth Jacobs (Registrar as well as pilot) and I signed up 14 folks. They had been in residence here from 1 to 14 years. Most just never got around to it, others thought it cost money, and a few didn't want to register for fear they would be called*

up for jury duty as jurors are selected from voters' lists. Ah, there is nothing like a free ride. I feel if you vote you have the right to complain. If you don't—well you are just part of the problem.

In September:

I spend as much time campaigning as possible. One or 2 days a week I am in the office and I must do some of the homestead chores if the place is not to be entirely reclaimed by the wilderness. The one thing that all the speakers were unanimous about was the need for campaigning. Well, I have been campaigning furiously and since it got me through the Primaries, I will not change my tactics for the Nov. elections. I rather enjoy it visiting many places that have attracted me as I tooled about my medical chores over the years. And almost without exception one hears, "Thanks for stopping by" or "You're the first live candidate that ever stopped here," or "Lots of luck in the campaign."

. . . One of the nice things about campaigning is that I can visit places that are attractive along the roads. One can hardly go in and just say that the place is attractive, but as a politician one is asked in, shown the place, and more often than not given a cup of coffee and some fattening food. I enjoy it. I have faced down all but one dog and he meant business for he was apparently guarding two small children playing in the yard. But, as you probably know, most dogs are cowards and if you look them in the eye, they will leave you alone.

In another letter:

No matter how many times Betsy and I make the long trip between AP and ANC we never cease our oohing and ahing at the wonders of nature displayed no matter what time of the year the journey takes place. Yesterday we came back from ANC having spent 2 days up there at a Republican Symposium devoted to the worthwhile theme "How to Win An Election." The effectiveness of the talks was somewhat marred for me by the sound of the light planes landing and taking off from the Lake Hood Seaplane Base.

Doc Fritz won the 1982 election handily and was honored by the opportunity to represent his Kenai Peninsula district in the Alaska State House of Representatives:

> *The four days in my life that were most important to me: the day I got married; the day I got out of medical school; the day I soloed an airplane; and the day that I was sworn in. I take it seriously and I am tremendously moved when I put my hand up and say I will defend the constitution of this native Alaska and the United States.*

In an interview shortly after being elected, Doc Fritz noted how his past efforts to support the health and wellbeing of Alaska Natives helped his most recent campaign:

> *I know one thing, for instance, one of the pluses; two native groups endorsed me as candidate for this last election and one guy said, "You thought we were—you helped us before we became people in 1968, or whenever it was the Native Claims Settlement Act was enacted [1971]. I consider that a big compliment, that I was without racial bias in those days, when, well she is just a Native or hell with it. I maintain I'm color-blind. If you want to be a bastard and you've got a black hide well you are. But it isn't because you got a black hide, or brown or yellow or anything else. I maintain I have a right to my own opinion, irrespective of race or color.*

Even after listening to all those tapes on salesmanship, Milo's candor was largely undiminished.

Following his election to what would be his third and final two-year term in the Alaska Legislature, "Idylls of the King" seemed to be in remission. Milo wrote Larry from Juneau in January 1983:

> *Betsy was with me down here for the inaugural festivities, and I think that she had a good time. Anyway, she got the opportunity of seeing where I work, where I live, and how the system works. Also, she was present during the swearing in ceremonies, which I always find very moving and think of Dad, who would have been so proud to see me as an elected portion of the government.*

Since moving to Alaska in 1940, Milo had seen it undergo tremendous change—especially in medical care—and Doc Fritz had been a significant part of that change which continued apace. His shorthand summary: "The airplane, the jet saved many lives. Drag them in from the bush by helicopter—that's the invention that surpasses anything—then you would shove them on a jet and get them to care."

Milo had been out of office for eight years and the technological advances that had become available to the House of Representatives and government in the meantime were striking. Milo alluded to those changes in a letter to Larry from Juneau:

> *Things have changed greatly since I was here last time. They have become more complex and computer oriented. . . . The office is about the size of a large telephone booth, but you can't have everything.*
>
> *. . . In this incarnation, I am very lucky in having an aide and a secretary, besides that, being the co-chairman of the committee on Health, Education, and Social Services, we have three more staff that do the research and get together the day's agenda on Monday, Wednesday, and Friday when the committee meets. In addition, I serve on something called the Committee on Community and Regional Affairs presided over by a cute little lady whose handling of the gavel is reminiscent of Willie Mayes knocking a home run over the bleachers behind second base.*

A passage in a March letter to his brother cites more changes that Milo witnessed:

> *One of the marvels of the age here in Alaska is the telecommunications conference network. It is an impressive thing to sit here in Juneau and talk to people and listen to their testimony on a bill from such far-away places as the Pribilofs, Kodiak, Nome, Barrow, Shishmaref, Golovin, Unalakleet, Talkeetna, Anchorage, Homer, Seldovia, Yakutat, Pelican, Hydaburg, Elfin Cove and many more. In this way we hear people with the clipped accents of the Eskimo, Scandinavian-American accents of fishermen, teachers, reindeer herders, lawyers, tug-boat skippers, miners, farmers and others from different walks of life. And this network will be considered primitive to what will be common in a very short time—video network so we can see to whom we speak and listen to.*

FOLLOWING HIS FINAL TERM IN THE LEGISLATURE, Doc Fritz's medical practice was "practically extinct," but he wasn't ready to retire yet and continued to see patients at his Anchor Point office several days a week. He occasionally also did locum tenens—temporarily filling in for colleagues in other practices. By 1985, a shortage of physicians was becoming a thing of the past, even on the Kenai Peninsula. "Now that there are excess doctors, if [the ophthalmologist in Soldotna] leaves his office long untended another will move in and both will starve to death."

Milo's last itinerant clinic was in 1974 and John Spahn had retired to the Seattle area in the years since, so they saw each other only rarely. In the spring of 1985, a month after visiting his old friend, Milo wrote Larry, "John went to bed last Friday and never woke up," continuing:

> John died of a heart attack and I went down Sunday for the memorial services. The little memorial chapel was filled with standing room only and your favorite brother had to deliver a eulogy extempore. This was not hard to do as I simply stated, all that he had done for nothing for the forgotten folk in the backwoods of Alaska when some bureaucracy had neglected to forward the necessary "authorization," whether it was for a pair of glasses, an operation, or an examination. John would always say in effect, "Don't worry about it, I'll send you a bill."
>
> This occurred hundreds of times. And often the person to whom he was going to send the bill was 5 years old or 85 and deaf and unable to speak or understand the least bit of English. But by doing this he got glasses to many that were sorely in need of them. And he saved their pride before their peers since the clinics were always "open," that is people were encouraged to observe to take away the awe and the mystery. I can just imagine old St. Peter saying, "Welcome aboard, John. You're here a little sooner than I expected. But that's all right we have the room. And say, when you are settled there is this little angel who needs a new pair of glasses. He hasn't any money, and his folks aren't here. I was wondering if you would fill his prescription or take the measurements from his old beat-up glasses."
>
> "Send him right in, St. Peter. Don't worry about a thing. I'll send him a bill."

SIX MONTHS LATER, MILO DECIDED that the time had come to give up medicine entirely, writing Larry:

> On the 17th of September I saw my last two patients be-
> cause I do not see as sharply as I must to properly examine
> the inside of the human eye and somehow it has been just
> stealing over me that I ought to quit while I am ahead. The 3
> weeks stint of locum tenens I did for my colleague in Soldotna
> was really my last hurrah. But I have no regrets. I did what
> I most enjoyed doing for over 51 years and one has to quit
> sometime. I will still get occasional calls for advice when doc-
> tors disagree but for all practical purposes it is finished.

Several years after his retirement from medicine, Doc Fritz was again reminded of the monumental changes in medicine he had seen when he hauled down his old *Textbook of Medicine*. It was, he noted, "published in 1931—the second edition—long before there were steroids, antibiotics or sulfonamides, CAT scans, magnetic resonance imaging and all the other wonders that have developed since those olden days. But the writing was good. And there used to be TB uncontrolled as well as syphilis and gonor-rhea. Good old days."

As his life wound down at Anchor Point, Milo was still able to draw on the black humor that had been a trademark of his throughout his life. As he wrote his aging younger brother, who was also dealing with the ravages of life and who would precede him in death, Milo fended off the darkness with bursts of his inimitable wit:

> Yesterday an angler off Homer came home with a
> 394-pound halibut. When landing a fish like that is the time
> to die. How much happiness can one stand?

And in another letter to Larry:

> The other day a mother moose and her days-old calf vis-
> ited us. Of course, our cur, utterly oblivious to the demands
> of hospitability yapped at them as they ate grass along the
> bluff. He'd run up and stop just short of where the mother
> moose could have stomped him, so finally Mama and baby
> walked into a clump of alders. But the goddam dog kept right
> on yapping. I went out to get him with a short leash, had
> him clipped on, and the mother moose, apparently fed up as
> I was, charged out of the alders after the dog. I dropped the

*leash and skipped into the house with an agility that would
have amazed you. After a while I peeped out thinking that I
would find a dead dog. But no luck, he did not have a scratch
on him. But he didn't yap any more.*

*It would have been a fitting end for me. There is no better
way for an old Alaskan to go than to be stomped to death by
a moose.*

FOR TWO YEARS BEFORE MILO DIED, Jonathan lived with them. Milo had
found homestead chores increasingly difficult and, grudgingly, allowed
Jonathan back into their lives and home. By then, Jonathan had more
or less given up on trying to eke out a living as a carpenter in Denver,
Las Vegas, Anchorage, and perhaps other places in recent years. In 1982,
Jonathan had (unsuccessfully) spent seven weeks in Fairbanks drying out.
By 1998, Jonathan was in need of a home. They were a family again. In several letters from Aunt Betsy, she alludes to more harmonious, if sad, times
together prior to Milo's death.

*Jonathan was so much help caring for Milo. He really
turned to and was very kind and attentive to Milo's needs.
. . . In the end Jonathan helped prepare Milo for his journey
and even carried him out to the waiting van. Since then, he
has taken very good care of me. He does most of the cooking,
he does the heavy cleaning, the shopping, etc.*

*. . . [Milo] was up, dressed and about until the last month.
After a week in the hospital, I brought him home. It is a com-
fort to me that I could care for him those last days. A com-
fort that I had that last conscious moment when I could say
goodbye and kiss him before the very strong medications in
the transdermal patches took over. The last few days he was
not conscious.*

*. . . We were best friends for sixty-six years, married for
sixty-three and Milo had a full ninety-one years spreading
joy, love, better health for many who could not afford care,
originating and getting passed some much-needed legislation. A very full life.*

A week after Milo's death on August 31, 2000, Governor Tony Knowles,
ordered state flags lowered for two days—Sept. 7 and Sept. 8—in memory

of Milo H. Fritz, "doctor, former state legislator and pioneer, and in recognition of his service to the people of Alaska."

The following week, Senator Ted Stevens honored his friend and former colleague by reading his tribute to Milo into the Congressional record, which begins: "Alaska lost one of its true pioneers when Dr. Milo Fritz died;" and concludes: "He left a legacy of caring and hard work and love of people and of his profession that will be hard to match. He gave his all, over and over again."

THE MACHETANZ MURAL
– *TRUE PIONEER*

*The Anchorage Native Primary Care Center
is exactly the place for the mural.*

—BETSY FRITZ

THOSE "GOOD OLD DAYS" OF THE 1940S, 50S AND 60S, those decades when Fritz itinerant clinics were bringing badly needed medical care to Native villages, were captured on canvas by the well-known Alaska artist Fred Machetanz in his painting, *True Pioneer.*

The mural, which was acquired by the Southcentral Foundation, an Alaska Native-owned health care nonprofit, depicts the Fritz clinics in a montage of scenes from around Alaska. Machetanz painted various scenes of Doc Fritz, Betsy, and John Spahn arriving in bush villages by the various means available to them then—umiak, single-engine plane, dog sled—and carrying out the pioneering medical work that, by mid-century, made Doc Fritz a legendary figure throughout Alaska. Near the center of his painting, Machetanz portrayed a teenage Native girl standing with her scrubbed and gloved hands clasped, not in prayer, but in preparation for assisting Doc Fritz in a medical procedure.

Also depicted is noted dog sled racer Jimmy Huntington, the original "Huslia Hustler"—a reference to that tiny village on a tributary of the Yukon River that hosted a Fritz clinic in 1961. Afterwards, Patterson Keller, Huslia's Episcopal Priest wrote an article describing the clinic from the perspective of the villagers. His article included these observations:

> For four days anybody who had the courage to say what was really wrong with them got real treatment for real ills. Some were told that nothing could be done, but they still held up their heads for they had the courage to hope and were grateful that someone had spent real time on them and had not merely said, "Maybe next year," or, "We got no money for that kind," or, "Write a letter."
>
> . . . If you watched the rectory for a while over these four days you would see people of the town slipping quietly in to present fish and meat, canned goods and baked things to be cooked for these visitors. . . . Food was given happily by people whose sons and daughters went under the knife and by those who would soon be able to hear much better and by those who for the first time in their lives would be able to look through real glasses made for their eyes that did not come from the ten-cent store.

The Machetanz mural hangs in Southcentral Foundation's Anchorage Native Primary Care Center, a gleaming modern facility in the heart of the Alaska Native Medical Center; the painting was unveiled in 2006—nearly six years after Milo's death.

The unveiling ceremony was a major event that drew many well-wishers, as well as TV coverage. Betsy, the guest of honor, looked poised and elegant in a tailored black jacket and skirt, a chic scarf draped about her neck, her hair professionally coifed. "We came to Alaska in 1940," Betsy told one newscaster in her soft, clear voice, "and Milo was sent over the whole state—every bit of the state—to do eye, ear, nose, and throat work."

The event also brought family members to Anchorage—my sister Barbara, flying in from Los Angeles, and my mother Helen, eighty-nine, who flew in from the East Coast. By then, Betsy was living on her own at

Anchor Point. Six months earlier, Jonathan had succumbed to a stroke or heart attack at age sixty-four.

The unveiling reunited Betsy with several former staff members from the Fritz Anchorage office—Milo's head surgical nurse Johnny Childs and office manager Helen Gamble, who like Betsy, attended in a wheelchair. Helen, too, was interviewed. She regarded Dr. Fritz as a missionary. "Sometimes he got paid," Helen said, "sometimes he didn't, because he really was not interested in money. He was interested in people's health, how he could make people see better."

The program included remarks by Alaska Native health care leaders, Yup'ik dancing, and a video presentation by Senator Ted Stevens, who said he was pleased that the painting by Fred Machetanz had found a permanent home, "where hundreds or, more likely, thousands of Alaskans will see it." He was also "grateful to Southcentral's generosity, which will ensure that these great men—Dr. Milo Fritz and Fred Machetanz—will not be forgotten by our state's people," continuing:

> As some of you know, Milo and I served together in the state legislature in 1966. While I went on to Washington, DC two years later, he stayed on in the legislature ensuring that the state government was aware of our rural health problems.
>
> . . . Now as a legislator, Milo was the same kind of perfectionist as when he practiced medicine. He had a commitment to the processes of democracy that few people really understand. He'd come to his House of Representative's desk every morning at 5:30 a.m. so he could read each bill before the regular session began. As the young people say today, "Milo was awesome."
>
> I also have special memories of traveling with Milo to remote villages even before he was in the legislature. Among them was a trip I took with him more than forty years ago when we flew to a village somewhere near Bethel. As a pilot myself, I admired Milo's skills while maneuvering his small Piper Tri-Pacer plane. The plane was loaded with medical equipment, a generator and supplies to treat all matter of ailments from tonsillectomies to tooth decays and other health problems too numerous for me to recall now. It was an unforgettable experience. Just watching him work was an

unforgettable experience. Actually, just knowing Milo was an unforgettable experience.

. . . Milo ensured that people in urban areas, particularly those in government, understood the importance of bringing health care to rural Alaska.

Milo was a great, complicated, brilliant, and interesting guy who will never be matched. For me, however, the most important thing I can say today, "He was my friend."

Betsy demurely basked in all the attention that day, though no doubt wishing that Milo had lived long enough to receive those accolades, himself, and to see how his "mad dream" of bringing modern medicine into the country, to scattered bush villages, was at last being realized. Since 1999, a year before Milo's death, the Southcentral Foundation has jointly owned and managed the Alaska Native Medical Center, which serves the entire Alaska Native and American Indian population of the state—over 100,000 people. As was made clear the day of the unveiling, Alaska Natives themselves are now the ones in charge of designing the systems and delivering the health care needed by their communities. At the conclusion of the twentieth century, the medical "good old days" of the Last Frontier were gone; Milo's "mad dream" for Alaska was no longer "mad," no longer just a dream.

THE BOOK

We are the pioneers of our own histories,
drawn to the horizon as if it waited just for us
The way the young are drawn to the future,
the old to the past.

—LINDA PASTERN

MILO'S INTENTION HAD ALWAYS BEEN TO WRITE A BOOK about his "Alaska Adventures" after the move to Anchor Point. A year into retirement he wrote Larry:

> When I came down here it was to write. Betsy has 14
> file cases of letters and papers and copies of things I wrote
> and sold. But when we finally got here, I could not write for
> I found that I would have to practice in order to eat and so
> the precious opportunity and all the written material is of no
> use. I can't do it and believe me I have tried.

A campaign of encouragement by family and friends—including Ted Stevens and Dr. Phillips Thygeson, who suggested a California-based medical historian who had chronicled Phil's life—went nowhere, despite

Betsy's efforts to organize their "paper history," in boxes and files, year-by-year. "I picked at random the year 1959 and now it is nearly finished." Betsy wrote, offering my parents a thumbnail sketch in a 1990 letter:

> That year, in addition to our heartbreaking situation with Pieter, Milo did 582 operations, he was a Delegate to the AMA both sessions, gave his paper at the Academy Mtg. in Oct., took a class in nasal surgery, made the memorable Easter Offering trip to Chaneliak with John Spahn in his plane in marginal weather, attended the annual meeting of the Alaska Medical Association in Juneau, published nine articles and slept through Jonathan's graduation. So having been in New York, Hartford, CT, Merion, PA, Atlantic City, Chicago, Dallas, Phoenix, Juneau and Chaneliak he was away from home for some time all together. I forgot he also took a course in instrument flying in Oklahoma too. It is no wonder he is worn out.
>
> Sometimes he would do two mastoidectomies in a morning and then see an office full of patients in the P.M. Other times it was surgery of a shorter nature but as difficult and an unbelievable number of patients. We must have been very efficient in getting them in and out because he was the one who treated them and they all got first class care—no shortcuts.
>
> . . . Then of course there were Medical Society Meetings each month and Medical Staff meetings each month.
>
> . . . This is only one year.

"The Book" proved too daunting an undertaking, However, their intension was to leave the Fritz papers to the University of Alaska library in Anchorage where their decades of historical Alaska material would be available to researchers. "It will all be in order for anyone who wishes to write up the nightmare. I bet there are times they will not believe what they read," Betsy wrote. "I hardly do myself."

Milo's accumulating health issues, including a diagnosis of type 2 (adult-onset) diabetes, high blood pressure, and then cataracts, contributed to his physical woes and a sense of his own mortality. But in 1991, the need to have cataracts removed from one, or possibly both eyes, presented an opportunity for a prolonged visit with Larry and Helen, retired in Chestertown, Maryland, where there was a skilled ophthalmologist. It

also presented an ideal opportunity, I thought, for an oral history interview with Milo during the relaxed recovery period afterwards—if he was
willing. He was. Six years after seeing his last patient, talking about medicine seemed to offer Doc Fritz a welcome tonic.

Despite Aunt Betsy's misgivings about Uncle Milo's memory lapses,
his declining energy level, and diminished cognitive abilities that had
made writing his autobiography too challenging, it turned out that Milo
was very able to talk about his life in medicine with clarity, enthusiasm,
and humor. The oral history interview that we did together over two days
seemed to be a gratifying experience for my uncle. There was no need to
come up with exact dates and details—the overview, the memories, his
own unique phrasing was what I was hoping for. All that he delivered
with gusto. Uncle Milo seemed to enjoy the shared project, viewing it as
an indication of my appreciation of him and his legion accomplishments.
Which, of course, it was.

Our fond farewell was at Dulles airport. In order to save Uncle Milo's
strength for the fatiguing journey back to Alaska, he opted for a wheelchair to transverse the expansive terminal. After wheeling my uncle as
far as I was allowed to go, we hugged and said our goodbyes. As I watched
Uncle Milo, composed and straight-backed in his chair, recede down a
long airport corridor, I knew I was seeing the last of an extraordinary
man whose heroic life and spirit of generosity had touched me as well as
a huge swath of Alaskans to an extent I was only beginning to adequately
appreciate.

Milo offered these thoughts summing up a life dedicated to practicing
medicine in his beloved Alaska:

> I don't know how many eye examinations I did but it was
> in the tens of thousands. I have seen over 58,000 people as
> patients and that does not include those I saw in the years
> I was on active duty with the Air Force. . . I enjoy the prac-
> tice of medicine as much now as I did 51 years ago when I
> started.
>
> . . . I would not live anywhere but here where life is so
> fascinating and exciting and where so diverse a bunch of
> people live together in relative harmony, peace, and a mea-
> sure of prosperity. How wonderful it is even to me, a biased
> enthusiast, is always brought home after a few days outside

where the Brownian movement of crowds in airports and cities seems so senseless. I loved the place from the day I got here on 29 Jan. 1940 and that love has become more and more a part of me the longer I survive.

EPILOGUE—LAST WORDS

*Our resident eagles are soaring back and forth today
interrupting their graceful paths of flight to plummet down
on some unsuspecting fish at 125 mph. They don't worry
about past or future. Just what can I do now.
Maybe they have something.*

—MILO FRITZ

URING MY FINAL, WEEK-LONG VISIT with Aunt Betsy in 2008, the
weather at Anchor Point cycled through three seasons—summer,
fall, and winter. By Sunday evening, there was a dusting of snow and warn-
ings about patches of black ice on the road to Homer.

After our eventful week together of making the arrangements necessary for her final wishes to be carried out, Aunt Betsy seemed weary, but
also very much at peace. She was glad I came, she told me. And she asked
me to come back . . . maybe in the spring.

The day before I was to leave, Aunt Betsy and I sat in her sunroom
the entire morning, alternately conversing and sitting in companionable
silence as we watched the timeless pull of the tides, the eagles soaring

against the sky, the play of light on the water and on the mountains across Cook Inlet. It was a powerfully mesmerizing scene, one that had captivated Milo when he first set eyes on it during World War II and fantasized about it as an ideal, if utterly unattainable, place to live. Betsy had come to share Milo's dream. They had paid dearly, in so many ways, to make that dream a reality, but that was all behind my aunt now. Over the years, Aunt Betsy told me, she had seen the eruptions of four volcanoes—Spur, Redoubt, Augustine, and Iliamna—from that outpost at Anchor Point. Now, she took pleasure in the subtleties of the ever-changing scene as she waited for "Milo to come for her."

As Milo's wife and stalwart partner for over 63 years, Betsy was an intimate part of what Milo referred to as the "triumphs and tragedies" of his roller coaster life. His appreciation of Betsy was unqualified. As Milo stated simply, "Without her, it wouldn't have been possible."

Carol took one last photo of Aunt Betsy and me. We said our goodbyes. There were no tears. We both put on a brave face, but I think we both sensed the finality of the parting. On that early October morning in 2008, I drove slowly away from my aunt's home through an inch of new snow. Winter had arrived. The little hand-hewn cabin with its soft-red door and window trim was now wearing the light snowfall from overnight and looked especially charming against the background of a few noble spruce trees and the chilly immensity of Cook Inlet. I had to stop and take a picture. Even at the time, that quintessential Alaska scene that I was admiring and documenting seemed to represent the end of an era. And it was. That image still exists, the cabin doesn't.

I did return to Anchor Point in the spring, after getting the dreaded but not unexpected call from Carol on April 15. Milo, it seemed, had finally come for Betsy in the wee hours of the morning while she was sleeping.

My sister Lenore joined me at Anchor Point in early May. We worked together, helping Carol with the enormous task of clearing out the house before it became the property of its new owner. Barbara arrived a few days after we left—a tag team effort. We had thirty days to see the contents off to their new homes: Native art to the Anchorage Museum, books and archives to the University of Alaska Consortium Library in Anchorage; Betsy's genealogy library and the meticulously researched documents, which had consumed years of her time, to the Daughters of the American Revolution. My aunt had designated her hometown of Tioga, Pennsylvania as the final resting place for her remains and those of Jonathan and Pieter. In sad irony, they were the final leaves on that branch of the Fritz-Berry family tree.

There had been no memorial service at the time of Milo's death. His intent was to save Betsy the bother and the expense. He did request that his ashes be scattered off the bluff at Anchor Point after "he passed in his dinner pail." After dedicating nearly sixty years to Alaska and the medical needs of the land's wide-ranging communities, Alaska became Milo's spiritual and well as physical home. "I would never voluntarily leave Anchor Point or Alaska," he stated. On a fine day in early May 2009, Lenore, Carol, and I stood on the promontory at Anchor Point with Milo's urn, poised to carry out his final wishes.

When conditions are right, you can see those four volcanoes among the snowy peaks of the mountains on the far shore—Mt. Spur and Mt. Redoubt to the north, Mt. Augustine to the south, and Mt. Iliamna, fifty miles west across the expanse of Cook Inlet. That day, conditions were right. Eagles on the wing, so often admired and described by Uncle Milo over the years, moved across the sky. In recent days, I had also become aware of an eagle who often sat for long stretches of time, perched atop a skeletal pine tree on the bluff—a watchful, solitary sentinel.

The three of us, emerging from our various sorting tasks inside the house, paused to take it all in—eagles, mountains, woods, tides—a vista both ever-changing and timeless. I could understand why Uncle Milo wanted to be an eternal part of this awe-inspiring Alaska tableau. We offered up a prayer and a few words of appreciation to the man whose spirit of service and embrace of adventure had touched something deep within each of us. The words we spoke were inadequate, but our very presence at that far side of the continent spoke eloquently of the gratitude we felt for this remarkable man. We took turns tipping the urn, releasing Milo's ashes into the expanse.

Dr. Milo H. Fritz hoped to be remembered as that "dashing flying surgeon from Alaska." He proved to be that and more—a man of great vison and generosity whose mission in life was to serve others, often at his own expense, and whose goals were based upon what was needed, not necessarily what was possible or merely acceptable. Pushing his pioneering efforts into the medical unknown was a constant battle with formidable foes—among them inertia and the passage of time. Through it all, Doc

Fritz sallied forth, armed with his sardonic mantra: "Don't do anything, something might happen." It was a heroic endeavor. Much of Milo's heroism included quietly bearing the weight of despair while coming to terms with his own shortcomings and inability to achieve his lofty goals—the burden of being human. Perhaps, for Milo, that was the true cost of being a hero.

I like to think that Uncle Milo's restless spirit has finally slipped those "surly bonds of earth," and is back in the Alaska skies where he spent so many happy hours piloting airplanes. And, just as Milo pictured his friend John Spahn in his afterlife fitting angels with eyeglasses, I like to picture my uncle rising upward on thermals, playing tag with the eagles, riding the wind out along the Aleutian chain, maybe circling over the vast land he loved and the Alaskans he served for so many years . . . ceaselessly, devotedly, eternally making rounds. My hope is that Doc Fritz has finally been released from the weight of his burdens that caused him to "collapse into bed" night after night. I like to imagine the old bush pilot in a place that is perpetually CAVU—ceiling and visibility unlimited—all his mad dreams achievable.

ACKNOWLEDGMENTS

WRITING A BOOK IS MOSTLY SOLITARY WORK, however, my efforts were enhanced and my life greatly enriched by some wonderful people.

Thank you to historian Adam Goodheart who generously took the time to sit and discuss possible approaches to this book at a stage when I was grappling with the enormity of the Fritz archives and casting about for direction. Adam's suggestion of moving away from a straight biography to a memoir-biography hybrid came at just the right time and proved well suited to the material.

Arlene Schmuland, head of archives and special collections at the University of Alaska Anchorage Consortium Library, was a delight to work with and gave me an appreciation for the tremendous and often unsung work that archivists and librarians do. My thanks to Arlene for guiding my research efforts so as to make the best use of my time, and to the other librarians and staff throughout the University of Alaska library system whose assistance was invaluable.

I was surprised and delighted when Jenny Benjamin, director of Truhlsen-Marmor Museum of the Eye at the American Academy of Ophthalmology, tracked me down over ten years ago to ask if I was willing to make my oral history interview with Dr. Milo Fritz available to

AAO members (of course!) In the years since, Jenny has been a wonderful source of enthusiasm and support. Despite her many responsibilities at AAO and its new museum in San Francisco, Jenny graciously offered to be a beta reader, which I greatly appreciated.

Monica Shah, deputy director for conservation and collections at the Anchorage Museum and her predecessor, Suzi Jones, have been very supportive of this book about Milo's life. My thanks to them and the curators and staff members at the Museum's state-of-the-art research facilities who were very engaged and helpful.

I owe much to members of my writing group who, for more than a decade, challenged me to make my writing better. I am especially grateful to the dedicated stalwarts who continued providing mutual feedback until our various writing projects were ready for publication: Laura Ambler, Helen Delaney, Brent Lewis, Mala Burt, Marcia Moore, Anne McNulty, and Gerald Sweeney.

It was my good fortune to have the talented author and editor Andromeda Romano-Lax as developmental editor for this book. Co-founder of 49 Writers, Andromeda knows Alaska well, and thanks to her sensitivity to the material and insightful guidance, the resulting book is much stronger.

My thanks to Judy Bittner, Alaska's state historic preservation officer, for her professional guidance and for graciously reacquainting me with Anchorage after a multi-decades-long absence.

Also thanks to Alaska artist Kristin Link for creating a map of Alaska that so beautifully dovetails with the book's text.

Ultimately, the manuscript appealed to Phil Garrett and his fine staff at Epicenter Press, the perfect home for this story about an extraordinary Alaskan.

Special thanks to my conscientious beta readers—Laura Ambler, Jenny Benjamin, Lenore Budd, David Butwin, Karl Fritz, and Barbara Schaff—who were so generous with their time, areas of expertise, and thoughtful suggestions.

Numerous writers—many of them Alaskans—have shared their publishing knowledge and experiences with me at pivotal points along this book's path to publishing. My appreciation to: Steve Solomon, Peter Jensen, Amy Abrams, Jerry Zolten, Kate Blackwell, Peter Fish, Lael Morgan, Dana Stabenow, Connie Godwin, Deb Vanasse, Leigh Newman,

Peggy Shumaker, Nancy Lord, X̱'unei Lance Twitchell, and Hank Lentfer.

I am greatly indebted to two other Alaskans, Ted and Cathy Stevens, who greatly supplemented my general knowledge of Alaska, giving me the historical perspective to take on this book project. My longstanding friendship with them, which blossomed from our mutual affection for Milo and Betsy Fritz, has helped keep my ties to Alaska vibrant over the years. My heartfelt gratitude to them for their many kindnesses and for sharing their knowledge and love of Alaska with me.

My family members, near and far, have helped immeasurably throughout my lengthy research and writing process with their documents, memories, and support. I am particularly appreciative of my father (always my toughest critic), who took the time to thoughtfully critique many of my early writing efforts—despite his conclusion that I would never be able to support myself as a writer.

Special thanks to Richard Schwartz, who has been the wind at my back during the homestretch of this project.

Lastly, I will be forever grateful to Paul Mims, my high school creative writing teacher, who played a key role in my development as a writer and also introduced me to the work of Joseph Campbell, specifically, *The Hero with a Thousand Faces.*

SELECTED SOURCES

Author Note:

This book, which chronicles the life of Dr. Milo H. Fritz through a mixture of memory and archives, is a work of nonfiction. The memories— mine, my uncle's, and those of my aunt and others—are as accurate as memories can be and, whenever possible, have been further verified and cross-referenced. Much of the archival material used in researching this book was drawn from the Betsy and Milo Fritz family papers in the Archives and Special Collections of the Consortium Library at the University of Alaska Anchorage and used by permission.

Additional archival material came from my own sources—diaries and letters I kept over the years, an oral history I conducted with my uncle in 1991—as well as letters and other documents from my parents and other relatives. Any quoted material is verbatim from these or other documented sources and so certain segments reflect common usage at the time. Elsewhere in the text, in sensitivity to Alaska's Native peoples, who were such an integral part of Doc Fritz's life and work, the language reflects current Indigenous terminology and place names.

Alaska Bound. (1948, April 2). [Clipping from a local newspaper, probably *Pelham Sun*].

Alaska Story: A New York Otologist's Flying Mission. (1958, July 30). [Special Picture Supplement of visit from Dr. Thomas Rambo]. *Scope*.

Albrecht, Earl. (1983, May). *An Oral History with Dr. Arthur Wilson/ Interviewer: Kenneth G. Kastella, Medicine in Alaska oral history project transcripts.* Alaska and Polar Regions Department, Rasmuson Library, University of Alaska, Fairbanks, Alaska.

Elizabeth Fritz honored by Alaska Nurses Association (n.d.) [clipping from a Tioga, Pennsylvania or Elmira, New York newspaper.]

Fair, C. (2010, December 23). Almanac: Mounting a Redoubt rescue effort. *The Mouth of the Kenai.*

Fair, C. (2011, January 5). Almanac: Rescuers Risk Ravages of Redoubt— Fritz recounts chilling backcountry tale. *The Mouth of the Kenai.*

Faith, W. (2003, April 1). *Bob Hope: A Life in Comedy.* De Capo Press.

Fritz, E. (ca. 1990) *Fritz Family History.* [Unpublished manuscript] Copies in possession of Linda Fritz.

Fritz, E. (ca. 1990). [Notes for biography of Dr. Milo Fritz received from Lloyd Crow.] Copies in possession of Linda Fritz.

Fritz, E. (ca. 1990). *1948 Trip to Alaska.* [Unpublished manuscript]. Betsy and Milo Fritz family papers, Archives and Special Collections, Consortium Library, University of Alaska Anchorage.

Fritz, E. (ca. 1990). *Christmas 1934.* [Unpublished manuscript]. Betsy and Milo Fritz family papers, Archives and Special Collections, Consortium Library, University of Alaska Anchorage.

Fritz, E. (ca. 1990). *Fritz Family History and Milo Fritz Biography.* [Unpublished manuscript]. Betsy and Milo Fritz family papers, Archives and Special Collections, Consortium Library, University of Alaska Anchorage.

Fritz, E. (ca. 1990). *Milo Fritz Biography, Part II.* [Unpublished manuscript]. Betsy and Milo Fritz family papers, Archives and Special Collections, Consortium Library, University of Alaska Anchorage.

Fritz, E. (ca. 1990). *The House that Jon Built.* [Unpublished manuscript]. Betsy and Milo Fritz family papers, Archives and Special Collections, Consortium Library, University of Alaska Anchorage.

Fritz, E. (ca. 1997). *Oly.* [Unpublished manuscript]. Betsy and Milo Fritz family papers, Archives and Special Collections, Consortium Library, University of Alaska Anchorage.

Fritz, E. (ca.1990) *Bits, Pieces and Debris* [Unpublished manuscript of Elizabeth Berry Fritz's story of Berry Family] Betsy and Milo Fritz family papers, Archives and Special Collections, Consortium Library, University of Alaska Anchorage.

Fritz, E. 1940. [Correspondence to Henry and Amelia Fritz]. Copies in possession of Linda Fritz.

Fritz, E. 1996-2006. [Correspondence to Helen Fritz]. Copies in possession of Linda Fritz.

Fritz, M. (1943, October 2). Ambulance Case on Mount Redoubt. *The Saturday Evening Post.*

Fritz, M. (1959, March). Julius Lempert's Contribution to Alaskan Ophthalmology. *Alaska Medicine.*

Fritz, M. (1960, November 30). *Alaska Territorial Medical Association Bulletins,* 1-5.

Fritz, M. (1961, December). A Voyage of the Yukon and Its Tributaries. *The Alaskan Churchman.*

Fritz, M. (1961, December). A Yukon Clinic. *Northwest Medicine.*

Fritz, M. (1962, February). He Also Dispenses Spectacles. *Guildcraft.*

Fritz, M. (1963, August). Tanana Revisited. *Northwest Medicine.*

Fritz, M. (1964, July 2). Dear Folks. [Unpublished letter giving Milo's personal account of the Good Friday Earthquake]. Betsy and Milo Fritz family papers, Archives and Special Collections, Consortium Library, University of Alaska Anchorage.

Fritz, M. (1966, March). Nome Clinic. *Alaska Medicine.*

Fritz, M. (1968, September). An M.D. in Politics. *Alaska Medicine.*

Fritz, M. (1982). *An Oral History with Dr. Milo H. Fritz/Interviewer: Kenneth G. Kastella, Medicine in Alaska oral history project transcripts.* Betsy and Milo Fritz family papers, Archives and Special Collections, Consortium Library, University of Alaska Anchorage.

Fritz, M. (1991, July 30). *An Oral History with Dr. Milo H. Fritz/Interviewer: Linda Fritz.* Betsy and Milo Fritz family papers, Archives and Special Collections, Consortium Library, University of Alaska Anchorage.

Fritz, M. July 1, 1934-June 30, 1936. [Correspondence to Henry and Amelia Fritz]. Copies in possession of Linda Fritz.

Fritz, M. 1939-1940. [Correspondence to Henry and Amelia Fritz]. Copies in possession of Linda Fritz.

Fritz, M. 1980-1993; 1997-1999. [Correspondence to Larry and Helen Fritz]. Copies in possession of Linda Fritz.

Fritz, M. 1988. *Liber Oncel Rudolf.* [Unpublished manuscript]. Betsy and Milo Fritz family papers, Archives and Special Collections, Consortium Library, University of Alaska Anchorage.

Keller, P. (1961, December). An Offering. *The Alaskan Churchman.*

Machetanz Painting Unveiled in the Primary Care Center. (2006, May/ June). *Anchorage Native News.*

Stevens, T. (2000, September 14). *Tribute to Dr. Milo Fritz.* [Read into *Congressional Record*] https://www.govinfo.gov/content/pkg/CRECB-2000-pt13/pdf/CRECB-2000-pt13-Pg18124.pdf

Stevens, T. (2006, May 10). *Remarks honoring Dr. Milo Fritz's contributions to rural medicine.* [CD of speech shown at Machetanz Unveiling Ceremony]. Betsy and Milo Fritz family papers, Archives and Special Collections, Consortium Library, University of Alaska Anchorage.

Thomas, C. 2005. *History of Fritz Side of the Family.* [Unpublished manuscript by Charlotte Eleanor Chandler Williams Thomas; original account is from Paula Fritz Hayes as told to Eleanor Margaret Hayes Chandler as told to Thomas.] Copies in possession of Linda Fritz.

Thygeson, P. (1987). *A Link With Our Past.* Ophthalmology Oral History Series. An oral history of Phillips Thygeson, MD, conducted by Sally Smith Hughes. Regional Oral History Office, University of California, Berkeley in cooperation with The Foundation of the American Academy of Ophthalmology.

Wilson, A. (1982, November). *An Oral History with Dr. Arthur Wilson/ Interviewer: Kenneth G. Kastella, Medicine in Alaska oral history project transcripts.* Alaska and Polar Regions Department, Rasmuson Library, University of Alaska, Fairbanks, Alaska.

Tamzin Biles

Editor, writer, and award-winning essayist LINDA FRITZ, author of *Answering Alaska's Call*, was introduced to Alaska and the joys of adventurous travel at age sixteen. Originally from suburban Philadelphia, Linda jumped at the chance to spend the summer in Alaska when offered employment as a nurse's aide for her uncle—Doc Fritz, Alaska's legendary flying doctor. While working in clinics and traveling throughout Alaska with her aunt and uncle, Linda absorbed the land's vastness and the can-do spirit of Alaskans—experiences that have influenced her life and writing ever since.

Following graduation from Penn State, where she studied journalism and consumer studies, Linda's dual interests in travel and magazine journalism led to an eclectic career path as a market researcher, writer/editor for *Sunset* and *Diversion* magazines, management consultant, and freelance writer that took her around the U.S.

After a hiatus to raise a family on Maryland's Eastern Shore, Linda was editor of the literary journal *Delmarva Review* for several years before taking on the writing challenge that had been gestating for decades: a book about the heroic life of Milo Fritz.

Visit her website, lindafritz.org.

CPSIA information can be obtained
at www.ICGtesting.com
Printed in the USA
JSHW032225130623
43189JS00005B/34